SAN FRANCISCO:

MISSION TO METROPOLIS
SECOND EDITION

The Mission Dolores shares with the present Officers' Club in the Presidio the distinction of being the oldest buildings in San Francisco; both were founded in 1776. Orginally called the Mission San Francisco de Asís, it received its present name from a small lake in the vicinity called *Laguna de Nuestra Señora de los Dolores*—Lagoon of our Lady of Sorrows. *(Redwood Empire Association.)*

SAN FRANCISCO:

MISSION TO METROPOLIS
SECOND EDITION

by Oscar Lewis

Howell-North Books • San Diego, California

1980 PRINTING

Printed and bound in the United States of America

Library of Congress Catalog Card No. 66-23944

ISBN 0-8310-7129-X

1 2 3 4 5   84 83 82 81 80

Published by Howell-North Books
11175 Flintkote Ave., San Diego, CA 92121

BOOKS BY OSCAR LEWIS

The Big Four
Bonanza Inn *(with Carroll D. Hall)*
Silver Kings
Sea Routes to the Gold Fields
High Sierra Country
California Heritage
Bay Window Bohemia
The Town That Died Laughing
Sagebrush Casinos
Here Lived the Californians
The Autobiography of the West
Fabulous San Simeon
George Davidson: Pioneer West Coast Scientist
Hearn and His Biographers
The War in the West: 1861-1865
This Was San Francisco
Sutter's Fort: Gateway to the Gold Fields
I Remember Christine *(novel)*
The Uncertain Journey *(novel)*
The Lost Years *(fantasy)*
Hawaii: Gem of the Pacific *(juvenile)*
The Story of California *(juvenile)*
The Story of Oregon *(juvenile)*
San Francisco: Mission to Metropolis

Preface

Few cities of modern times have had a history as varied and eventful as San Francisco. Although it was founded less than two centuries ago—which makes it one of the "youngest" of the world's major cities—it has been the scene of a greater number of picturesque and exciting and significant happenings than scores of far older communities. For the City by the Golden Gate has always had qualities that differ from those of other cities—qualities that from the beginning have drawn to her shores an uncommonly large number of men and women unable—or unwilling—to follow conventional patterns of behavior.

That characteristic is illustrated in the circumstances of the city's long-delayed founding. It was not until 1769—less than eight years before the colonies on the far side of the continent threw off the yoke of England—that the first white men laid eyes on San Francisco Bay. And when, in the spring of 1776, the sites of the mission and the presidio, the first buildings to be erected on the San Francisco Peninsula, were chosen, the Continental Congress—which three months later was to adopt the Declaration of Independence—was already in session at Philadelphia.

During the first seven decades of its existence the village of Yerba Buena remained a remote frontier outpost, its handful of residents neglected and all but forgotten by their nominal rulers at Madrid and Mexico City. During by far the greater part of that period its contacts with the outside world were limited to the exploring ships, whalers, or trading vessels that at long intervals dropped anchor in the harbor.

Then, as the first half of the nineteenth century drew toward a close, came a series of dramatic events, each following close on the other, that raised the village from its obscurity and focused on it the attention of the world: On June 14, 1846, a group of Yankee settlers from the Sacramento Valley took over the town of Sonoma and announced the establishment of the short-lived California Republic; three weeks later, on July 9, United States troops under Commodore John D. Sloat occupied the Mexican capital at Monterey; and on July 11, John B. Montgomery, captain of the U.S.S. *Portsmouth*, completed the occupation of the northern half of the province by raising the American flag above the plaza at Yerba Buena.

On January 24, 1848, gold was discovered on the south fork of the American River, and eight days later, on February 2, the signing of the Treaty of Guadalupe Hidalgo ended the war with Mexico and ceded California to the United States. By the end of 1849 the former village of Yerba Buena—which at the time of the conquest had had fewer than four hundred inhabitants—had become a city of thirty-five thousand.

The next half dozen years were crowded with incident. The burgeoning city was six times swept by fire and six times rebuilt. A long struggle to put down violence and establish a respect for law and order culminated in the Vigilance committees of 1851 and 1856. Sand hills were leveled and used to fill in the shallows of Yerba Buena Cove. Streets were laid out, paved with redwood planks, and lined with scores of substantial buildings of brick or stone, which housed banks, wholesale and retail firms, newspaper offices, theaters, schools, and other facilities befitting the city's position as the financial, commercial, and cultural capital of the West Coast.

But unlike the happenings in some cities, the stirring events of San Francisco's past did not all take place during its formative years. Its periods of tranquility have been both infrequent and brief. Hardly had the yield of the Sierra gold fields begun to slacken when the discovery of the surpassingly rich Comstock Lode bolstered the city's sagging economy and ushered in a second period of lavish spending: for hotels, office buildings, banks, and theaters in the downtown area, and, on the heights above, a cluster of baroque wooden mansions. By the time the output of the Nevada silver mines in turn had begun to decline, the great ranches of the interior valley had come into full production, and the port of San Francisco took on new life as each year immense quantities of California wheat were shipped to the markets of the world.

Each decade thereafter had its memorable events: In the 1880s the bitter anti-Chinese agitation and labor disputes; in the 1890s, the first of the city's three world fairs and, as the decade ended, the Klondike gold rush and the war with Spain, followed by the period of growth and prosperity that marked the first years of the new century and ended abruptly on the morning of April 18, 1906. Next came the rebuilding of the ruined city and, in rapid succession, a thorough political house-cleaning, a second world fair, and the First World War. Coming down to recent times, the city witnessed the booming 1920s and the depression-ridden 1930s, the building of the bay bridges, and the Second World War. Finally, it has been called on to cope with the opportunities and challenges of the past twenty years, a period that brought about changes and problems that have affected virtually every phase of the economic and social life of its people.

One who undertakes to compile a history of a city with so diverse a background as San Francisco's faces several difficulties. The first is the problem of holding the narrative down to a moderate length while omitting nothing essential. A second is that of striking a proper balance—that is, of avoiding the temptation to dwell overlong on certain picturesque or dramatic happenings and to slight others that, although less colorful, are of equal or perhaps greater importance. On the other hand, the historian's task is made easier by the fact that San Francisco is one of the most thoroughly documented American cities; hence, there is no lack of material from which to draw. For from its beginning San Francisco has been written about more frequently and at greater length, and from a wider variety of viewpoints than almost any other city on the continent.

Since the amount of material relating to the city is already so large as to constitute an embarrassment of riches, why, it might be asked, should one add to it? The answer is that although numerous books relating to San Francisco are now in print (many of which make entertaining and rewarding reading), all deal with special phases of the subject and none presents the over-all picture. The present work attempts to provide an inclusive (but not over-long) factual account of the city's evolution from its earliest beginnings to the present—one that suggests the venturesome spirit and the qualities of tolerance and light-hearted gaiety that have won it a unique place among the cities of the world.

Suggestions for those who wish to read further about the subject will be found in the list of books at the end of this volume.

OSCAR LEWIS

San Francisco, 1966

This air view of the tip of the San Francisco peninsula shows the dramatic changes that have taken place there since the mission and presidio were founded in 1776. Today a world-renowned city of more than three-quarters of a million occupies the site.

Contents

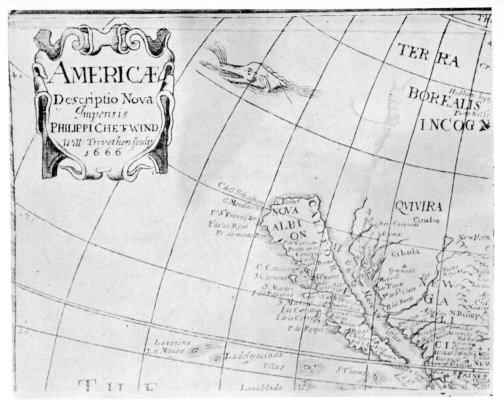

These early maps show California as an island, as it was often depicted by map makers of the 17th century and earlier.

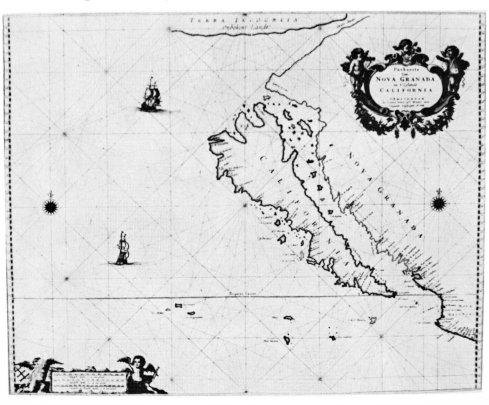

I

Discovery and Settlement

1. THE ELUSIVE BAY

The first voyage of Columbus ushered in an age of exploration that enormously extended the boundaries of the known world. Yet by a curious combination of circumstances, close to three centuries were to pass before the first white men set foot on the shores of San Francisco Bay.

The fact, however, that the discovery of that great land-locked harbor was so long delayed does not mean that California itself shared the same fate. Indeed, the first ship passed along its coast only fifty years after Columbus' little fleet set sail from Cadiz. This was the *San Salvador*, commanded by Juan Rodriguez Cabrillo, a Portuguese explorer sailing under the flag of Spain.

Cabrillo and his party left Navidad, on the west coast of Mexico, in the fall of 1542 and proceeded up the coast, keeping close to shore and charting and conferring names on headlands, inlets, islands, and other landmarks. The expedition penetrated as far as Point Arena (which its cartographer christened Cabo de Fortunas), then having encountered rough weather and adverse winds, turned about and again headed south. During the return voyage Cabrillo suffered a broken arm, from the effect of which he died. He was buried on San Miguel, one of the Channel Islands off the Southern California coast, on January 3, 1543.

Following the commander's death, the *San Salvador's* pilot, Bartolomé Ferrelo, resumed the survey, sailing up the coast to a point opposite the present California-Oregon border. Like Cabrillo before him, Ferrelo twice passed the entrance to San Francisco Bay without seeing it; however, his charts show the Farallone Islands which lie opposite the Golden Gate, about 30 miles offshore.

Thirty-seven years passed before the next ship appeared off the coast. This was the *Golden Hind*, flagship of the English freebooter Francis Drake. Drake's ship, heavily laden with booty captured during the sack of Spanish ports and from treasure-laden galleons on the west coast of South America, reached Northern California waters in June, 1579. Its commander, who was anxious to get his rich booty safely back to England, well knew that if he attempted to return by way of the Strait of Magellan, his victims would be on the lookout for him. He accordingly decided to cross the Pacific and attempt to reach his home port by rounding the Cape of Good Hope.

The *Golden Hind* headed north to take advantage of the prevailing winds that would speed its progress across the ocean. On arriving off the California coast, however, Drake decided to beach his ship—which had already been two years at sea—and put it in condition for the long return voyage. The precise spot on the California coast where he first sighted land is unknown, though it was probably in the vicinity of Humboldt Bay. From there he proceeded southward, searching for what the ship's chaplain, Francis Fletcher, described as "a convenient and fit harborough."

The place where the party landed was, according to most authorities, the inlet now known as Drake's Bay, which lies in the lee of Point Reyes, some twenty-five miles north of the Golden Gate. One reason for believing that this bay was the landing place is Chaplain Fletcher's reference to "white bancks and cliffs" along the shore, which he likened to the chalk cliffs of Dover, and which are to be found only in that part of the California coast. During their six weeks' stay, the party was received with friendliness by the native Indian tribe, the Coast Miwoks, whose members frequently visited the strangers' camp.

Before setting sail for England on July 23, 1579, Drake christened the land New Albion, claimed it in the name of his sovereign, Queen Elizabeth, and "caused to be set up . . . a plate of brasse fast nailed to a great and firm post; whereon is graven her graces name, and the day and year of our arrival here, and the free giving up, of the province and kingdom . . . into her majesties hands . . . ; together with her highnesse picture and arms in a piece of sixpence current English monies, shewing itself by a hole made of purpose through the plate."

By one of the fortunate accidents of history, this venerable "plate of brasse," after having dropped from sight for more than 350 years, was recovered in the summer of 1936 at a spot only a few miles from where it had originally been nailed to its "great and firm post." For some time after its recovery the question of whether the plate was genuine was widely debated. But after examinations by experts in Elizabethan language and calligraphy, and a chemical analysis of-the metal, the authenticity of the plate was established beyond a reasonable doubt.

After leaving the California coast Drake succeeded in bringing the *Golden Hind* back to England, and as a reward for having circumnavigated the globe (and for delivering his booty into the royal treasury) was knighted by his grateful queen.

Not so fortunate was the Portuguese navigator Sebastián Cermeño, who was the next visitor to the California coast. For Cermeño left behind property far more valuable than Drake's brass plate; that is, his ship, the

Drake's "Plate of Brasse," now in the Bancroft Library.

San Augustin, together with its cargo of silks, porcelains, spices, and other products of the Orient. In the early 1590s Cermeño had been commissioned by Luis de Velasco, Viceroy of New Spain, to make a trading voyage to the Far East. His orders were that on his return across the Pacific, he was to touch on the California coast and there locate a safe harbor where ships in the Oriental trade could break their long eastward voyages and take on supplies before continuing southward to their home ports on Mexico's west coast.

Cermeño left the Philippines on July 5, 1595. Four months later he sighted land in the vicinity of Point Reyes and, as Drake had done sixteen years earlier, rounded the point and dropped anchor in the crescent-shaped bay. During the next few weeks the crew camped on the beach while needed repairs were made on the ship, and a small launch that had been carried in knockdown form on the deck was taken ashore and assembled. This was fortunate because in late November a violent storm broke the *San Augustin* from her mooring and carried her ashore. Both ship and cargo were lost, along with several of the crew. The survivors, about seventy, set out for the south in their open launch. After a grueling voyage of seven weeks they succeeded in reaching their home port of Acapulco. In recent years a party of archeologists examining Indian campsites in the Point Reyes area in search of relics of Drake's visit, came on a number of hand-wrought ship's spikes and bits of Chinese pottery, which from their age and design are believed to have come from the wreckage of the *San Augustin.*

Seven years after Cermeño's ill-fated visit, one of the officers of the lost ship, Sebastián Vizcaíno, led an expedition north to continue the search for a harbor where the Manila galleons might safely put in. Like others before him, Vizcaíno failed to discover the Bay of San Francisco—which would have provided an ideal solution to the problem—however, he charted the coastline more carefully and in greater detail than his predecessors and named many of its physical features. On December 2, 1602, he put in at Monterey Bay and took formal possession of the land in the name of the Spanish king. An account of the expedition, written by Father Antonio de la Ascensión, has much to say of the beauty of the country and the richness of its resources.

The departure of the Vizcaíno party was followed by a long pause in the story of the exploration of Alta California. During those years the conquest and colonization of South and Central America had occupied the chief attention of Spanish authorities at Madrid and Mexico City. Consequently, more than a century and a half passed before interest in the lands to the north revived. This came about because other European nations were extending their holdings in the New World, and in the process were drawing ever closer to California. By the middle of the eighteenth century Russia had established itself on the Alaskan peninsula and was moving southward, and England had begun to press its claim to the territory, a claim based on Francis Drake's visit in 1579.

In the mid-1760s the Spanish king, Charles III, belatedly realized that if his hold on Alta California were to be maintained, steps must be taken to establish permanent colonies there and to man them with a military force strong enough to repel foreign aggression. As a first step in carrying out that plan, a numerous party of soldiers and civilians was assembled in Mexico and, early in 1769, began the long trek to the north. The expedition was divided into four parts, two of which were to travel by land, and two by sea. Don Gaspar de Portolá, a captain in the Spanish army, was named governor of Alta and Baja California and placed in over-all charge of the enterprise. It was a difficult journey for all four parties, but particularly so for those who went overland. For the latter had to pass over hundreds of miles of rugged countryside, much of it waterless and without sustenance for man or beast. However, in June the four travel-weary groups had reassembled at San Diego Bay. On June 16 Father Junípero Serra, who had traveled with one of the overland parties, blessed the site of the Mission San Diego de Alcalá, first of the twenty-one missions Franciscan priests were to establish in California during the next half century.

Portolá's stay at San Diego was brief. His real objective was Monterey Bay, where Vizcaíno had landed, and which Father de la Ascensión had described in glowing terms 167 years earlier. Accordingly, Portolá continued northward, taking with him the men and animals that were physically able to travel. The route followed by this first party of white men to travel by land up the California coast, paralleled the shore line most of the way, turning inland only at points where the mountains rose directly from the edge of the sea. To avoid one such barrier — presented by the Santa Lucia range — the group crossed over to the Salinas Valley.

It was that change of direction that led indirectly to the party's discovery of San Francisco Bay. For by following an inland route Portolá approached the Bay of Monterey from the east rather than the south. The result was that he failed to recognize the landmarks depicted on the Vizcaíno chart and passed on up the coast, continuing his search for the elusive bay.

During the last week of October the party approached ever nearer the unknown body of water that lay ahead. By the 23rd they had reached the lower end of the San Francisco Peninsula; on the 27th they crossed Purísima Creek, and on the 29th camped beside a second stream, the Pilarcitos, which flows into the ocean a little distance north of the present town of Half Moon Bay. There they again found their way blocked, this time by the steep cliffs on the seaward side of Montara Mountain. While most of the party rested in camp, Portolá sent several men up the western shoulder of the mountain to learn what lay ahead. From the spot where they stood after reaching the top the bay itself was not visible, being hidden from their sight by the ridge of hills that lay to the east. They did, however, have a clear view of the Farallone Islands and of the coastline as far north as Point Reyes.

The men's report of what they had seen was a keen disappointment to the expedition's commander. For both the Farallones and Point Reyes were clearly indicated on Vizcaíno's chart, and both were far to the north of the bay he was seeking. Realizing at last that he had overshot the mark, Portolá made camp beside San Pablo Creek while he debated what his next move would be. His decision was to continue up the coast as far as Point Arena before returning to San Diego. Accordingly, on November 1, he sent his chief scout, Sergeant José Ortega, and several companions to spy out the country ahead and find a feasible route to be followed by the main party.

Ortega's little group made their way up the shore line toward the tip of the San Francisco Peninsula. They proceeded along what is now the ocean beach, passed Seal Rocks and, a short distance beyond, found their progress blocked by an arm of the sea that extended inland and formed the outer entrance to the Golden Gate. Following along the edge of the cliffs, the group reached the crest of a ridge of hills and stared in surprise at what they saw. Spread out before them and extending for miles to the north and south and east was a great body of water: it was the Bay of San Francisco.

On returning to the main camp on November 3, Ortega and his companions learned that during their absence a party of hunters had climbed

The discovery of San Francisco Bay by members of the Portolá expedition on November 2, 1769, is depicted in this painting by Walter Francis.

Mount Montara and from there had viewed the southern arm of the bay and the Santa Clara Valley beyond.

Curiously, Portolá and his men failed to recognize the significance of their discovery. To them this body of water was merely an obstacle that prevented their further progress up the coast. Discouraged, they turned about and retraced their steps to Monterey — which they this time recognized — then continued on to the south. The bedraggled party reached San Diego on January 24, 1770; they had been absent more than five months.

2. JUAN BAUTISTA DE ANZA

When Portolá returned to San Diego, he found the party he had left behind in sorry condition, with their supplies almost exhausted, and many suffering from illness. Up to that point the plan of founding permanent settlements in the new land had met with little success, and discouragement and discontent were widespread. However, the timely arrival of two shiploads of men and material from Baja California relieved much of the distress, and the spirits of the party revived.

With the coming of spring Don Gaspar led a second group north to Monterey Bay. This time he was accompanied by two Franciscan priests, Father Junípero Serra and Juan Crespi. For the plan was to found not only a military post beside the bay, but a mission as well. The company arrived at Monterey toward the end of May, 1770, and on June 3 dedicated the sites of the two establishments. The ceremony marking the founding of the mission is said to have taken place beneath the identical oak under which Sebastián Vizcaíno had stood when he took possession of the country in the name of the Spanish king more than a century and a half earlier.

Once the building of the Monterey outposts was under way, Portolá returned to San Diego, leaving his lieutenant, Pedro Fages, in charge. Under the latter's direction San Francisco Bay was further explored. In the fall of 1770 Fages led a party northward, seeking, as Portolá had done the previous year, a practicable route to Point Reyes. After passing through the Salinas and Santa Clara valleys, the group proceeded up the east side of the bay to the spot where Berkeley now stands. From the crest of the Berkeley hills they saw that their way was barred by the arm of San Pablo Bay, whereupon they abandoned their plan of continuing farther and returned to Monterey.

Lieutenant Fages, however, was not easily discouraged and made a new attempt two years later, in 1772. This time he was accompanied by Father Crespi, whose diary preserves a detailed account of their travels. From it we learn that the party camped overnight near present-day Hayward, passed the sites of Mills College and Oakland, and paused beside Strawberry Creek, which flows through the campus of the University of California. From high on the Berkeley hills they viewed the broad panorama of the bay, then continued on, skirting the shore of San Pablo Bay. Then, finding that body of water too wide to cross, they also returned to Monterey.

Spain's program of colonization, in Alta California, as elsewhere in its New World possessions, followed a set pattern. This consisted in founding three types of settlements: military posts called presidios, missions designed to convert the natives and train them in the ways of civilization, and pueblos serving the needs of European settlers and of the domesticated Indians.

The bringing in of the settlers who would cultivate the land and make it productive got under way in 1774. In the spring of that year a large party of civilian emigrants, together with soldiers to protect them and livestock and tools needed to establish themselves in their new homes, set out from the town of Tubac in the province of Sonora in northern Mexico. Their leader was Juan Bautista de Anza, a captain in the Spanish army and a veteran of the frontier. Something of the importance attached to that enterprise by the officials at Mexico City may be gathered from the fact that when Anza set about assembling his party he personally selected those members best qualified to stand the hardships of the long overland journey and the primitive conditions awaiting them at its end.

The party's march through hundreds of miles of barren and inhospitable country constitutes a feat of endurance rarely equaled in the early West. The group left Tubac on September 29, 1775, and reached the newly founded San Gabriel Mission, near present-day Pasadena, early the following January. After a brief pause there, Anza led them up the coast to Monterey, then returned to Sonora and prepared to pilot another and larger party over the same route. By the time this second expedition reached Monterey plans had been completed for a second move: that of founding a mission and a presidio on the shore of San Francisco Bay.

In that venture too the tireless Captain Anza played a leading part. Leaving the remainder of his party, which numbered some 240 men, women, and children, to recuperate from their journey, he and a few companions set off up the coast. They arrived at the tip of the San Francisco Peninsula on March 28, and, after a thorough inspection of the terrain, Anza had two crosses set up. One, near the southern entrance to the harbor, marked the location of the future presidio. The second cross, designating the place where the mission would be built, lay about three miles to the southeast. That accomplished, he and his companions--Father Pedro Font, Lieutenant José Moraga, and eleven soldiers—passed around the southern end of the bay, followed its east shore to a point beyond the Carquinez Strait, then returned to Monterey, which they reached on April 8. The captain then returned to Sonora and resumed his duties as commandant of the presidio at Tubac.

Of his parting from those he had led through so many hardships and dangers he wrote:

In the fall of 1775 Captain Juan Bautista de Anza led a party of 240 colonists from Sonora, Mexico, to California. After a long and exhausting march the expedition reached the site of the future city of San Francisco on March 28, 1776, as shown in a painting by Walter Francis.

As I mounted my horse in the Plaza [at Monterey] the greater part of the people I had brought from their country, and particularly the women, remembering the treatment, good or bad, they had experienced under my command, were dissolved in tears, which they shed publicly, not so much because of their banishment as because of my departure, and with embraces and wishes for my happiness bade me farewell, giving me praises I did not deserve. I was deeply moved by their gratitude and affection, which I reciprocate, and I testify that from the beginning up to today I have not seen any sign of desertion in any of those whom I have brought from their country to remain in this distant place; and in praise of their fidelity I may be permitted to make this memorial of a people who in the course of time will come to be very useful to the monarchy in whose service they have voluntarily left parents and country, which is everything one can abandon.

Thus passed from the scene this indomitable figure whose courage and resourcefulness helped make possible the establishment of the first permanent settlements on the San Francisco Peninsula.

3. MISSION AND PRESIDIO

Although the sites of the presidio and mission were chosen and marked in late March of 1776, more than six months passed before their building began. The delay was caused by serious opposition to the plan that had meanwhile developed. Fernando de Rivera y Moncada, who had succeeded Portolá, had all along contended that the soldiers and civilians of the Anza parties were needed at the settlements already established and that the founding of those to the north should be put off until some future time. Anza, who was acting on orders from his superiors in Mexico, rejected Rivera's suggestion that his party be broken up and distributed among the existing presidios and missions.

As a result of the ill-feeling between the two men, Rivera, after Anza's departure, ignored the urging of Lieutenant Moraga and the mission priests that they be permitted to carry out the original plan. It was not until several months later that Rivera received instructions from Mexico City that forced him to yield. His enabling order, however, which was issued on May 8, provided for the founding of a presidio only. His failure to authorize the building of a mission was ignored by the churchmen, and when Lieutenant Moraga led the first party of settlers north in mid-June they were accompanied by Father Francisco Palou. The group arrived at the tip of the peninsula on June 28, camped overnight at the site of the mission, and there on the following day Father Palou conducted the first Mass.

Moraga and the soldiers of the party camped on the site where the presidio would be built, and while waiting for the arrival of other members of the expedition—who were making the trip aboard the supply ship *San Carlos*—then set about preparing the ground for the first buildings. It was during this period that the wife of one of the soldiers gave birth to a daughter—the first white child to be born within the boundaries of the future city.

The Spanish supply ship *San Carlos,* the first vessel to ply the waters of the bay, entered the Golden Gate in the fall of 1775. She was under command of Lieutenant Juan Manuel de Ayala.

The Officers' Club at the Presidio is one of the two oldest buildings in San Francisco, the other being the Mission Dolores. Both
structures date from the 1770s. Since this photograph was taken
the building has been restored to conform more closely to its
original appearance. *(The California Historical Society.)*

The *San Carlos,* which had been more than two months at sea on the
passage up from Monterey, eventually put into port in mid-September.
Men and supplies were landed, and on the 17th cannon boomed from the
deck of the little craft, while the flag of Spain was raised above the make-
shift headquarters of the new military post. Thus the founding of San
Francisco's first settlement was officially celebrated. Three weeks later, on
October 9, Father Palou dedicated a temporary church beside the Laguna
de los Dolores (the Lake of Sorrows). This, sixth in order of founding of
the California missions, was christened San Francisco de Asís in honor of
the patron saint of the Franciscan order.

The original mission building served until 1782 when work began on
a new and larger church, which was completed nine years later. This building, standing today and known as the Mission Dolores, and the commandant's house at the presidio, comprise the city's only remaining links with
its earliest beginnings. Dolores is small as compared with others of the
mission chain, but is one of the best preserved and retains many features
characteristic of California mission architecture. Its four-foot-thick walls
are made of adobe bricks, protected from the weather by a coating of
plaster. The red-tile roof is supported by hand-hewn redwood timbers held
together with thongs of rawhide and by pegs made from the wood of man-
zanita shrubs.

Both the mission and the commandant's house (the latter now serves
as an officers' club) fell to partial ruin during the final years of the Mexican
regime, and both were later rebuilt. Of the two, the mission was least
changed by the restoration. Although the cluster of buildings of which it
was the center—living quarters for the padres and their Indian charges,

workrooms, shops, and warehouses—have long since disappeared, the church itself remains much as it was originally, both inside and out.

It is a long, narrow building with a high wooden ceiling that still bears traces of once bright decorations applied by the mission Indians under the direction of the priests. A number of objects dating from the Spanish-Mexican period are still in use. In the peak of the roof hang three brass bells cast in Mexico during the middle of the eighteenth century.

In the city's first cemetery, which adjoins the mission to the south, are the graves of many closely identified with San Francisco's beginnings. Among the headstones still to be seen are those of Luís Argüello, first governor of California under Mexican rule, Francisco de Haro, first *alcalde* of the village of Yerba Buena, and James Casey and Charles Cora, two criminals who were hanged by the Vigilance Committee of 1856.

4. INDIAN TRIBES

The mission was established to Christianize the Indians of the region and train them in the ways of civilization. This, as events were to prove, was no easy task. For the natives of the area were singularly unenterprising members of their race. They lived in small villages on the banks of streams or beside the ocean or bay, their shelters rude huts made of tule reeds or the skins of animals. Their food was fish, mussels, seaweed, or small animals, which they either ate raw or broiled over campfires. Their handicrafts were limited to fashioning the implements necessary to their survival: bows and arrows, fish nets and spears, mortars and pestles for grinding acorns or the seeds of wild grasses, baskets woven of rushes, and braided snares used to trap birds or small animals.

Four tribes lived about the bay: the Coast Miwoks in present-day Marin County, the Wintuns on the north shore of San Pablo Bay, the Yokuts south of the Carquinez Strait, and the Costanoans on the east and west sides of the bay's southern arm, including the San Francisco Peninsula. When the *Golden Hind* had anchored in Drake's Bay in 1579, the first party to go ashore had seen "several huts on the waterside." On drawing near they had observed that there was "a fire in the middle of each house, with the people lying around it upon rushes." Francis Fletcher, the ship's chaplain, had added: "The men go quite naked, but the women have a deerskin over their shoulders, and round their waist a covering of bulrushes after the manner of hemp."

Fletcher's account continues:

The people bringing the admiral a present of feathers and cauls of network, he entertained them so kindly and generously that they were extremely pleased, and soon after they sent him a present of feathers and bags of tobacco. A number of them coming

In their frail boats fashioned from tule reeds the Indians of the region were skilled at navigating the often rough and dangerous waters of the bay. This drawing was made in 1816 by Louis Choris.

to deliver it, gathered themselves together at the top of a small hill, from the highest point of which one of them harangued the admiral, whose tent was placed at the bottom. When the speech was ended they lay down their arms and came down, offering their presents, at the same time returning what the admiral had given them. The women remaining on the hill, tearing their hair and making dreadful howlings, the admiral supposed them engaged in making sacrifices, and thereupon ordered divine service to be held, at which these people attended with astonishment.

The natives thus described were the Coast Miwoks. For our first glimpse of the Costanoans, we are indebted to a second English visitor, Captain Woodes Rogers, who visited the coast in 1709.

They lived in huts of boughs and leaves, erected in the form of bowers, with a fire before the door, around which they lay and slept. The men were quite naked and the women had only a short petticoat reaching scarcely to the knee, made of . . . grass, or the skins of pelicans or deers. . . . The men are straight and well built, having long black hair, and are of a dark brown complexion. They live by hunting and fishing. They use bows and arrows, and are excellent marksmen. The women, whose features are rather disagreeable, are employed in making fishing lines, and in gathering grain (doubtless what grew spontaneously), which they grind upon a stone. The people are willing to assist the English in filling water, and would supply them with whatever they could get; and are a very honest people, and would not take the least thing without permission.

As this description makes clear, the Costanoans were friendly and docile by nature. When the mission was first established they willingly became wards of the padres, accepting the food and clothing and shelter offered them and submitting to the discipline of mission life. But after they had been indoctrinated into the white man's religion and put to work making adobe bricks, tilling the newly laid-out fields, or tending the mission herds, they soon became restless. At the local mission, as at others up and down the coast, many slipped away and returned to their ancestral hunting grounds.

The defection of their Indian charges was, however, but one of the problems faced by the local padres. For almost from the beginning it had become clear that the Mission Dolores was not destined to grow and prosper to the extent of many others of the chain. The steep hills and sandy soil of the upper peninsula were manifestly unsuited to large-scale argriculture, and early efforts to grow corn, grain, and other crops had such meager results that the effort was soon abandoned. Thereafter only enough was produced to supply local needs. This was true, too, of that other mainstay of the mission economy, the raising of cattle. For the region's brush-covered hills and valleys offered too little forage to support herds of any size. The result was that many locally recruited and trained neophytes were transferred to the Santa Clara Mission, which had been established in 1777; later some were also sent to San Rafael and Sonoma, the northernmost missions of the chain.

5. NATIVE HANDICRAFTS

Although the Mission Dolores never became as large or prosperous as many other California missions, it long remained the most important settlement north of Monterey. Its population was comparatively small, yet it much exceeded that of the presidio—the garrison of which rarely numbered more than twenty soldiers—and while few crops or cattle were raised there, a wide variety of other activities were carried on. A book entitled *Voyage Pittoresque Autour du Monde,* published in Paris in 1822, gives an excellent description, both in pictures and text, of life at the mission during its period of greatest activity. The author-artist, Louis (Ludovic) Choris, a Russian of German descent, visited the bay in the fall of 1816 aboard the Russian exploring ship *Rurik.*

Choris described the mission community as "a fair-sized village" with a population of about fifteen hundred Indians, who were supplied with food, clothing, and shelter by the padres and in return worked in the mission shops, cultivated the gardens and truck farms, or watched over the horses and cows that grazed on the neighboring hills. The crops included corn, wheat, peas, beans, and potatoes. Food was prepared in a community kitchen, to which a member of each family came at mealtime to receive the family allotment. The natives lived in small barracks-like buildings, each of which sheltered two or more families. Besides working in the community fields and gardens, each family was assigned a plot of land for its own use. These the families cultivated during their free time. Among the products they raised were onions, garlic, cantaloupes, watermelons, and pumpkins; some plots were also planted to fruit trees and berry and grapevines.

Choris reported that the number of Indians at the mission varied with the seasons, being largest during the winter months and declining sharply each spring when many rejoined their tribes and resumed their former way of life. Some returned in the fall, often bringing with them new recruits, while others, having regained their freedom, refused to surrender it again, and the mission fields and workshops saw them no more.

The Russian visitor concluded that although some neophytes were content with their lot, most of them were unable to adjust to an environment so different from what their ancestors had known for many generations. "After several months spent in the missions," he wrote, "they usually begin to grow fretful and thin, and they constantly gaze with sadness at the mountains which they can see in the distance." He believed that only those who had been born at the missions, or had spent the greater part of their lives there, were long content to remain and practice the simple skills taught them by the padres.

At the time of Choris' visit the weaving of woolen cloth was one of the chief industries at the local mission. He described a large workroom in which twenty looms were being operated, most of them by squaws. There were also two gristmills. These, which were operated by mulepower, produced flour for the mission and the presidio. When there was a surplus it was sold to the masters of ships that from time to time entered the harbor. As time passed, a considerable trade with such visitors was built up by the padres, who bartered the products of the mission fields and shops for goods brought aboard the trading ships that were making regular visits.

The Indians were permitted to retain many of their native customs. After Mass on Sunday mornings they gathered in the open space before the chapel and held their tribal dances.

> Half the men [wrote Choris] adorn themselves with feathers and girdles ornamented with feathers and bits of shells that pass for money, or they paint their bodies with regular lines of black, red and white. . . . Others sift the down from birds on their hair. The men commonly dance six or eight together, all making the same movements and all armed with spears. Their music consists of clapping of hands, singing, and the sound made by striking split sticks together, which has a charm to their ears. The women dance among themselves, but without violent motions.

Another favorite amusement was gambling. A number of games were played; the commonest of which consisted of tossing bits of wood at designated spots on the ground, their position on landing determining the winner. On this and other tests of skill or luck they cheerfully wagered whatever they possessed: weapons, tools, ornaments, even their food and clothing.

Choris considered native crafts of the Costanoans and Coast Miwoks inferior to those of the tribes farther south, whose finely wrought baskets he greatly admired. Natives of the bay region were, however, highly skilled at making spears and bows and arrows, and at fashioning arrowheads. The last-named were made from pieces of glasslike obsidian rock. From it the native artisans, using stone implements, fashioned the slender, symmetrical heads, chipping their edges and points to a razorlike sharpness. Because their ancestral hunting grounds bordered on the bay, the local tribes were expert boatsmen. Their frail canoes, made of tule reeds, lay so low in the water that their occupants often sat in water halfway to their knees while they plied their two-bladed oars.

6. A NEGLECTED OUTPOST

The Secularization Act of 1833 put an end to the missionaries' long and determined effort to Christianize the natives. That act removed the neophytes from the supervision and guidance of the padres, and all except a small part of the church land was thrown open to settlement. The result was disastrous to the Indian charges. Many who had spent their entire lives as wards of the church, were unable either to revert to the habits of their ancestors or to become useful members of the white man's world. At home in neither environment, they drifted aimlessly about. Some remained in the vicinity of the deteriorating mission establishments or congregated in the seaport towns, where they lived in squalor, falling easy victims to the vices of the Europeans. Others found a dubious refuge at the cattle ranches that sprang up on the former mission lands, and there were held in a condition not far removed from serfdom.

Duflot de Mofras, an attaché of the French Embassy at Mexico City, visited the Mission Dolores in 1841. He found the mission property falling to ruin, its fields overgrown with weeds, and its herds of cattle, horses, and sheep long since dissipated. Of the four hundred Indians who had lived there eight years earlier, less than fifty remained. These occupied the few buildings that still stood and gained a precarious livelihood by raising corn, potatoes, and other vegetables. No priest was then in residence at the Mission, though from time to time services were held by a Father Marcado, who came up for that purpose from Santa Clara.

De Mofras found the local presidio in an even worse state of disrepair than the mission. Most of the buildings grouped about the original quadrangle, once used as storerooms, workshops, and living quarters for the soldiers, were deserted, their roofs and adobe walls fallen to ruin. Only the commandant's house and one barracks were still occupied. This northernmost of the military posts in Alta California had never been strongly held. From the beginning the main military force in the province had been concentrated at Monterey, the capital. After Mexico had gained its inde-

The Mission Dolores, as it was in the early 1840s, was drawn by an unknown artist. The mission cemetery, where many of the city's pioneers are buried, is shown on the left.

pendence from Spain in 1821, the number of troops stationed at the San Francisco presidio had declined steadily. At the time of de Mofras's visit the garrison consisted of only "a sublieutenant and five soldiers and their families."

When the British sloop-of-war *Blossom* had dropped anchor in the bay sixteen years earlier, in 1825, the deterioration of the presidio was already far advanced. Its small garrison was in sorry straits, their pay more than ten years in arrears, and the men and their families dependent on the mission for food, clothing, and other necessities. The *Blossom's* captain, Frederick William Beechey, described the presidio as "little better than a heap of rubbish and bones, on which jackals, dogs and vultures were constantly preying." He added that the entire presidio had been built "in the humblest style," and that only the commandant's house and the chapel had their adobe outer walls whitewashed. His account continues:

Viewed from a distance or near, the establishment impresses a spectator with any other sentiment than that of its being a place of authority, and but for a tottering flagstaff upon which was occasionally displayed the tricolored flag of Mexico, three rusty field-pieces, and a half-accoutered sentinel parading the gateway in charge of a few poor wretches heavily shackled, a visitor would be ignorant of the importance of the place. The neglect of the government of its establishments could not be more thoroughly evinced than in the delapidated condition of the buildings in question; and

such was the dissatisfaction of the people that there was no incli-
nation to improve their condition, or even to remedy many of the
evils which they appeared to have the power to remove.

Yet another visitor to the bay, whose ship, the *Rurik,* preceded that of
Captain Beechey by nine years, was Otto von Kotzebue, captain of the
Russian Imperial Navy. The *Rurik,* which was on an exploring expedition,
arrived in the fall of 1816 and remained several weeks. The diary of Adel-
bert von Chamisso, the expedition's naturalist, makes clear that relations
between the two bay settlements were sometimes badly strained. During
the *Rurik's* stay visits were exchanged between the ship's officers and the
soldiers at the presidio, who were commanded by Lieutenant Luís Argüello.

> We ate on shore [wrote Chamisso] in a tent, and our friends
> at the presidio were always promptly on hand. This condition of
> things rose spontaneously. The misery in which they languished,
> forgotten and deserted for six or seven years by Mexico, their
> motherland, did not permit them to be hosts; and the need felt to
> pour out their hearts to someone, drove them to us, with whom
> they live easily and comfortably. They spoke with bitterness of the
> missionaries, who, with all the lack of provisions, yet lived having
> an abundance of the produce of the earth. Now that their money
> was spent, the missionaries would deliver to them nothing without
> a requisition, and even then only that which was absolutely indis-
> pensable to their sustenance; this not including bread or meal; so
> that for years, without seeing bread, they lived on maize.

The discontented soldiers blamed their plight in part on the failure
of their commander to insist that the mission authorities provide them with
more and better supplies. Chamisso continues: "A soldier went further, and
complained to us that the commandante would not permit them to press
natives from the opposite shore, in order to force them to work for the
soldiers, as they did for the missions. Discontent rose too because the new
governor at Monterey, Pablo Vicente de Solá, since his entry upon the
duties of his office, set himself in opposition to smuggling, which alone had
provided them with the most indispensable necessities."

But despite the hardships and neglect they were called on to endure,
residents of the isolated communities beside the bay did not find life altogether intolerable. Lighthearted and fun-loving by nature, these sons and
daughters of Spain contrived to while away the tedium of existence with
music, fiestas, and other diversions of their homeland. One favorite amusement, to which they resorted on fete days, was bull-and-bear fights. These
were held in the open space before the mission and were witnessed by the
entire population of the peninsula, Indians and whites alike.

Such contests required days of preparation. First, a party of horsemen was dispatched to the interior to capture a bear. This they accomplished by killing a horse or bullock for use as bait. They then concealed themselves nearby, and when the victim appeared, the *vaqueros*, who were all skilled in the use of the lasso, roped it and, after tying it securely, placed it on a sled and dragged it to the mission. Meanwhile a wild bull had been captured in somewhat the same manner. On the day of the contest the two were tied together with a long rope and placed in a stockade. The contest between the two enraged beasts was usually brief, but while it lasted the excitement of the spectators was intense.

When foreign ships put into the harbor bull-and-bear fights were usually staged for the entertainment of the newcomers. These did not always enjoy the spectacle. Wrote one visitor: "Unwilling and bound as the animals were, the spectacle had in it nothing great or praiseworthy. One pitied the poor beasts, who were so shamefully handled." Another commented: "These battles were the everlasting topics of conversation with the Californians, who indeed have very little else to talk about."

For well over a half century the mission and the presidio remained the only settlements on the peninsula, or indeed anywhere on the shores of San Francisco Bay. During that period both enjoyed a brief season of growth and activity, then went into a long decline, victims of the indifference and neglect of the authorities at Mexico City and Monterey. The time came, however, when it became evident that the region's isolation from the rest of the world was soon to end. For with the growth of maritime trade on the Pacific the fame of the great landlocked harbor had spread, and each year a larger number of ships passed through the Golden Gate. From the 1830s on, the ships of the New England whaling fleet put in to take on wood, water, and other supplies before beginning the long cruise back to their home ports. Later in that decade the Boston traders began paying regular calls to barter manufactured goods from the East for hides and tallow produced on the outlying cattle ranches. Meanwhile a thin trickle of settlers, the advance guard of hundreds who were to follow, had begun making their way westward across the plains and mountains into the rich valleys of the interior.

II

Yerba Buena

1. FRONTIER VILLAGE

Except for the Spanish supply ship *San Carlos*, the first vessel belonging to a European nation to enter San Francisco Bay was that of the English explorer George Vancouver. Vancouver had reached the Pacific Northwest in the summer of 1792 and, after spending several months in the vicinity of the island that now bears his name, had continued down the coast, and on the evening of November 14 passed through the Golden Gate. In the gathering darkness he failed to see the presidio buildings on the hillside near the harbor's entrance and proceeded several miles down the bay, then dropped anchor to await the coming of daylight. Next morning he discovered that his ship was lying off a small cove sheltered from the wind by two promontories and with a sandy beach on which small boats could land. It made an excellent anchorage.

No buildings were visible on the shore, and the only sign that the place might be inhabited was a few cattle grazing on the hillsides. Soon, however, a party of horsemen rode down to the beach. Vancouver sent a boat to take them aboard; when they arrived on deck he learned that they were from the mission and the presidio. They had come to welcome him and his men and to offer such hospitality as their limited resources permitted. He learned, too, that the spot where he had anchored was called Yerba Buena Cove. (The name Yerba Buena — meaning "good herb" — had been given it because of an aromatic shrub that grew about the shore.) During their stay in the harbor Vancouver and his party were frequently entertained at both local settlements. From the commandant at the presidio he received permission to set up a tent on the beach while taking on water, wood, and other supplies. This tent was the first shelter on the site of the future city.

Although more than forty years were to pass after Vancouver's departure before the first permanent building was put up on the shore of the cove, during the interval several other ships stopped there, their masters choosing the place in preference to the more exposed anchorage opposite the presidio. Among the earliest of these ships were the Russian frigate *Predpriatie* and the American schooner *Tarter*, which arrived in 1823 and 1824.

Yerba Buena (now San Francisco) in the spring of 1837. This picture is from a lithograph based on a drawing by Jean Jacques Vioget.

One reason why ships of other nations chose to put in at San Francisco Bay rather than at Monterey was that they could thereby avoid the heavy duties the Mexican authorities had imposed as a means of discouraging trade with foreigners. It was in the hope of preventing smuggling at this northern port that in 1827 Governor José Maria Echeandía had ordered a detachment of soldiers stationed at the cove. There is no evidence, however, that this order was ever carried out.

As the 1830s advanced the long-dormant economy of the bay area began to stir. As the former mission lands and other fertile areas were taken over and as the herds of the *rancheros* multiplied, a larger number of ships entered the lucrative hide and tallow trade. San Francisco Bay became a regular port of call for the trading ships. Their usual procedure was to anchor off Yerba Buena Cove and remain several weeks while small boats were dispatched to landing places up and down the bay to pick up cargo for the return voyage. Meanwhile the *rancheros* came aboard and selected the merchandise they were to receive in return for their hides and tallow: food, clothing, manufactured articles of many sorts, as well as such luxuries as jewelry, musical instruments, wine, and liquor.

A graphic description of Yerba Buena Cove as it was in the winter of 1835-36 is to be found in Richard Henry Dana's *Two Years Before the Mast*, first published in New York in 1840. Dana, then a youth of twenty, spent three weeks there as a member of the crew of the Boston trading ship *Alert*. The *Alert* arrived on December 4 and anchored in what Dana described as a "little harbor, or bight, called Yerba Buena." One other ship was in the cove, a Russian brig that had come down from Sitka to spend the winter and take on a cargo of tallow and grain.

Although the Secularization Act had been passed two years earlier, it had not yet been put into effect in the northern part of the province. Hence, while the Mission Dolores was already nearly deserted, other missions in the area were still active, and it was from these that the *Alert* obtained the bulk of her cargo.

How that business was conducted was thus described by Dana:

A few days after our arrival the rainy season set in, and for three weeks it rained almost every hour. . . . This was bad for our trade, for the collecting of hides is managed differently in this port than in any other on the coast. The Mission of Dolores, near the anchorage, has no trade at all; but those of San Jose, Santa Clara, and others situated on the large creeks or rivers, which run into the bay, and distant between fifteen and forty miles from the anchorage, do a greater business in hides than any in California. Large boats, or launches, manned by Indians, and capable of carrying from five to six hundred hides apiece, are attached to the Missions, and sent down to the vessels with hides, to bring away goods in return. Some of the crews of the vessels are obliged to come and go in the boats, to look out for the hides and goods. These are favorite expeditions with the sailors in fine weather; but now, to be gone three or four days, in open boats, in constant rain, without any shelter, and with cold food, was hard service.

The view of Yerba Buena Cove as seen from the deck of the *Alert* was described by the young Easterner in these words:

Beyond, to the westward of the landing-place were dreary sandhills, with little grass to be seen, and few trees, steep and barren, their sides gullied by the rain. Some five or six miles beyond the landing-place, to the right, was a ruined Presidio, and some three miles to the left was the Mission of Dolores, as ruinous as the Presidio, almost deserted, with but a few Indians attached to it, and very little property in cattle. Over a region far beyond our sight there were no human habitations, except that an enterprising Yankee, years in advance of his time, had put up, on the rising ground above the landing, a shanty of rough boards, where he carried on a very small retail trade between the hide ships and the Indians.

2. PIONEER TRADERS

The "enterprising Yankee" mentioned by Dana was William A. Richardson, an Englishman who had arrived in 1822 as first mate of the British whaler *Orion*. When his ship left he had remained behind and, although foreigners were ordinarily prohibited from taking up permanent residence in the province, had obtained permission from Governor Pablo Vicente de Solá to remain — largely, it was said, because of his knowledge of navigation and carpentry. The following year Richardson adopted the Catholic faith and was baptized at the local mission; in 1825 he married a daughter of Ignacio Martínez, the commandant at the presidio. In 1830 he became a naturalized citizen of his adopted land and, after spending several years in the southern part of the province, returned north in 1835. There he went into the business of transporting goods between Yerba Buena Cove and other points on the bay.

The boats Richardson used in that venture he acquired in the following manner: Sometime in the late 1820s the padres at the San Francisco and Santa Clara missions bought two thirty-ton schooners from the Russians — whose colony at Fort Ross, some seventy miles up the coast, had been founded in 1812 — intending to use the vessels in trading operations with foreign ships. Because the ships were manned by inexpert Indian crews who failed to keep them in repair, they developed leaks and eventually sank beside their docks. Richardson later made a deal with the priests by which he agreed to raise and repair the vessels and, in return for a promise to carry the mission goods free, was given permission to use them and their Indian crews in his own trading ventures.

Having launched the first commercial boat service on the bay, the energetic Richardson acquired from the provincial governor a grant of land on the Marin shore. There, in the inlet now known as Richardson's Bay, he did a brisk trade with the ships of the whaling fleet, which by then were visiting the harbor in considerable numbers, and which found the place convenient to replenish their supplies of wood and water. By 1837 — the year after Dana's visit — Richardson had become a dominant figure in the economy of the bay area. That same year Governor Alvarado appointed him to the office of Captain of the Port.

In 1835, to facilitate his expanding trading operations, Richardson had put up on the shore of Yerba Buena Cove the "rough board shanty" described by Dana. However, it did not long remain the only building on the site of the future city. In the summer of 1837 its owner added a second and more pretentious building. This was the Casa Grande, a one-story adobe that stood on the rise of the hill to the west of the anchorage, near what is now the intersection of Clay Street and Grant Avenue. It served both as a trading room and as living quarters for Richardson and his family.

At the time the Casa Grande was built, a movement was already under way that was to have far-reaching consequences. For by the mid-1830s it was apparent that the authorities in Mexico City could not indefinitely keep their rich northern possession shut off from contact with the rest of the world. Since the secularization of the missions pressures to break down the government's long-standing policy of isolation had been mounting. This was because the decline of the missions and the rise of the cattle ranches had drastically changed the economy of the province. Hides and tallow were the only marketable products of the ranches and, since there was no domestic demand for either, the industry could exist only if foreign markets were found.

Word of the growing commercial activity of this northernmost of the California ports soon reached the settlements in the southern part of the province. Early in 1836 an Ohio-born merchant, Jacob P. Leese, who was living at the pueblo of Los Angeles, came north to look into the possibility of opening a second trading post at Yerba Buena. On his way up the coast Leese stopped at Monterey and induced Nathan Spear and William Hinckley, two merchants of that town, to join him in the venture. On reaching the bay, Leese made a careful survey of the area before selecting a site for their store. Like others before him, he found the mission and the presidio badly run down. The presidio had only a single inhabitant, an elderly soldier named Joaquin Piña. At the mission a few families made a meager living cultivating the former gardens and running a few cattle on the nearby hills. Leese's choice fell to Yerba Buena Cove, and he applied to the local *alcalde* for a grant of land there. This was a necessary procedure because some years earlier the Mexican congress had passed an act providing for the establishment of pueblos — or towns — adjacent to several of the California missions. Although official authorization for the founding of the local pueblo had not yet been received, residents of the mission had organized a town government and, at an election held on November 27, 1835, had elected one of their number, José Estudillo, to the office of *alcalde*.

One of Estudillo's duties was that of granting town lots to qualified applicants. However, when Leese made his application, no one was certain what were the boundaries of the pueblo, or whether it embraced the land adjacent to the cove. Estudillo accordingly turned down Leese's request and instead offered him land at either the mission or the presidio. This was unsatisfactory to Leese, who returned to Monterey and presented his case to the new governor, Mariano Chico, who issued the necessary order. Leese returned and chose a site adjoining that of Richardson's Casa Grande. There he put up the town's third house, which was completed in the summer of 1836 — in time for a house-warming party the American-born Leese held on July 4. According to tradition, the festivities lasted three days and nights.

Later that year Leese's wife (who was a sister of General Mariano Vallejo) gave birth to a daughter — the first white child to be born at the pueblo.

The following year, 1837, Leese and his partners obtained from Ignacio Martínez, who had meanwhile succeeded Estudillo as *alcalde,* the grant of a 100-*vara* lot (a *vara* is approximately 33 inches) on what is now the west side of Montgomery Street between Clay and Sacramento. This property, which was on level ground close to the beach, was better suited to their purpose than the site Leese had chosen earlier, and there the partners erected their trading post. It was the little town's largest building: a two-story frame structure with dormer windows on its upper floor. There Leese lived and conducted the business until 1841. The owners then sold the building, together with a hide warehouse that occupied part of the lot, whereupon Leese moved to Sonoma. There he joined his brother-in-law in the management of the latter's large holdings.

The buyer of Leese's Yerba Buena property was the nearly 200-year-old Hudson's Bay Company that had long held a virtual monopoly on the Canadian fur trade. In the 1820s it had extended its operations southward by establishing a trading post on the Columbia River. The factor in charge there was Dr. John McLoughlin, and when the company took over the Yerba Buena store in 1841, McLoughlin chose his son-in-law, William Glen Rae, to manage it. For a time the venture prospered, and Rae, who is often mentioned as generous and hospitable, became one of the important men of the village. Gradually, however, the manager's openhandedness and conviviality brought on business reverses. This, plus the fact that he had participated on the losing side in one of the province's frequent political squabbles, led to his suicide in 1845. Following his death, the company closed its Yerba Buena trading post, though it continued to maintain a local agency until after the American conquest.

3. THE VIOGET SURVEY

During the period between the building of the first house on the cove in 1835 and the sale of the Leese trading post to the Hudson's Bay Company six years later, the village of Yerba Buena enjoyed a moderate but steady growth. Eugène Duflot de Mofras, a French visitor to the place in 1841, found some twenty houses grouped about the shore and on the adjacent hillsides — all of them, he stated, belonging to "foreigners . . . and used mainly to store goods coming by ship." The growth continued. A census taken in 1844 listed the trading posts of the Hudson's Bay Company, of Leese's former partners Spear and Hinckley, and of merchant William A. Leidesdorff, a native of the Dutch West Indies and (later) an American vice consul; also several grocery stores — one operated by a former sea captain named Jean Jacques Vioget, one restaurant, two grog shops, one blacksmith, and three carpenter shops.

San Francisco as it appeared in 1846-47. The ships in the foreground are anchored in Yerba Buena Cove; beyond are the
streets and buildings of the early town, with Twin Peaks visible
at the upper left.

At the time Richardson and Leese built their houses beside the cove,
no one seemed to have foreseen that others might follow them; accordingly,
they were permitted to select their sites more or less at random. Richardson,
as stated earlier, put up his Casa Grande near the present junction of Grant
Avenue and Clay Street, and Leese's original house adjoined it on the south.
Both buildings faced on a little-used trail that extended from what is now
the intersection of California and Kearny streets to the vicinity of Pacific
and Stockton streets, where it joined a wagon road over which the solid-
wheeled carts of the period passed in traveling between the mission and the
presidio.

    The trail between the Richardson and Leese houses and the beach was
called Calle de Fundacion (Foundation Street) and became the settlement's
first thoroughfare. However, when others began applying for lots in the area,
it grew clear that a village was in the making there, and the need for a
formal plan became evident. Accordingly, in 1839, the *alcalde*, Francisco

de Haro, commissioned the grocer Vioget — who among his other accomplishments had a knowledge of surveying — to prepare a map laying out streets and property lines. Vioget's survey covered the district bounded by Montgomery, Sacramento, Dupont (now Grant Avenue), and Pacific streets, and fixed the pattern for the later city.

For some time after Vioget had completed his survey the future town existed only on paper. Its streets were unmarked and, of course, unimproved, and it was not until the owners of lots were required to fence their property that its design began to grow clear. Montgomery Street, which lay closest to the water, became the main thoroughfare, its location and direction being determined by the Leese trading post, still the most imposing building on the cove. This street, which ran parallel to the beach, extended from just beyond today's Sacramento Street on the south to the base of Telegraph Hill. At a point near the intersection of Jackson and Montgomery streets a bridge was built across an inlet of the cove known as the Laguna Salada.

Among the buildings put up on or near Montgomery Street during the next several years was Kent Hall, the residence of Nathan Spear, which was so named because it was built with materials bought from the master of the British bark *Kent*. A bit farther to the north was William Hinckley's residence; both it and Kent Hall fronted on the west side of Montgomery Street between Clay and Washington. Farther south, a short distance beyond California Street, was the home of Leidesdorff. He built the first house on the east side of Montgomery Street, fronting on the beach, a warehouse in which he stored hides, tallow, and other merchandise; the building stood near the present corner of California Street and the narrow street that bears his name. Leidesdorff's trading post was a two-story adobe on the southwest corner of Kearny and Clay streets, facing the block-square plaza — now Portsmouth Square — that was the focal point of the Vioget plan. A year or two later Leidesdorff retired from the mercantile business, and the building became the City Hotel, the town's first. It remained a popular gathering place until it was destroyed in one of the fires of the early 1850s.

In 1844 the growing activity of the port caused the authorities at Monterey to put up the town's first government-owned building — the Custom House, which stood in the northeast corner of the plaza near the line of today's Washington Street. Like the City Hotel, it was built of adobe bricks, largely by Indian labor, and followed closely the style of the California missions, with thick walls, tile roof, and porches extending across the front and along one side.

The Custom House was built and manned in the hope of preventing foreign trading ships from evading the payment of taxes on goods landed at Yerba Buena. Despite that precaution, however, widespread smuggling continued, not only there but at all California ports. One tax-dodging device used by the traders was to stop at one of the islands off the southern coast

The adobe Custom House, depicted in this early painting, stood near the northwest corner of the old Spanish plaza (now Portsmouth Square). It was destroyed in the fire of May 3, 1851.

when they first arrived, and unload most of their cargoes. They then proceeded to Monterey, paid the tax on what remained and, having received clearance papers, picked up the goods that had been cached and sold them at the various coastal settlements.

Throughout the early 1840s the town continued to grow moderately. By 1845 it had spread beyond the confines of the Vioget Survey, and the *alcalde*, José Sánchez, authorized an increase of its area by extending existing streets and adding new ones. The pleasant informality with which the affairs of the little community were conducted is suggested by the fact that the "Alcalde's Map," as the new street plat was called, was kept beneath the bar of one Robert Ridley, on Kearny Street between Sacramento and Clay. The names of the owners of lots were written on it and, since their ownership changed frequently, much handling and many erasures soon rendered the map all but unreadable.

The Alcalde's Map more than doubled the size of the original town. Streets were extended as far as Sutter on the south, Stockton on the west, and Green Street on the north. Montgomery Street over most of its length was too close to the water to permit further extensions in that direction; however, new streets were laid out on both sides of the curving shoreline of the cove.

4. CALIFORNIA IN TRANSITION

While the village was taking shape beside the bay, matters that were to have a profound effect on its future were being discussed at places far distant from California. For by then it was recognized in the capitals of several great powers that Mexico's hold on its remote and neglected northern possession was growing weaker, and the question of into whose hands the prize would fall was being considered.

Within the province itself dissatisfaction at the weakness and vacillation of the home government had been mounting among many old-time Spanish-Mexican families. One source of resentment was the fact that the officials sent to govern the province were frequently incompetent, knew nothing of the country and refused to give local residents a proper voice in its affairs. The dissatisfaction of the Californians eventually reached a point where some were openly advocating the severing of all ties with Mexico and the setting up of an independent republic.

Meanwhile England, France, and Russia were secretly laying plans to add this area — one of the largest and richest undeveloped lands on the continent — to their colonial empires. England, whose claim to California dated from Francis Drake's visit in 1579, was already firmly entrenched in the Puget Sound region and hoped to extend its holdings southward to include not only the Oregon country but California as well; the establishment of the Hudson's Bay Company's trading post at Yerba Buena in 1841 was generally regarded as part of that plan. Count Nikolai Rezanov's account of his visit to San Francisco Bay in 1806, and the founding of the Russian outpost at Fort Ross six years later, left little doubt that Russia, too, had designs on the territory. And the French diplomat Eugène Duflot de Mofras, in his book published in Paris in 1844, openly urged his countrymen to move in ahead of their rivals and capture the prize.

Meanwhile officials at Washington were keeping a watchful eye on developments and laying plans of their own. From the mid-1830s on, the subject was frequently discussed in Congress and on the editorial pages of Eastern newspapers — the general opinion being that since Mexico must soon relinquish its hold on California, the national interest made it imperative that it pass to the control of the United States rather than to a European power. Among the arguments advanced to support that view were that many citizens of the United States had already settled in the province, with more arriving each year; that to permit a foreign power to occupy the West Coast would threaten the security of the nation; and that San Francisco's great landlocked harbor must eventually become the center of the country's expanding trade with the Orient.

The last argument was the chief reason why, in 1835, on President Jackson's orders, and with the consent of Congress, the U. S. minister at Mexico City was authorized to offer the Mexican government $500,000 for the northern half of the province. However, nothing came of that or of other attempts to acquire the territory by peaceful means during the administrations of Jackson and of his successors, Van Buren, Harrison, and Tyler. In the meantime relations between the United States and Mexico had deteriorated steadily.

When James K. Polk took office in 1845 it was evident that events were approaching a climax. Since early in 1842 England, France, and the United States all had warships stationed on the west coast of South America: the French at Valparaiso, and the British and Americans at Callao, with the commanders of each closely watching the movements of the others. In May, 1842, the French fleet slipped out of the harbor, leaving no word of its destination. Four months later the British commander received orders from London and hurriedly departed, again without disclosing what his next port of call would be.

To the American commander, Commodore Thomas Catesby Jones, the departure of the British ships seemed to call for prompt action. After consulting with the U. S. chargé d'affaires at Lima, he set sail for California on September 7. En route, one of his three ships, the *Dale*, put in at Panama with a dispatch to be forwarded to Washington telling of his intentions. The other two ships, the *United States* and the *Cyane*, proceeded to Monterey, which they reached on September 18. There Jones, who had assumed that the two countries were at war, sent a message ashore demanding the surrender of the town. Monterey's defenses, according to one authority, consisted of only "29 soldiers, 25 militia, with 11 cannon, nearly all useless and lacking ammunition, and 150 muskets." Hence, no attempt was made to put up even a token resistance, and on the morning of September 20 a detachment of 150 marines and soldiers landed, raised the American flag above the Custom House, and took formal possession of the town. Two days later, on learning that no word had reached California indicating that the two nations were at war, Jones was forced to conclude that he had acted too hastily. He accordingly ordered the American flag lowered, summoned the landing party back aboard their ships and, after apologizing to the Mexican officials, sailed away.

Jones's premature action did nothing to improve relations between the two countries. At Washington the belief that Mexico was negotiating for the sale of California to England was strengthened by reports from the U. S. minister at Mexico City and from Thomas O. Larkin, the Massachusetts-born merchant who was serving as U. S. consul at Monterey. At the time President Polk took office Larkin was instructed to use every effort to uncover and report on the activities of agents of foreign powers in California, and to urge the inhabitants, native Californians and Americans alike, to oppose, by force if necessary, any attempt to take over the province.

Mexican officials at Monterey had long been aware that they would be powerless to defend the province in case of an attack. The central government was too much occupied with problems closer to home to send troops or military supplies, and California's depleted garrisons and antiquated weapons would have been useless against a determined aggressor.

A further complication was that from the beginning 1840s the number of foreigners, chiefly Americans, entering the province and, despite regulations to the contrary, taking up permanent residence there, had been increasing rapidly. Moreover, among the Californians themselves, sentiment against the newcomers was divided. Years of neglect and indifference had weakened their loyalty to the mother country, and many among them favored the transfer of the province to the United States. The already involved situation was further complicated by the division of the native families into hostile groups, each seeking to gain control of the government. In the series of small and largely bloodless skirmishes that followed, both factions welcomed the help of the Yankee settlers, many of whom had grown up along the frontier and were expert riflemen.

On their part, the Americans were willing to join in such local plots and counterplots — knowing that if the faction they supported should win, they would be liberally treated by grants of land and other favors. But in the confused state of affairs it was anybody's guess which side had the best chance of victory. During the campaign that followed Juan Bautista Alvarado's revolt against Governor Manuel Micheltorena in 1845, a number of Americans and other foreigners joined both "armies." However, when the opposing forces eventually met near Los Angeles on February 20, the foreigners prudently withdrew and let the Californians decide the issue among themselves. In the "Battle of Cahuenga Pass" that followed, casualties were light: on one side a horse was killed, and on the other a mule was wounded.

Later that year Governor Micheltorena made a final attempt to stem the flow of Yankees arriving over the Sierra trails and from the Oregon country to the north. One such group was rounded up, taken to Monterey, and ordered to leave at once. The prisoners protested that they had not known their entry into the country to be illegal, and pointed out that they could not recross the mountains because the trails were blocked by snow. Reluctantly, Micheltorena granted them permission to stay until spring.

In the spring of 1846, however, events of much greater importance were in the making, and no attempt was made to carry out the governor's order.

5. BEAR FLAG REVOLT

By the mid-1840s immigration had increased to the point where the number of foreigners in the province exceeded that of the Spanish-Mexicans. Of the non-Californians, a large majority were from the United States. These were made up of two distinct groups. One consisted of long-time residents, men who had arrived by sea a decade or more earlier, in many cases had taken out Mexican citizenship, married into the California families, and as merchants, traders, or landowners had come to wield considerable influence in local affairs. Because they enjoyed close business and social relations with the native Californians, they had come to share their viewpoints and to support their policies, though this was sometimes more for expediency than conviction.

The second and more numerous group was of a different sort. They were products of the frontier, hunters or trappers who had drifted in from beyond the mountains and, attracted by the temperate climate, the abundance of wild life, and the large areas of fertile, unoccupied land, had elected to stay. For the most part they had remained in the interior, avoiding the coastal areas where they would be subject to the authority of the Mexicans, and ignoring the latter's feeble attempts to expel them.

John C. Frémont, captain of Topographical Engineers, U. S. Army, arrived in California early in 1846 as head of an exploring expedition. His conduct during events leading up to, and including, the American conquest has long been a matter of controversy. *(The Bancroft Library)*

The presence of this group was strongly opposed by the provincial authorities and by the holders of land grants in the interior, whose property the newcomers had pre-empted. On their part, the settlers, schooled in the free-and-easy traditions of the frontier and impatient of restraints of any sort, resented what they considered unwarranted interference with their freedom to come and go as they pleased.

Such was the situation when John C. Frémont, captain of Topographical Engineers of the U. S. Army, reached California on his second expedition early in 1846. Frémont's party, ostensibly on an exploring mission, consisted of about sixty men — surveyors, guides, and helpers; all were well armed and well mounted, having with them some two hundred horses. Frémont left most of his party in the San Joaquin Valley, continued on to Monterey, and asked Governor José Castro's permission to spend the winter in California. Castro, concerned at the presence of an armed party of that size in the province, demanded to know the reason for their visit. Frémont replied that theirs was a purely scientific mission and that he planned to leave as soon as the trails to Oregon became passable. With some reluctance Castro agreed to permit him to stay until spring, provided he and his men remained in the Central Valley.

Frémont rejoined his party — which had meanwhile left the San Joaquin Valley and camped near San Jose — and, instead of returning inland, led them southward into the Salinas Valley. On learning of this, Castro charged Frémont with breaking his agreement and brusquely ordered him and his party to leave the province at once. Instead of complying, Frémont and his men withdrew to the top of nearby Gavilan Peak and made ready to resist any attempt to oust them.

Thereupon Castro, acting in his capacity as lieutenant colonel of the Mexican Army and commander-in-chief of the Department of California, issued this proclamation:

Fellow Citizens: A band of robbers commanded by a Captain of the U. S. Army, J. C. Frémont, without having respect to the laws and authority of the Department, daringly introduced themselves into the country and disobeyed the orders of your Commander-in-Chief and of the Prefect of the District by which he was required to march forthwith out of the limits of our Territory, and without answering our letters he remains encamped at the farm "Natividad" from which he sallies forth committing depredation, and making scandalous skirmishes.

In the name of our native country I invite you to place yourselves under my immediate orders at headquarters, where we will prepare to lance the ulcer which (should it not be done) would destroy our liberties and independence, for which you ought to sacrifice yourselves as well as your friend and fellow-citizen,

Headquarters at San Juan   José Castro
8 March 1846

But Castro's promised attack failed to materialize, and after waiting three days Frémont and his men broke camp and proceeded by easy stages to Sutter's Fort.

Events now followed one another in rapid succession. After a brief stay at the fort, Frémont and his party set off for Oregon. Soon after he left, Archibald H. Gillespie, a lieutenant of the U.S. Marines, reached Monterey aboard the warship *Cyane*. Gillespie carried secret instructions from Washington. After conferring with the U.S. consul, Larkin, and other American residents at Monterey, he hurried north to intercept Frémont, whom he overtook at a point just within the Oregon border. What was the information he passed on to Frémont, and whether he bore official orders from President Polk, has never been definitely established. Consequently the question of whether Frémont's later actions were in accordance with instructions from the President, or were undertaken on his own responsibility — or on the advice of his influential father-in-law, Senator Benton of Missouri — has ever since remained one of the intriguing mysteries of California history.

In any event, Frémont and his men turned about and retraced their steps, setting up camp near the Sutter Buttes in the middle of the Sacramento Valley. There he remained for several weeks, seemingly undecided as to his future course. In Monterey Frémont's return was looked on by the Mexican officials as an act of war. Meanwhile, rumors that a strong force of Castro's troops were moving against the settlers in the valley caused much excitement among them. Many made their way to Frémont's camp and urged him to help repel the expected attack. Frémont, however, was reluctant to engage American soldiers against what so far as he knew was still officially a friendly nation. On the other hand, he did nothing to dissuade the others from themselves taking action; indeed, there is ample evidence that he encouraged them to do so.

The first hostile act of the settlers was to capture a herd of horses being driven from Monterey to Sonoma, which they believed were to be used by Castro's troops in their campaign to drive the Yankees from the country. That maneuver went off so well that their leaders were encouraged to make a second and bolder move — the capture of the town of Sonoma.

Soon after daybreak on June 14, 1846, a nondescript party of thirty-three horsemen dressed in the leather shirts and leggings of the frontier, rode up to the home of forty-six-year-old Mariano G. Vallejo, the town's leading citizen. When Vallejo asked the reason for their early morning visit, the party's leader announced that they had taken possession of the town and had come to place him under arrest. Vallejo, who had always been friendly with the Americans, had some difficulty comprehending what this unexpected development meant. Nonetheless, he invited three of the leaders inside and, with his brother Salvador, and Victor Prudon, a French resident of the valley, sat down to work out the terms of the capitulation. Following the hospitable custom of the day the host had several bottles of fiery California brandy placed before his guests. The result was that the negotiations continued so long that the impatient group outside twice sent emissaries inside to speed the procedure. The first, John Grigsby, was no more successful than the others, and, after a second long wait, William B. Ide was dispatched on the same errand. Ide, who later reported that he had found his fellow negotiators in a pleasantly mellow mood, prudently refused Vallejo's *aguardiente*, and the matter was finally concluded.

The Bear Flag, emblem of the short-lived California Republic, was raised above the plaza at Sonoma on June 14, 1846. (*The Society of California Pioneers.*)

Thereupon Ide assumed command and dispatched Vallejo, his brother, and his brother-in-law, Jacob Leese, under guard to Frémont's headquarters, which had meanwhile been moved to Sutter's Fort. Ide then drew up a proclamation announcing the formation of a "republican government" and setting forth the benefits that would accrue to the Sonomans under the new regime. Another member of the party, William Todd, had meanwhile designed a flag for the new republic. This consisted of a crudely drawn grizzly bear and a star, painted red on a white background, with a red stripe along its lower edge bearing the words "California Republic." The flag was hoisted to the top of a pole in the plaza, Ide's proclamation was read to the curious crowd of townspeople who had gathered, and the new government began to function.

6. THE YANKEES TAKE OVER

Like numerous other California revolutions of the 1830s and early 1840s, the Bear Flag rebellion was conducted with a maximum of oratory and a minimum of bloodshed.

On learning of the events at Sonoma, Castro again issued an eloquent appeal to his countrymen to take up arms and drive the Yankees from the province. At the pueblo of Los Angeles a second official, Andrés Pico, brother of the governor Pio Pico, likewise called on loyal residents to come to the defense of their sorely beset country. These fervent appeals, however, found only an indifferent response. By then many Californians had become weary of the dissension among their leaders and refused to bestir themselves in what they regarded as a lost cause. Castro was able to muster only 160 men, and in the south the response was even smaller. When Pico's "army" set out from Santa Barbara to help drive out Frémont and the Bear Flaggers, it numbered less than a hundred. The single engagement of the campaign, the so-called Battle of Olampali, was fought on the Marin peninsula near present-day San Rafael. After a brief exchange, during which two Californians were killed and a number of horses captured, the Mexicans withdrew to the east side of the bay. Meanwhile Frémont, who until then had maintained a nominal neutrality, announced his support of the settlers' revolt and, having forwarded his resignation from the Army to Washington, prepared to join forces with them.

It soon became clear that the Bear Flag Revolt had been an ill-timed exploit, and that it had alienated many Spanish Californians who had been friendly to the American cause and who favored, or at worst were reconciled to, the transfer of the province to the United States. To have the territory forcibly taken over by a band of settlers who were illegally in the country and who had refused to leave was, understandably enough, bitterly resented by the native population.

The irony of the situation was that had the Bear Flaggers delayed taking action for only a brief time, it need never have happened at all. For on May 12, 1846 — more than a month before the seizure of Sonoma — the long-threatened war with Mexico had broken out. When the news reached Commodore John D. Sloat, commander of the U.S. ships in the Pacific, then at Mazatlan, he at once set sail for Monterey. On July 9, he sent a landing party ashore at that port. No opposition was offered as the flag was raised and the province declared a part of the United States. Then in a conciliatory message to the townspeople Sloat promised them full freedom of movement and a minimum of interference with their domestic affairs.

Six days later, on July 15, Sloat turned over his command to Commodore Robert F. Stockton, whose ship, the *Congress*, had just arrived after a voyage around the Horn. Stockton proved a more aggressive leader than Sloat and less concerned with preserving the good will of the Californians. He at once mustered the Bear Flag group, and other settlers who had joined them, into the Army, placed Frémont in charge with Gillespie second in command, and hurried off to the south to complete the occupation of the province. This, too, was accomplished without bloodshed. Stockton entered Los Angeles on August 13, announced that all California was now in American hands, and returned to Monterey, leaving Gillespie and a detachment of fifty soldiers to maintain order.

To leave so small a force behind proved a serious mistake of judgment. Hardly had Stockton and the bulk of his men left when the Spanish Californians, incensed at what they considered unduly severe restrictions placed on their movements, armed themselves, ambushed and took prisoner twenty of Gillespie's troops, and laid siege to the others. Although Gillespie was surrounded by a much larger force, he managed to dispatch a messenger to Monterey with word of his plight. He then withdrew to a hill behind the Los Angeles plaza and fortified it in preparation for an attack. The messenger reached Monterey after a hard ride of five days, but before relief could be sent, the encircled party was forced to surrender. They were permitted to march to San Pedro after agreeing to leave the province on the first available vessel.

Their ship was on the point of sailing when reinforcements arrived from the north. Gillespie and his men disembarked and joined the newcomers; then the combined force, numbering about three hundred, set about the reconquest of the south. This proved an unexpectedly difficult task. As they marched inland the troops were harrassed by bands of mounted Californians, who circled about them night and day and used a single small cannon with such effect that the expedition had to be abandoned. The force returned to San Pedro, having suffered the loss of four men killed and six wounded. The Californians, encouraged by their successes in the Los Angeles area, stepped up resistance elsewhere in the south. At San Diego,

Santa Barbara, and several other points companies were formed and prepared to join in the guerrilla war.

The men of Gillespie's command remained at San Pedro waiting further reinforcements, which were approaching from two directions. Frémont with three hundred men was marching down from Monterey, while the troops of Colonel Stephen W. Kearny, having completed the occupation of New Mexico, were hurrying overland from the southeast. The Kearny contingent entered California with men and animals near exhaustion from their long march across the desert, and soon after their arrival were met by a large force of mounted Californians led by Andrés Pico. The engagement that followed, the Battle of San Pasqual, was the bloodiest ever fought on California soil. When it was over, Kearny remained in possession of the field and thus technically the winner, but the victory was gained at the cost of eighteen men killed and seventeen wounded, while the Californians lost only a few wounded.

Kearny's command eventually reached San Diego, which had meanwhile been occupied by a naval unit under Stockton. After several weeks to rest and regroup, the combined force, now six hundred strong, set off to retake Los Angeles. This time they met no serious resistance. On July 10, 1847, Captain Gillespie again raised the flag he had lowered four months earlier. Three days later the signing of the Cahuenga Capitulation officially ended hostilities and completed the conquest of the province.

The terms of the Cahuenga agreement were liberal. The Californians were given assurance that their individual freedom and property rights would be respected, and that none would be punished for having taken up arms against the Americans. In return they agreed to obey the laws of the victors, to surrender their firearms and artillery — which consisted of two small cannon — and to give no aid to Mexico in the war with the United States. A little more than a year later the Treaty of Guadalupe Hidalgo brought the Mexican War to an official close and formally ceded California to the United States.

The treaty was signed on February 2, 1848. Nine days earlier James W. Marshall had picked up the first flakes of gold from the tailrace of the sawmill Captain Sutter was building in the Sierra foothills.

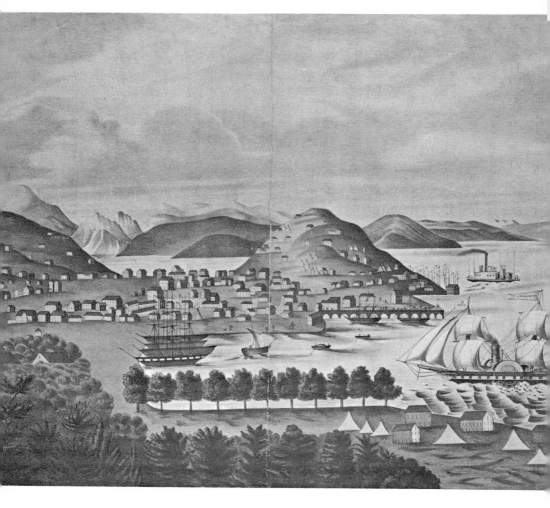

This fanciful view of San Francisco in 1848 shows, right foreground, one of the side-wheel steamers of the Pacific Mail Steamship Company entering Yerba Buena Cove, with the buildings
of the growing town in the middle distance and Telegraph Hill
rising abruptly in the background.

III

Discovered — Gold!

1. LAND TITLES

The village of Yerba Buena played only a minor role in the conquest of California and its transfer to the sovereignty of the United States. Although the Bear Flag incident, that prelude to the actual conquest, took place less than fifty miles distant, the settlement by the bay was not directly involved; indeed, few of its residents were in sympathy with the aims of the Bear Flaggers, and they accordingly lent them no support.

This was so because the village was then enjoying a brisk trade with the owners of the outlying cattle ranches and with the masters of the whalers, trading ships, and other vessels that put into the harbor. The local merchants and traders, all of whom were foreign born, were on friendly terms with the Mexican authorities and in many cases had married into California families and taken out Mexican citizenship. Although most of them favored the territory's eventual transfer to the United States, they were meanwhile content to maintain the status quo. The action of the group of settlers from the Sacramento Valley — most of whom were newcomers to California — was looked on as an ill-advised and irresponsible exploit that could delay and perhaps permanently end negotiations the villagers knew to be in progress for the purchase of the province by the United States.

From the time the first houses were put up beside the cove in 1835 until the American flag was raised above the plaza eleven years later, the townspeople had been left largely to their own devices, with a minimum of official supervision. To be sure, in 1834 an *ayuntamiento*, or town council, had been appointed by the provincial governor to administer the affairs of the pueblo, and Francisco de Haro had been named *alcalde* to preside over its deliberations. But the duties these officials were expected to perform were neither many nor onerous, for in 1838 the *ayuntamiento* ceased to meet, and although *alcaldes* were regularly elected, the office was regarded primarily as a means of honoring its holder, and the duties were correspondingly light.

One consequence of the informality with which the affairs of the town were conducted was the celebrated "land grant cases." These were a series of long-drawn-out lawsuits to establish title to property within the boundaries of the town, some of which were not settled until more than a decade after the Americans took over. This litigation was so protracted because, when the California missions were first established, each mission was granted an extensive area of contiguous land on which to plant crops and run cattle. Thus for more than half a century after the Mission Dolores was founded, virtually the entire peninsula from the Golden Gate southward to San Francisquito Creek — a distance of thirty miles — was mission land. Only the presidio, comprising about 1,500 acres at the tip of the peninsula, was exempted.

In 1835, two years after the passage of the Secularization Act, the first considerable tract of mission land passed to private ownership. This was the 2,200-acre Rancho Laguna de la Merced near the southern boundary of the present city, which was awarded to José Galino. Later that year Francisco de Haro received title to the 8,926-acre San Pablo Rancho, which adjoined the Galino grant on the south. A third major grant was that of the 16,000-acre Buri-Buri Rancho lower down on the peninsula which was awarded Francisco Sánchez in 1838. In 1840 José C. Bernal received title to 4,500 acres in the Hunters Point–Islais Creek area; Bernal Heights in the southeastern part of the city perpetuates the grantee's name. Another, the San Miguel grant, comprising 4,443 acres extending southward from the mission-district hills, was given José Noe in 1845. Noe, like de Haro and Sánchez, was an early *alcalde*. The one foreign-born resident to receive land on the upper peninsula was Jacob P. Leese, General Vallejo's brother-in-law, who, as stated earlier, was then operating a trading post on Yerba Buena Cove. Leese's grant, made in 1841 and consisting of 8,880 acres, adjoined that of José C. Bernal to the south.

All these grants were confirmed by the authorities at Monterey. Several other persons applied for peninsula lands during the early and middle 1840s. Some of these applications were rejected and others were still under consideration when the United States took over in July, 1846. Among the latter was that of Francisco Guerrero and H. D. Fitch, who had applied for two square leagues (approximately 14,000 acres) between Yerba Buena Cove and the presidio. A second application, filed by Joaquin Piña, asked for a square league on the ocean front near Point Lobos, and a third, which included most of the present industrial district south of Market Street, was sought by one Peter Sherreback.

This is a sampling of the grants — some valid, others of doubtful legality, and still others fraudulent — on which title to lands in or near the future city was based at the time of the American conquest. The question of whether to reject or confirm these various claims presented a complex and confusing problem, but it was one with which the new rulers of the province were obliged to cope. For in his proclamation issued at Monterey on July 6,

Commodore Sloat had assured the Californians that "all persons holding titles to real estate, or in quiet possession of all lands under color of right shall have their titles and rights guaranteed to them." The Treaty of Guadalupe Hidalgo reaffirmed the promise that land titles in the ceded territory would be respected "to the same extent they would have been valid had the territories remained under Mexico."

On the San Francisco peninsula the situation was further complicated by the fact that records pertaining to land grants were far from complete, that their boundaries were poorly defined and sometimes overlapped, and that many persons who arrived after the conquest disregarded the claims of the grant holders and settled wherever they chose. How these complex matters were eventually resolved is told in Chapter Five.

2. YERBA BUENA BECOMES SAN FRANCISCO

Toward the end of June, 1846, the U.S.S. *Portsmouth* entered the Golden Gate and dropped anchor off Yerba Buena Cove. For some days thereafter she remained with her guns trained on the village, while no one was permitted to go ashore, and a watch was maintained on deck day and night. Finally, on July 8, her commander, Captain John B. Montgomery, received a dispatch from Commodore Sloat stating that Sloat had taken possession of Monterey and ordering him to occupy Yerba Buena.

Next morning a detachment of seventy soldiers and marines landed, marched to the plaza, and stood at attention while Montgomery raised the American flag on the pole above the Custom House. Gunners on the *Portsmouth* fired a twenty-one-gun salute, Montgomery read Sloat's proclamation announcing the annexation of California, and when he had finished, the onlookers retired to Vioget's bar around the corner and drank a toast to the success of the new regime. With these formalities Yerba Buena passed from the control of Mexico to that of the United States.

Montgomery's orders directed that he take possession of other northern settlements as well. He accordingly dispatched a party of marines under Lieutenant Joseph Warren Revere to Sonoma and Sutter's Fort, both of which were occupied without resistance. Meanwhile at Yerba Buena the change-over from Mexican to American rule was being completed. Montgomery named Lieutenant Henry B. Watson military commander of the port and installed him and a small force of marines in the Custom House, then set about recruiting a company of volunteers from among residents of the town. On August 26 he appointed another of his officers, Lieutenant Washington A. Bartlett, to serve as the first American *alcalde* of the little community.

Bartlett's appointment was confirmed by the voters at an election held on September 15. One of his first official acts was to order an extension of

Lieutenant Washington A. Bartlett of the U.S.S. *Portsmouth* in 1846 became the town's first *alcalde* under American rule. It was during Bartlett's term in office that the name of the settlement was changed from Yerba Buena to San Francisco.

the Vioget Survey of 1838. This was undertaken by Jasper O'Farrell, an Irish surveyor who had arrived in California four years earlier. O'Farrell's survey, which increased the area of the town to about eight hundred acres, laid out streets as far as present-day Post Street on the south, Leavenworth Street on the west, Francisco Street on the north, and eastward for some distance beyond Market Street. Over the greater part of the newly-surveyed district the streets were extensions of those already in existence. Hence, they followed the pattern of the Vioget Survey, by which the streets intersected at right angles without regard to the contour of the land. O'Farrell's one variation from the earlier plan was Market Street, a hundred-foot-wide thoroughfare that extended from the shore of the cove in a southwesterly direction to the vicinity of the Mission Dolores.

Market Street served to break the uniformity of the older pattern, being so laid out that the streets on the north and west entered at acute angles, while those on the opposite side met it at right angles. Therefore, at only a few points was it possible to cross directly from the old part of the town to the new. At the time, however, that presented no difficulty, for the closely built-up section still centered on the plaza, and there were few houses on the far side of Market. Not until several decades later, after the growth to the south and southeast had made Market Street the city's most heavily traveled thoroughfare, did this lack of facilities for easy cross-town traffic present a serious problem — a problem that has continued to this day.

O'Farrell's 1847 survey corrected one minor error in that of his predecessor. For the streets originally laid out by Vioget failed to intersect at true right angles. Correcting this variation, which amounted to two degrees, caused some of the buildings on the older streets to project beyond the new property lines. The alteration, which became known as the "O'Farrell Swing," gave a certain irregularity to the streets of the original town, some of which were not adjusted until after the fire of 1906.

Until the O'Farrell Survey was officially adopted, few of the streets had names. The new map remedied that deficiency by conferring on them the names of men who had been prominent in California both before and during the American conquest. Montgomery, Kearny, Stockton, Dupont, Frémont, Jones, and Taylor honored officers of the U.S. Army and Navy. Sutter and Vallejo streets were named for distinguished Californians, and Howard, Bryant, Brannan, Folsom, Harrison, Leavenworth, and Hyde streets commemorated pioneer residents of the town.

It was during Bartlett's term as *alcalde*, too, that the name of the town itself was changed. In the town's first newspaper, the weekly *California Star* — which had been founded earlier that month — this notice appeared on January 30, 1847:

> Whereas, the local name of Yerba Buena, as applied to the settlement or town of San Francisco, is unknown beyond the district; and has been applied from the local name of the cove on which the town is built: Therefore, to prevent confusion and mistakes in public documents, and that the town may have the advantage of the name given on the public map,
>
> It is hereby ordained that the name of San Francisco shall hereafter be used in all official communications and public documents or records appertaining to the town.
>
> Washington A. Bartlett,
Chief Magistrate.

By the middle of 1847 population had increased to the point where the administrative procedures inherited from the Mexicans no longer sufficed. Accordingly, in July Colonel R. B. Mason, the military governor, wrote to George Hyde, who had meanwhile succeeded Bartlett as *alcalde:*

> There is wanted in San Francisco an efficient town government, more so than is in the power of the *alcalde* alone to put in force. There may soon be expected a large number of whalers in your Bay, and a large increase of population by the arrival of immigrants; it is therefore highly necessary that you should, at an early day, have an efficient town police, proper town laws, town officials, &c., for the enforcement of the laws for the preservation of order, and for the protection of persons and property.
>
> I therefore desire that you call a town meeting for the election of six persons, who in connection with the *alcalde* shall constitute the town authorities until the end of the year 1848.

The election was held on September 13, and the six councilmen entered on their duties. A record of what they accomplished during the next several weeks has been preserved in an eight-page pamphlet entitled "The Laws

of the Town of San Francisco," which was issued later that year from the
press of the town's second newspaper, the *Californian*.

The first ordinance, enacted only three days after the town officials took
office, was designed, in the words of the act, "To prevent the desertion of
seamen." It reads:

> Be it ordained . . . that if any person within the limits of this
> Town, shall entice or advise any Sailor or other person employed on
> board of any vessel within this harbor or bay, to leave the vessel on
> which he or they may be employed, upon conviction thereof, shall
> be fined not exceeding five hundred dollars, nor less than twenty,
> and be imprisoned not exceeding three months.

Similar fines and prison terms were imposed on persons who "shall
feed, harbor or employ" runaway sailors without permission from the *alcalde*. A third section provided that sailors who deserted their ships would,
upon conviction, be sentenced to "hard labor on the public works for a
period not exceeding six months."

The councilmen made this their first order of business because the
town's prosperity depended in large measure on trade with the whalers,
merchantmen, and other vessels visiting the port. Hence it was desirable
that friendly relations with the masters of such craft be maintained. One
source of complaint by the latter was the practice of early-day innkeepers of
persuading the crews of newly-arrived ships to desert, then of exacting substantial fees for supplying new crews when the ships were ready to sail. The
fact that wages and living conditions differed from ship to ship made it
easy to persuade sailors that they could improve their lot by jumping their
present ships and signing on elsewhere. Another common practice was for
shipmasters who planned to stay in port for any length of time to dismiss
their crews so as to avoid feeding and paying them wages during the interval.

Other measures adopted by the 1847 town council throw further light
on local conditions. Under the heading "Police Regulations," it was provided
that each councilman "constitute himself a conservator of peace within the
limits of the town" and "preserve the peace and morals of the place"; for
these services he was to receive no compensation. Cash fines or labor on
public works were imposed for a number of offenses. These included assault,
forcible entry into houses, and theft; also, "the firing of a gun within one
mile of Portsmouth Square" and "the killing or maiming of carrion fowls."
Yet another regulation read: "Be it ordained . . . that from and after the 12th
day of November, 1847, all property owners desiring to dig wells upon their
premises, or who now may have them dug, shall, under penalty of fifty dollars fine, carefully close and fence, or box, them in."

Rules were adopted, too, for the licensing of merchants and other businessmen. An annual fee of $25 was imposed on sellers of "goods, wares and

merchandise, real estate and every description of property," whether by private sale or public auction. Those selling spirituous liquors were charged $50 every six months and in addition were required to put up a bond of $250 as a guaranty that they would conduct "an orderly house." Those found guilty of violating this provision were liable to fines of not more than $25 or less than $10 — one-half of which would be paid the informer.

One purpose of such fines and fees was to raise funds for needed civic improvements. Among the first of these was the building of a municipal wharf over the shallow waters of the cove, to which ocean-going ships could moor while loading and discharging cargo.

Another means of financing public works was the sale of town lots. During the first months after the Americans took over, however, the revenue from that source was small because a considerable area of land fronting on the cove was reserved for use by the federal government. Accordingly, representations were made to Governor Kearny that by withholding the property from private ownership the government was preventing the proper development of the harbor. Evidently this argument proved effectual, for on March 10 Kearny issued this decree:

I, Brigadier-General S. W. Kearny, Governor of California, by virtue of authority vested in me by the President of the United States of America, do hereby grant, convey, and release unto the town of San Francisco, the people, or corporate authorities thereof, all the right, title, and interest of the Government of the United States, and of the Territory of California, in and to the beach and water lots on the east front of said town of San Francisco . . . except such lots as may be selected for the use of the United States Government by the senior officers of the Army and Navy now there: Provided the said ground hereby ceded shall be divided into lots and sold by public auction to the highest bidder, after three months' notice previously given; the proceeds of said sale to be for the benefit of the town of San Francisco.

In response to Kearny's order Edwin Bryant, who was then serving as *alcalde,* set June 29 as the date of the auction. His announcement of the sale reflects his confidence in the future of the town. Its final paragraph reads:

The site of the town of San Francisco is known to all navigators and mercantile men acquainted with the subject to be the most commanding commercial position on the entire eastern coast of the Pacific Ocean, and the town itself is, no doubt, destined to become the commercial emporium of the western side of the American continent. The property offered for sale is the most valuable in, or belonging to, the town, and the acquisition of it is an object of deep interest to all mercantile houses in California and elsewhere engaged in the commerce of the Pacific.

The land included in the sale consisted of about 450 lots, each 15½ *varas* wide by 50 *varas* deep (approximately 43 by 137½ feet). They were all "beach lots" — that is, they lay between the high- and low-water marks, the slope of the beach being so gradual that the entire area was submerged when the tide was in. Delay in completing the arrangements caused the auction to be postponed for several weeks. The bidding began on July 20 and continued three days. A little less than half the lots were sold, at prices ranging from $50 to $100. Following Kearny's instructions, the area between Sacramento and Clay streets was withheld from sale for possible future use by the federal government. Six years later when the land thus reserved was up at auction, lots less than half the size of those sold in 1847 brought more than a hundred times as much. Later in 1847 a second sale was held, this time of lots 50 *varas* square, facing newly laid-out streets in and near the present retail shopping district. They were offered at $12 each, plus a recording fee of $3.62½.

3. EIGHTEEN HUNDRED AND FORTY-SEVEN

During the first two years under American rule more than a score of new buildings were put up in the vicinity of Portsmouth Square. Among them were a second hotel, several stores, half a dozen bars and gambling houses, a church, a school, and the offices of the two weekly newspapers. A census taken in the summer of 1847 established the total number of houses in the village at 157, one-quarter of which were built of adobe bricks and the remainder of wood; most of the latter were one-room cabins. The population at that time — seventeen months after the Americans had taken over — was 469, not including military and naval personnel, or residents of the Mission Dolores. Of the townspeople, more than half were natives of the United States; there were also about forty each of Spanish Californians, Indians, and Kanakas, plus a sprinkling of Europeans, New Zealanders, and South Americans.

The 1847 census was taken, on orders of the military governor, by Lieutenant Edward Gilbert of the U.S. Army. In rendering his report, Gilbert too drew a bright picture of the town's future. On the question of whether it or its chief rival, Monterey, was likely to become California's leading seaport, he wrote:

> In conclusion I cannot suppress a desire to say that San Francisco is destined to become the great commercial emporium of the North Pacific coast. With the advantages of so hearty and intelligent a race of pioneers, it can scarcely be otherwise. Notwithstanding these conclusions . . . I have heard it said that Monterey is des-

tined to outstrip it. That Monterey can never surpass San Francisco, I think the following will clearly establish: 1. San Francisco has a safer and more commodious harbor than Monterey; 2. The waters of the bay afford an easy method of communication and . . . transportation between the town and the hundred lateral valleys, which are destined soon to become granaries and hives of plenty; 3. It also has a ready means of communication by water with large and rich valleys of the San Joaquin, the Sacramento, and the American Fork, as all of these rivers are tributaries to the bay. So far as my information goes, Monterey, although it has a fine country at its back, has none of the facilities for reaching and transporting the products which San Francisco possesses in regard to the country that surrounds it. This, allowing for all other things being equal, would give San Francisco an insuperable advantage.

When this forecast was made, however, commerce on the bay and its tributaries was anything but heavy. A single ship, a twenty-ton sloop belonging to Captain Sutter, carried all the freight passing between San Francisco and Sutter's Fort at the confluence of the Sacramento and American rivers. Half a dozen other small craft — including a steam launch, the *Sitka*, belonging to William A. Leidesdorff — were ample to handle the traffic on the bay. Ocean-borne traffic, however, was more brisk, and was increasing year by year. The ships of the whaling fleet were then making San Francisco Bay a regular port of call, as were merchantmen in trade with the Hawaiian Islands and with ports in California, Oregon, and the west coast of Mexico. During the year ending March 30, 1848, eighty-six vessels entered the Golden Gate. Among them were sixteen whalers, four naval craft, and eight from the Hawaiian Islands — the balance were from West Coast ports or around-the-Horn traders from the far side of the continent.

Although the flow of newcomers into California increased noticeably during the first two years after the conquest, their total number was small, and of these comparatively few remained in San Francisco. The largest single party, a group of about two hundred Mormons led by Elder Samuel Brannan, appeared unannounced in the harbor on the last day of July, 1846, only three weeks after Captain Montgomery had taken possession of the town. The Mormon company had set off from New York early that year, intending to found a colony somewhere in California. The ship, the *Brooklyn*, was loaded with tools, farm implements, and an assortment of other equipment, including the machinery for two flour mills, and a printing press. On learning that the country had become a part of the United States, the party abandoned their plan of establishing a colony, and their energetic leader entered actively into the life of the town. Within a few months Brannan had made himself one of its most influential citizens. One of his earliest enterprises was the founding of San Francisco's first newspaper, the *Cali-*

fornia Star, in whose columns he urged a number of civic improvements, including the establishment of the town's first public school.

Meanwhile growing numbers of emigrants were moving westward over the overland trails. Although the journey by land required the crossing of hundreds of miles of semi-arid countryside and passage over two mountain ranges, most parties came through safely. Early in 1847, however, word reached San Francisco that one large group, which had set out from Illinois the previous spring, had become snowbound while attempting a late crossing of the Sierra. This was the Donner Party, numbering eighty-seven men, women, and children, of whom less than fifty survived the ordeal. When news that the marooned party was in desperate straits reached San Francisco in early February, a mass meeting was held to lay plans to aid them. A fund of $1,500 was subscribed, and a group of twenty men volunteered to carry food and medical supplies to the starving party. Four separate relief parties struggled through the storms of the extraordinarily severe winter of 1846–47 before the last survivors were brought to safety down the western slope of the mountains.

4. "GOLD ON THE AMERICAN RIVER!"

During the first eighteen months after the U.S. flag was hoisted above the former plaza (which had been renamed Portsmouth Square), San Francisco's population doubled, the activity of the port increased substantially, and all signs indicated that the town was entering a period of moderate but steady growth. Yet when the year 1848 opened, San Francisco was still a small frontier settlement in a remote, sparsely settled land, separated by thousands of miles from the populous centers and, so far as anyone could foresee, destined to remain so for a long time to come. Even among those who were convinced of the port's future importance few would have been rash enough to predict that within two years it would be a city of thirty-five thousand, its name a household word throughout the world.

It was, of course, the gold discovery that brought about that transformation. It took some time, however, before the San Franciscans realized the full significance of that event. News of the first flakes of gold picked up in the tailrace of Captain Sutter's sawmill on the morning of January 24 did not reach the bay until more than three weeks later — and when it finally arrived it aroused only passing interest. The business of the little port was then brisk and the townspeople were far too much occupied with their own affairs to concern themselves with what might be happening at some distant point in the Sierra foothills.

Captain Sutter's eagerness to keep news of the discovery secret gave San Franciscans their first opportunity to see the metal that was to bring about such drastic changes in the town itself and in their personal fortunes. For Sutter had exacted from his workmen a promise to stay on the job until the mill was completed; meanwhile he had negotiated a treaty with the local Indians by which, in exchange for "a few shirts, handkerchiefs, and other articles of trifling value," he was granted a lease to twelve square miles of land surrounding the mill. Toward the middle of February he sent one of his employees, Charles Bennett, to Monterey in the hope of having the lease validated by Governor Mason.

Bennett carried with him several ounces of gold. On reaching San Francisco on his way to Monterey he showed it to a friend, Isaac Humphrey, and asked the other's opinion whether it was really gold. Humphrey, an experienced miner, unhesitatingly pronounced the samples genuine, and on Bennett's return from Monterey accompanied his friend back to the mill. They arrived on March 4 and found the workers there devoting all their spare time to washing gravel from the river bed. During the next several weeks so much gold was recovered that it was presently used as a medium of exchange at the trading post that had been established at Sutter's Fort.

But even in face of evidence that gold in considerable quantity was being mined on the American River, San Franciscans remained skeptical. When, in its issue for March 15, the *Californian* first announced the discovery, the news was relegated to a brief paragraph on the little paper's back page. Nine days later Edward C. Kemble, editor of the rival weekly, Sam Brannan's *California Star*, set off to make a personal inspection of the gold fields. On reaching Captain Sutter's settlement, which was called New Helvetia, Kemble was joined by the Captain himself. But as the pair neared the scene of the discovery the workmen caught sight of their employer and, putting aside their pans and rockers, resumed work on the mill. This seems to have had the desired effect, for Kemble returned to San Francisco and in the paper's next issue informed his readers that reports of the richness of the strike were "a humbug."

A few days later, however, a visitor from the diggings appeared at a San Francisco store, made a number of purchases, and by way of payment tossed a poke containing eight ounces of gold on the counter. After some haggling — for no one knew the true value of the metal — the customer was offered and accepted $8 per ounce in trade. The merchant then put the shining particles on display at his store, and in the face of this visible evidence, the doubts of the townspeople began to disappear.

During the next week a number of San Franciscans quietly slipped out of town and headed for the foothills. One of them was the exuberant Sam Brannan, and to Brannan goes credit for belatedly jarring the residents out of their lethargy. On his return from the diggings in mid-May he strode down Montgomery Street, holding aloft a small bottle filled with nuggets, and shouting at the top of his ample lungs, "Gold! Gold! Gold on the American River!"

Part of the large fleet of abandoned sailing ships is shown in this view from Rincon Point during early gold rush days.

Virtually the entire population joined in the rush that followed. In the stores stocks of picks, shovels, pans, and other mining tools were quickly exhausted, and when they were gone the owners padlocked their doors and joined the exodus. So rapidly did the fever spread that within a week after Brannan's dramatic announcement the town was all but deserted. In its issue for May 27 the *California Star,* whose editor had deprecated the importance of the find, reported that ". . . the stores are closed and places of business vacated, a large number of houses tenantless, various kinds of mechanical labor suspended or given up entirely, and nowhere the pleasant hum of industry salutes the ear as of late; but as if a curse had arrested our onward course of enterprise, everything wears a desolate and sombre look, everything is dull, monotonous, dead." Then, having unburdened himself of these gloomy reflections, he himself closed up shop and headed for the foothills.

Not long thereafter a sailing ship flying the Peruvian flag entered the harbor and anchored off the cove. Puzzled that no small boats put out to meet them and that no one could be seen on the beach, the captain went ashore to find out what was amiss. He had walked some distance along the deserted streets before he encountered someone who could enlighten him.

The authors of *The Annals of San Francisco,* a history of the city published in New York in 1856, thus pictured the scene at the time they too set off for the gold fields:

About the end of May we left San Francisco almost a deserted place, and such it continued during the whole summer and autumn months. Many ships with valuable cargoes had meanwhile arrived in the bay, but the seamen deserted. The goods at great expense had somehow been landed, but there was nobody to take care of them, or remove them from the wharves where they lay exposed to the weather. . . . The merchants who remained were in a feverish bustle. They were selling goods at high prices, but could get no hands to assist them in removing and delivering the articles. . . . Here, therefore, as at the mines, the prices of labor and all necessities rose exceedingly. The common laborer, who had formerly been content with his dollar a day, now proudly refused ten; the mechanic, who had recently been glad to receive two dollars, now rejected twenty for his day's services. It was certainly a great country . . . , every subject was as lofty, independent, and seemingly rich as a king.

What happened in San Francisco was duplicated in other California towns. Monterey, the capital, was next to feel the effects of the wholesale migration. In late spring Walter Colton, the town's mayor, reported that not only had the civilian population decamped, but the military and naval personnel had deserted in such numbers that Colonel R. B. Mason, the military governor, the naval commander, and Colton himself, had been reduced to cooking their own meals. "Picture us," wrote Colton, "in a smoking kitchen

Telegraph Hill, showing Fremont Hotel at center left, and tents of newly arrived gold seekers, is from a painting by an unknown artist made in 1849 or '50. (*Wells Fargo Bank History Room.*)

grinding coffee, toasting a herring, and peeling onions." Los Angeles and other southern communities next caught the fever, and soon it reached more distant points. The Hawaiian Islands played a major role in spreading the news abroad. For soon after the rush began, San Francisco merchants dispatched ships to Honolulu for goods to replenish their depleted stocks. Then as now, Honolulu was the crossroads of the Pacific, and ships touching there carried word of California's gold to Australia, China, and the countries of South and Central America.

By midsummer news of the discovery had reached the East Coast, usually in the form of letters from California residents to their home-town newspapers. As had happened earlier at San Francisco, the news at first aroused only mild interest. Toward the end of May, the former U. S. consul at Monterey, Larkin, sent a detailed account of the extent and richness of the mines to Washington, and although his message seemed to confirm the earlier reports, it was disregarded both in governmental circles and by the public at large.

It was not until Governor Mason's official report reached the capital in late November that the importance of the find was recognized. Mason's messenger, Lieutenant L. Loeser, carried with him "a small chest called a caddy containing about $3,000 worth of gold in lumps and scales" which were put on display at the War Office. President Polk's message to Congress on December 2 included this paragraph:

> It was known that mines of the precious metals existed to a considerable extent in California at the time of its acquisition. Recent discoveries render it probable that these mines are more extensive and valuable than was anticipated. The accounts of the abundance of gold in that territory are of such an extraordinary character as would scarcely command belief were it not corroborated by the authentic reports of officers in the public service, who have visited the mineral district, and derived the facts which they detail from personal observation.

5. THE RUSH BEGINS

The effect of President Polk's message was both prompt and dramatic. Throughout the eastern half of the country newspapers printed accounts of the new sensation, and, from Maine to the Mississippi and beyond, thousands made ready to join the exodus. On the eastern and southern coasts the majority chose to go by sea, and so great was the demand for passage that scores of ships were pressed into service, hastily refitted, and, crowded to their fullest capacity, dispatched on the months-long voyage around the Horn. Between December 14, 1848, and January 18, 1849, 61 ships sailed for California from Atlantic Coast ports. By February their number had increased to 130, and the sailings continued at that rate or higher for the remainder of the year.

Even more emigrants made the journey by land, though the overland migration did not get fully under way until the spring of 1849. Contemporary accounts tell of great crowds assembling at St. Jo, Independence, and other frontier towns, waiting until the grass on the prairie ahead was high enough to provide food for the animals. The trains of wagons moving westward were so numerous that they sometimes extended in unbroken lines as far as the eye could see. One emigrant's diary records that he counted 469 wagons on a single nine-mile section of the trail; another states that at night so many campfires were visible that from a distance they resembled the lights of a great city.

In its initial phases the overland journey presented no serious hardship. But after the caravans entered the parched and barren country beyond Salt Lake, their difficulties multiplied. While crossing the sandy desert country the wagons had to be emptied of all but the bare essentials to lighten the loads of the weary draft animals. So much goods was discarded along the way that to one observer the trail resembled the wake of a retreating army. After the desert was passed, a final ordeal faced the emigrants: the lofty Sierra Nevada had to be crossed before they could reach the promised land. Moreover, the trials of those who took the central route were paralleled by other thousands who followed the more southerly trail by way of Santa Fe.

Those who went by sea faced hardships equally severe but of a different nature. Passengers aboard the around-the-Horn sailing ships spent long periods in crowded quarters below decks, subsisting mainly on salt pork and hardtack, washed down with limited rations of brackish water. Others who made the crossing at Panama frequently had to face weeks of waiting on the Pacific side of the Isthmus before they could get passage north. During their enforced stay in the tropics hundreds fell victim to yellow fever.

But whether they traveled by land or sea, or whether they came from the eastern half of the United States or from foreign lands (for world-wide migration was soon under way), the hardships of the journey were borne with fortitude. For all were convinced that a fortune in California gold was awaiting them when they arrived.

6. BOOM TOWN

By late summer of 1848 many San Franciscans who had joined the first rush to the gold fields had returned, and the town became a very lively place indeed. Some had made their way back because they had failed to pick up quick and easy riches in the diggings, others because they foresaw that the business life of the town would be enormously stimulated by the shiploads of Argonauts that had now begun to arrive.

Sansome Street, 1850. An illustration from Frank Marryat's *Mountains and Molehills,* published in London in 1855.

They returned to find that startling changes had taken place. The harbor, in which a month or two earlier only an occasional whaler or merchant ship was to be seen, presented an animated picture. A dozen vessels were anchored in the roadstead and others were arriving daily. Small boats shuttled between ships and shore as passengers and goods were landed — the passengers (and usually the officers and crews as well) to hurry off at once to the diggings, and the cargoes to be dumped in disordered heaps on the shore.

In the town itself the few merchants who had remained behind were doing a land-office business. Such goods as they had to sell brought whatever they chose to ask, and to replenish their depleted stocks they paid comparable prices for merchandise arriving on incoming ships. Throughout California the rush to the foothills had caused normal activities to be suspended; fields were everywhere left unplanted and crops unharvested. Consequently virtually everything was soon in short supply. Food and other necessities had to be brought in from the Hawaiian Islands, Oregon, and other distant points.

The supply of coins in circulation was far too small, and gold dust became the usual medium of exchange. Its value ranged from $8 to $12 per ounce, though at times the supply was so plentiful that it brought $6 or less. Of that phase of the inflated economy, John Henry Brown, the town's first innkeeper, wrote:

Most people had an idea that gold dust would depreciate in value, judging by the quantity which was brought to the city; consequently, I would pay out the gold dust as fast as possible, fearing I might lose by keeping it. . . . Cash seemed to be money, but gold dust was looked on more in the light of merchandise. I have often purchased it for six dollars per ounce. At this time [the fall of 1848] the gamblers would not play for it. Those having no coin were obliged to come to the bar and sell their dust for eight dollars per ounce; and when I was short of cash I would pay only six. . . . The first shipment which I made was with Captain Newell of the schooner *Honolulu* which was going to the Sandwich Islands for goods. I remember giving Newell twenty pounds of gold in bottles with which to purchase goods, and he was to sell the balance of the dust and bring back what cash remained. I did not expect it was going to bring me over twelve dollars per ounce; but, to my great surprise, I did not ship any that brought less than sixteen dollars.

The value of real estate followed the same upward trend. During one period of several months the population doubled every ten days. San Franciscans who returned to town from a brief stay at the mines learned that their property had increased in value many times over. A lot facing Portsmouth Square that a year earlier had been bought for $16.50 was sold in late spring of 1848 for $6,000, and before the end of that year was resold for $45,000. A second lot that had cost its original owner $15, brought $40,000, and a third, which two years earlier had been traded for a barrel of whiskey, was sold by its bemused owner for $18,000.

The increase in rents in the area centering on Portsmouth Square was even greater. A one-story building at the corner of Kearny and Washington streets was leased to a banking firm for $6,000 per month; one-room offices brought as much as $1,000 per month, and one newly arrived attorney was obliged to pay $250 monthly for a tiny basement room. The profits of the gambling houses were so large that their operators could afford to pay fantastic prices for choice locations. One building on the Square rented for $180 *per day*, while space for a single faro table brought $30 for each twelve-hour shift.

Food, clothing, and necessities of all kinds were usually in short supply, and at times of extreme scarcity brought whatever the seller chose to ask. The high cost of goods and services during one such period was thus described by Walter Colton, a former U. S. Navy chaplain, who returned from a few weeks at the diggings in the fall of 1848:

But you are hungry — want a breakfast — turn into a restaurant — call for ham and eggs, and coffee — then your bill — six

dollars! Your high boots, which have never seen a brush since you
first put them on, have given out; you find a new pair that can
replace them — they are a tolerable fit — and now what is the
price — fifty dollars! Your beard has not felt a razor since you
went to the mines—it must come off, and your frizzled hair be
clipped. You find a barber; his dull shears hang in the knots of your
hair like a sheepshearer's — his razor he strops on the leg of his
boot, and then hauls away — starting at every pull a new fountain
of tears. You vow you will let the beard go — but by then one side
is partly off and you try the agony again — and what is the charge
for this torture — four dollars!

During September and October, 1848, eggs sold for $1 each and pota-
toes and onions for $1.50 per pound. The menu of one pioneer eating house
has been preserved. It reads: "Bean soup, $1; hash, low grade, 75¢; hash,
18-carat, $1; beef, plain, $1; beef, with one potato, $1.50; baked beans,
plain, 75¢; baked beans, greased, $1; two potatoes, 50¢; two potatoes, peeled,
75¢; rice pudding, 75¢." That was during the early weeks of the rush. Only
a few months later restaurants were featuring such delicacies as quail, duck,
antelope and deer steaks, and mountain trout, along with imported wines
and liquors, all at prices exceeding those of the most expensive present-day
establishments.

Bayard Taylor, correspondent for the *New York Tribune,* who arrived
in the summer of 1848, thus recorded his experiences on first coming ashore:

A furious wind was blowing down through a gap in the hills,
filling the streets with clouds of dust. On every side stood buildings of all kinds, begun or half-finished, and the greater part of
them were canvas shacks, open in front, and covered with all kinds
of signs, in all languages. Great quantities of goods were piled up
in the open air, for there was no place to store them. The streets
were full of people, hurrying to and fro, and of as diverse and
bizarre a character as the houses: Yankees of every possible variety,
native Californians in serapes and sombreros, Chileans, Sonorians,
Kanakas from Hawaii, Chinese with long tails, Malays armed with
their everlasting creeses, and others on whose embrowned and
bearded visages it was impossible to recognize any special
nationality.

We came at last to the plaza, now dignified by the name Portsmouth Square. It lies on the slant of the hill, and from a high pole
in front of a long one-story adobe building used as the Custom
house, the American flag was flying. On the lower side stood the
Parker House — an ordinary frame house of about sixty feet front
— and towards its entrance we directed our course.

Our luggage was deposited on one of the rear porticos, and we discharged our porters, after paying them two dollars each — a sum so immense in comparison to the service rendered that there was no longer any doubt of our having actually landed in California. There were no lodgings to be had at the Parker House — not even a place to unroll our blankets; but one of the proprietors accompanied us across the plaza to the City Hotel, where we obtained a room with two beds for $25 per week, meals being in addition $20 per week. I asked the landlord whether he could send a porter for our trunks. "There is none belonging to the house," said he; "every man is his own porter here . . ." Our room was a sort of garret over the only story of the hotel; two cots, evidently of California manufacture, and covered only with a pair of blankets, two chairs, a rough table and a small looking-glass, constituted the furniture. There was not space enough between the bed and the rafters overhead to sit upright. . . . Through a small window of dim glass, I could see the opposite side of the bay. The wind whistled around the eaves and rattled the tiles with a cold, gusty sound that would have imparted a dreary character to the place, had I been in a mood to listen.

This view, looking north toward Telegraph Hill, shows the piers extending into the waters of the Cove and, on the right, some of the numerous ships anchored in the roadstead.

IV

The Struggle for Order

1. HOUNDS AND SYDNEY DUCKS

The tens of thousands who poured into San Francisco during 1848 and 1849 caused an almost complete breakdown of existing facilities, both public and private. Means of feeding and housing the newcomers, and of protecting life and property, were quickly overwhelmed. The condition into which municipal affairs had fallen is made clear by this statement to his fellow townsmen by John W. Geary when he took over the office of *alcalde* in August, 1849:

> At this time we are without a dollar in the public treasury, and it is to be feared that the city is greatly in debt. You have neither an office for your magistrate, nor any other public edifice. You are without a single police officer or watchman, and have not the means of confining a prisoner for an hour; neither have you a place to shelter, while living, sick and unfortunate strangers who may be cast upon our shores, or to bury them when dead. Public improvements are unknown in San Francisco. In short, you are without a single requisite necessary for the promotion of prosperity, for the protection of property, or for the maintenance of order.

Geary, in cooperation with the newly elected town council, cast about for means of remedying that situation. The most pressing need was to raise funds to replenish the empty treasury. This was accomplished by the increased sale of town lots, by enforcement of the ordinance requiring businessmen to pay license fees, and by the levying of fines on those convicted of infractions of local laws. Most productive of these fund-raising devices was a drastic increase in the license fees charged gamblers; for the next several years this remained the city's largest source of revenue. The first uses of such funds were for the establishment of a municipal court, for the organization of a paid police force, and for the purchase of the brig *Euphemia* — which was anchored at the intersection of Battery and Jackson streets — for use as a city jail.

The newly formed law-enforcement agencies faced an onerous task. For, as the new *alcalde* had stated, conditions in the overcrowded town were

58

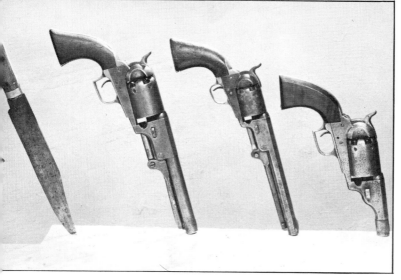

Weapons carried by the Argonauts. The derringer on the right was preferred by members of the gambling fraternity, while the miners favored Colt Navy revolvers. The Bowie knife, left, was useful both for defense and for extracting gold from rock crevices. (*Wells Fargo Bank History Room.*)

completely out of hand. Bands of hoodlums roamed the city, committing crimes that ranged from petty theft to murder, knowing that their victims had recourse to neither police nor courts. Notorious among such groups were the Sydney Ducks, most of them former convicts who had been deported from England to penal colonies in Australia and who had hastened to California at news of the gold strike. The Sydney Ducks were joined by others: former members of Stevenson's regiment of volunteer soldiers from New York, who had recently been demobilized; political hangers-on, many of them products of New York City's Tammany Hall, plus, in the words of historian John S. Hittell, "sharpers, gamblers, and cheating adventurers of every variety."

Throughout the winter of 1848-49 one such group, who called themselves "the Hounds," kept the city in turmoil. They formed themselves into semimilitary companies, established headquarters in a tent near Portsmouth Square, and made nightly forays against the town's foreign colonies. One of their favorite targets was the camp of the Chileans at the base of Telegraph Hill. On such raids they pulled down tents, beat the occupants, and, having helped themselves to whatever they wanted, set fire to whatever remained. The depredations of the Hounds reached a climax in mid-July, 1849. During the course of a raid on "Spanish Town" one of their number was shot and killed, whereupon they set about the destruction of the entire colony, plundering the tents and shooting down their occupants as they fled.

The following morning a group of citizens, shocked and alarmed at this latest outrage, met at Portsmouth Square. There funds were raised for the relief of the victims, and a call was issued for volunteers to help the police restore order. About 230 answered the call. The recruits were given firearms, divided into squads, and dispatched to round up the rioters. That afternoon twenty of the gang's leaders were arrested and placed on a warship in the harbor to await trial. Although the proceedings that followed were without official sanction, the customary legal procedures were observed. Prosecuting and defense attorneys were appointed, a grand jury heard the evidence, and at its end indicted the prisoners on charges of riot, conspiracy, robbery, and assault with intent to kill.

The trial was held the next day; the ringleaders were found guilty and sentenced to prison for terms ranging from one to ten years. Fines were imposed on others, and still others were required to post bonds to assure their keeping the peace. However, means of carrying out the prison sentences were lacking, and in the end such prisoners had to be released. Although the outcome of the trials seemed at the time to be a defeat for the forces of law and order, it served a valuable purpose. For it proved that by acting decisively and in concert the peaceable citizens could curb the excesses of the criminal element and bring violence and bloodshed to at least a temporary halt.

This lesson was not forgotten, as became clear two years later when a new wave of lawlessness threatened to engulf the city. During the interval the ranks of the Hounds had been augmented by criminals from many parts of the world. The groups congregated at Sydney Town, a spot on the slope of Telegraph Hill that later gained a dubious renown as the Barbary Coast. From there they nightly set out for other parts of the city, holding up passersby, looting homes and shops, and beating and sometimes murdering those who resisted. As had happened earlier, the law-abiding citizens were slow to move against the marauders. Only after it became obvious that the police and courts were unable, or unwilling, to control them were the citizens again spurred to action.

That came about when, toward the end of February, 1851, a merchant named Jansen was set on and brutally beaten. Two suspects were arrested, and when they were brought before a local judge for a preliminary hearing, some friends of the victim gathered in the courtroom and demanded that the prisoners instead of being dismissed (which was the customary procedure) be given a prompt and impartial trial. The judge disregarded the citizens' demands and turned the men loose. Thereupon the aroused group arrested them again, organized an impromptu court, and after hearing the testimony of the witnesses, demonstrated the impartiality of the proceedings by releasing the suspects for lack of sufficient evidence connecting them with the attack.

Following that brief flurry of activity, interest in cleaning up the city again subsided and the gangs from Sydney Town were soon operating as boldly as before. The circumstance that once more stirred the populace to action was a growing suspicion that the city's frequent fires were being set by the marauding gangs, who were taking advantage of the resulting confusion to rob and plunder. It was this, together with the growing arrogance of the criminals and the all but complete breakdown of the regularly elected law-enforcement agencies, that led to the organization of the first of the city's much-discussed Vigilance committees, that of 1851.

2. A CITIZENS' ARMY

The purposes of the new organization, which was founded on June 9, 1851, were thus stated in Article 1 of its constitution:

Whereas, it has become apparent to the citizens of San Francisco, that there is no security to life and property, either under the regulations of society as it at present exists, or under the law as now administered:

Therefore, the citizens, whose names are hereunto attached, do unite themselves into an association for the maintenance of the peace and good order of society, and the preservation of the lives and property of the citizens of San Francisco, and do bind themselves, each unto the other, to do and perform every lawful act for the maintenance of law and order, and to sustain the laws when fully and properly administered; but we are determined that no thief, burglar, incendiary or assassin, shall escape punishment, either by the quibbles of the law, the insecurity of prisons, or the laxity of those who pretend to administer justice.

Attached to the document were the signatures of about two hundred men, including many leaders in the business and professional life of the city.

The organization of the committee had hardly been completed when it was called on to act. On the evening of the following day, June 10, a burglar, John Jenkins, was surprised while breaking into a store on the Long Wharf. He had taken an iron safe from the store, lowered it into a rowboat, and was making off with it when he was arrested by two newly enrolled members and taken to the committee's headquarters, which were then situated at Sansome Street near Bush. A prearranged signal — the ringing of a bell on a near-by firehouse — summoned the members. About eighty men responded, and while a large crowd gathered outside, the prisoner was tried, found guilty, and sentenced to be hanged. When Sam Brannan, one of the committee's leaders, announced the verdict to those in the street, it was met with shouts of approval by most, though some protested that the trial had been conducted with undue haste. Shortly before 2 o'clock that same night the prisoner, closely guarded to prevent attempts to rescue him, was marched to Portsmouth Square. There a rope was thrown over a beam at one end of the Custom House and the order of the impromptu court was carried out.

The arrest of Jenkins and his speedy trial and execution were received with mixed feelings by the townspeople. The committee members made clear that they deplored the necessity of having to resort to extralegal methods to restore order, but that the officials charged with enforcing the law had failed to do so. On the other hand, there were those who maintained that the weakness and corruption of the police and courts posed a less serious threat to the security of the inhabitants than what they termed the "mob rule" of the Vigilantes.

Also ranged against the committee were the lawbreakers themselves and the city officials whose duties the Vigilantes had taken over. At an inquest held on June 12 a coroner's jury condemned the committee's action and held nine of its members responsible for Jenkins' death. The committee responded by publicly announcing that all its members assumed equal responsibility for its actions. The announcement summarized the reasons why the organization had been formed and repeated a pledge to disband as soon as its ends had been achieved. The temperate tone of that pronouncement, plus the high character of the men whose names were signed to it, did much to allay the misgivings of their fellows and to win them broad support.

A few days later the committee adopted a resolution inviting the public to cooperate by reporting robberies and other unlawful acts, and warning felons to leave the city voluntarily under penalty of being expelled by force. The final two paragraphs read:

> Resolved, That a safety committee of thirty persons be appointed, whose sacred duty it shall be to visit every vessel arriving with notorious or suspicious characters on board, and unless they can present to said committee evidence of good character and honesty they shall be reshipped to the places from whence they came. . . .
>
> Resolved, That all good citizens be invited to join and assist the Committee of Vigilance in carrying out the above measures so

---

The execution of Whittaker and McKenzie by the Vigilance Committee of 1851 drew a large audience.

necessary to the perfect restoration of peace, safety, and good order
in our community.

As a result of the committee's warning to lawbreakers to leave the city,
the number of passengers aboard the steamers bound for Sacramento,
Stockton, and other interior points increased markedly during the next few
days.

At its daily meetings the committee heard the complaints of residents
who had been robbed, assaulted, or otherwise injured, dispatched squads
to bring in the suspects, and having heard the evidence, either released
them, levied fines, or placed them aboard outgoing ships with instructions
never to return.

On July 11, a month after the execution of Jenkins, the death penalty
was imposed on a second prisoner. The victim this time was James Stuart, a
former convict from Sydney; Stuart was found guilty of murder and, two
hours later, hanged from a derrick on the end of one of the wharves. Again,
the regularly elected officials denounced the committee's action, and a grand
jury was appointed to recommend means of curbing its powers. The jury's
report, rendered later that month, ended with these words:

> The grand jurors, believing, whilst they deplore their acts, that
> the association styling themselves "the Vigilance Committee," at
> great personal sacrifice to themselves have been influenced in their
> actions by no personal or private malice, but for the best interests
> of the whole, and at the same time, too, when all other means of
> preventing crime and bringing criminals to direct punishment had
> failed, here dismiss the matter.

When opponents of the committee failed to have its leaders indicted
by the grand jury, they appealed to the authorities at Sacramento. On July
21 Governor John McDougal wrote the organization's leaders, pointing out
the dangers of such self-constituted tribunals and urging its members to "act
in concert with the civil authorities to detect, arrest and punish criminals."
His message continued: "It is my sworn duty to see that the laws are executed, and I feel assured that all good citizens will cordially cooperate with
me in its discharge." Despite the conciliatory tone of McDougal's statement,
it was evident that a major clash of wills between the two factions was in
the making. For although the Vigilantes repeated their promise to disband
when order had been restored, they refused to do so until they considered
their task accomplished.

The long-expected test of strength took place on August 18, when
agents of the committee arrested two suspected burglars, Samuel Whittaker
and Robert McKenzie, took them to headquarters, and after hearing the
evidence sentenced them to death. Early on the morning of August 21, a
squad of deputies from the sheriff's office appeared at the committee rooms,

overpowered the guards, and took the prisoners to the city jail. The ringing of the bell on the tower of the Monumental Volunteer Fire Company sounded the alarm, and the Vigilantes hurriedly assembled. Some members urged an immediate attack on the jail to retrieve the prisoners; however, calmer judgment prevailed and for several days no action was taken. Then, on the following Sunday, a party of Vigilantes, thirty strong, forced their way into the jail, recaptured the prisoners, returned them to the committee rooms, and carried out the sentence.

The execution of Whittaker and McKenzie was one of the committee's final acts. Soon thereafter the organization ceased to function. Although it was never formally disbanded, no further meetings were held and the administration of the law was left to the regularly elected officials.

During the ten weeks it had remained in session, the committee condemned and executed three men, forced scores of undesirables to flee the city, and, by its inspection of incoming ships, prevented the landing of many others. Its most important service, however, was to draw attention to the weakness and corruption of those charged with maintaining the peace, and to awaken a demand that a respect for law and order be restored.

3. A SEQUENCE OF FIRES

Another ever-present hazard during the late 1840s and early 1850s was fire. This problem, like that posed by lawlessness, called for the expenditure of much time and effort before it could be even partially solved.

The principal cause of the fires that periodically destroyed large sections of the early city was that most of the houses in the downtown area were built of wood and cloth. Another cause was the brisk winds that daily blew in from the ocean, and a third was the fact that wood stoves and kerosene or whale-oil lamps were the usual sources of heat and light. Still another cause was the Sydney Ducks, who set fires to divert attention while they carried on their looting operations elsewhere. Whatever their origin, the city's lack of an adequate water supply and proper fire-fighting equipment made it virtually impossible to check the flames once they had gained headway.

Between 1848 and 1851, six major fires swept the city. All caused heavy damages, rendered many homeless, and created acute shortages of food and other essentials. The first of the series broke out on Christmas Eve of 1848. It consumed all buildings on both sides of Kearny Street between Washington and Clay and caused a loss estimated at one million dollars. Among the buildings destroyed was the two-story Parker House, the largest and best known of the city's hotels, whose entire ground floor was occupied by gambling casinos.

A larger and more destructive fire, on May 4, 1849, leveled the two blocks bounded by Kearny, Clay, Washington, and Montgomery streets to

This view from the top of the California Street hill pictures the fire of June 22, 1851, which destroyed twelve square blocks in the heart of the city and caused a loss estimated at $3 million.

the east of Portsmouth Square, and, facing the Square to the north, a block bounded by Kearny, Washington, Dupont, and Jackson. Whereas the operators of bars and gaming rooms had been the chief losers in the earlier fire, in this one the losses, which amounted to nearly three million dollars, fell most heavily on merchants, bankers, agents for stage and steamship lines, and other business and professional men. Six weeks later, on June 14, yet another major blaze — the third in less than six months — consumed the four-block-square district between Clay, Kearny, and California streets and the bay; it, too, caused a loss of approximately three million dollars.

Meanwhile steps were being taken to protect the city from these recurrent disasters. After the fire of May 4, 1849, the town council appropriated funds for digging additional wells and building a reservoir. At the same time the council passed two ordinances. One required property owners to keep six buckets full of water about their premises at all times; the second levied heavy fines on those who refused to fight the fires or to help remove property in their paths. Yet another precautionary measure prohibited the further building of houses with walls or roofs of canvas. This last measure, however, had little practical effect, for the city at that time was constructed almost entirely of wood; the only fire-resistant buildings were a few adobes that dated from pre-conquest days.

It was not until less inflammable materials came to be widely used in rebuilding the burned-over areas that efforts to prevent fires, or to confine them to limited areas, began to bear results. Early in 1850 appeared the

The headquarters of the various volunteer fire companies had pumps, hose-carts and other equipment on their ground floors and handsomely fitted up clubrooms above. Pictured here are the buildings of the St. Francis Hook and Ladder Company No. 1 *(left)* and of the Knickerbocker Engine Company No. 5 *(right)*.

first buildings of a type that long remained characteristic of the business section of the city. These were narrow, two- and three-story structures of brick or stone. Each had iron shutters before its doors and windows which were folded back during the day and closed at night or when danger threatened. The shutters afforded a measure of protection against the two prime hazards of the period — fire and theft. The fact that several scores of these picturesque buildings were still in use more than a century later is evidence of their sturdy construction.

But that type of construction was just getting fully under way when the city suffered its most disastrous fire of all, that of May 4, 1851.

It really commenced [wrote John S. Hittell] a little before twelve on the night of the third of May, but was called the fire of the fourth. It swept away the entire business portion of the city. . . . The burned district was three quarters of a mile long and a quarter of a mile wide, and more than fifteen hundred houses were destroyed. Sixteen blocks were burned, including ten bounded by Pine, Jackson, Kearny and Sansome; five bounded by Sansome, Battery, Sacramento and Broadway; one bounded by Kearny, Montgomery, Washington and Jackson, and fractions of five other blocks. Many of the brick buildings supposed to be fireproof were unable to withstand the intense heat of half a mile of flame fanned by a high wind. Vast quantities of goods were destroyed. In some cases men stayed inside of the brick stores with barrels of water, intending to risk their lives in the hope of saving their buildings and goods. Twelve men were shut up in Naglee's building [Naglee was a pioneer banker] for three hours in the midst of intense heat and almost suffocating smoke, but they survived. Six who remained in the store of Taaffe, McCahill & Co. were not so fortunate.

A visiting English journalist, Frank Marryat, described the spectacle in these words:

No conception can be formed of the grandeur of the scene; for at one time the burning district was covered by one vast sheet of flame that extended half a mile in length. But when the excitement of such a night as this has passed by, one scarcely can recall the scene. The memory is confused with the recollection of the shouts of the excited populace — the crash of falling timbers — the yells of the burnt and injured — the maddened horses released from burning livery-stables plunging through the streets — helpless patients being carried from some hospital, as the swaying crowd, forced back by the flames, tramples all before it — explosions of houses blown up by gunpowder — showers of burning splinters that fell around on every side — the thunder of brick buildings as they fell into heaps of ruin — the blinding glare of ignited spirits.

This panoramic view from Telegraph Hill shows the city and bay in 1850. It is from a lithograph published in London in 1851.

Then and for more than a decade thereafter, San Francisco's fire-fighting facilities were owned and manned exclusively by volunteers. The first major blaze, that of Christmas Eve, 1848, had demonstrated the urgent need for pumps, hoses, ladders, and other devices, and of men trained in their use. Accordingly, at a mass meeting held in Portsmouth Square a few days later, three engine companies — the San Francisco, the Empire, and the Protection — had been organized, and funds had been raised to buy the necessary equipment and to provide quarters to house it.

The volunteer fire companies were in effect clubs, and membership in such organizations was looked on as a mark of social distinction. Their headquarters, which usually occupied the upper floors of the station houses, were often fitted out with card and billiard tables, a library, a bar, and other recreational facilities. As time passed, keen competition developed among the different companies. Each aimed to excel not only in the speed with

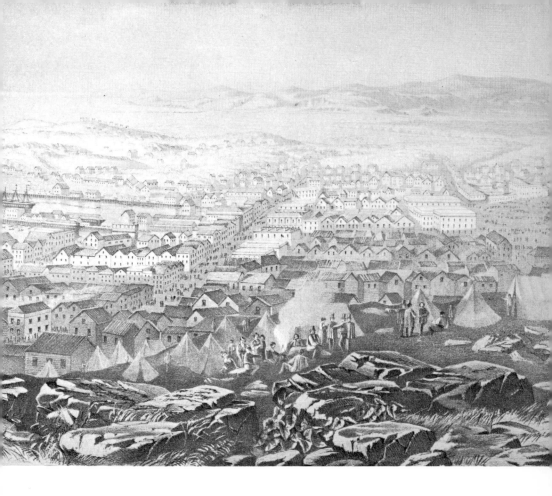

which they responded to alarms but in the quality of their equipment and the skill with which it was used. So strong did the rivalry become that there were occasions when two companies on arriving simultaneously at the scene of a fire fought pitched battles among themselves while the buildings they had come to save burned to the ground.

As the number of volunteer companies grew — by 1855 they totaled more than twenty — they came to wield considerable influence in civic affairs. Men who aspired to public office could hardly hope to win without their support, and the successful candidates were often chosen from the ranks of these companies. During the early years their political power was used in worthy causes. Later, however, many companies fell under the control of politicians who used them to further their own ends. It was mainly for that reason that, in 1866, the citizens voted to disband the volunteer companies. Thereupon a paid fire department took over the protection of the city.

4. VIGILANTES AGAIN

Between 1848 and 1852 the center of the city was several times rebuilt, each time on a more ambitious scale. Some of the reconstruction was financed with public funds, the balance by private capital. In 1852 the city purchased, for $200,000, the Jenny Lind Theater at Kearny and Washington streets and converted it into a city hall and court house. Other civic activities of the period included the laying of a three-mile-long "plank road" out Folsom Street to the Mission Dolores, and the improvement of port facilities by building new piers and docks. The last-named projects were paid for by the sale of waterfront property that until then had been reserved for possible use by the federal government.

New churches, schools, and theaters, the founding of a library, and the building of the first horse-drawn streetcar line were all evidences of San Francisco's swift transition from a frontier village to what by the standards of the day was a fully equipped modern city. Montgomery, Kearny, Washington, Clay, and other downtown streets were lined with substantial buildings of brick or stone. One of these, the four-story Montgomery Block (which was owned by a future Civil War general, Henry W. Halleck) was at the time of its completion in 1853 the largest building west of the Mississippi and remained so for more than a decade.

By the spring of 1854, however, it became clear that the city's five-year-long boom was slackening off. Gold production declined sharply as the richest of the placers were worked out, the number of arriving emigrants thinned to a trickle and then stopped entirely, and hundreds of miners, no longer able to support themselves at the diggings, flocked back to the city — where few jobs awaited them. The result was that San Francisco found itself in the grip of its first serious depression. For some months, however, this was looked on as no more than a temporary setback; few doubted that new strikes in the foothills, plus the rise of agriculture and the beginnings of industry would soon revive the state's sagging economy.

But news from the mines continued to be bad, and as gold dust became scarce and customers few, the local merchants — whose shelves were piled high with unsold goods, and who were without funds to pay for new shipments that were arriving by every steamer — were forced to close their doors. According to one account, by the end of 1854 more than one-third of the city's one thousand stores stood vacant. All types of businesses shared in the decline. During the next twelve months more than two hundred persons and companies went bankrupt. So many loans were defaulted that the city's leading financial houses were obliged to close. The failure of Page, Bacon & Company in February, 1855, and of Adams & Company soon after, completed the debacle.

The already gloomy situation was made more so by a realization that during the prosperous years when they had been occupied with their own affairs, the self-serving politicians had once again taken over the control of the city government and were enriching themselves at the expense of the taxpayers. The true state of affairs was revealed in dramatic fashion in the fall of 1854. On October 6 of that year Henry Meiggs, a member of the town council and the holder of much property in the North Beach area, slipped out of the Golden Gate aboard a chartered brig, the *American,* carrying with him several hundred thousand dollars in gold that he had accumulated by forging city warrants.

When the amount of Meiggs' peculations, and the means by which he had been able to amass so large a sum, became known, the citizens were both shocked and angered. Their anger was directed not so much against the fugitive himself as against those officials who had failed to detect and prevent the crime. The investigation that followed had not progressed far before it became clear that laxness and ineptitude in the conduct of the city business were not the only — or the most serious — shortcomings of the city-hall group. So many evidences of extravagance, favoritism in the award of city contracts, and close connections with gamblers and other underworld figures were uncovered that a full-scale campaign to clean up the city got under way.

One of the leaders in that movement was James King of William (so called to distinguish him from other James Kings in the city), a former banker who had recently founded a daily newspaper, the *Evening Bulletin.* The *Bulletin* entered an already crowded field — during that period the city seldom had less than a dozen newspapers — but from the beginning the little journal was widely read. In daily editorials its crusading editor denounced the city's wrongdoers, exposing corruption and chicanery wherever found. The police and courts were among his favorite targets, the one for failing to arrest known lawbreakers and the other for refusing to convict those brought to trial.

King's most forceful blows, however, were directed against what he termed the chief source of the city's woes — gambling and its attendant evils, including prostitution. Gambling had, of course, been a feature of San Francisco life from the beginning and, as in other frontier communities, had been looked on with tolerance by all but a few. Hence, by the time that attitude began to change, the owners of the gaming rooms were so firmly entrenched, and wielded so much influence in official circles, that attempts to outlaw them or to regulate their activities had uniformly failed.

The *Bulletin's* crusade was shrewdly conducted. To give his charges the appearance of impartiality, King opened his columns to spokesmen for the opposition and in parallel columns answered their arguments. During the heat of battle, the editor was accused, with some justice, of using unfair

The shooting of James King of William. It was the attack on this crusading editor that led to the formation of the Vigilance Committee of 1856. *(Frank Leslie's Illustrated Newspaper.)*

tactics, both by making unsubstantiated charges and by attacking individuals out of personal enmity. But despite his occasional excesses, the truth of his charges was widely recognized, and the *Bulletin's* campaign gained many supporters.

Two of the men King had been denouncing in particularly violent terms were a local gambler, Charles Cora, and James P. Casey, editor of a rival paper, the *Sunday Times*. Casey, who had served his political apprenticeship in the New York City wards, had recently been elected a member of the town council — a feat he had accomplished by stuffing several hundred ballots bearing his name into the ballot box of a precinct where he was serving as an election inspector. King learned of that exploit, exposed it in his paper, and added the charge that the new councilman was an ex-convict who had served a term in Sing Sing. Casey vehemently denied both charges and demanded that King print a retraction. Instead of complying, King made known his intention of producing documentary evidence supporting his claims, whereupon Casey threatened to shoot him on sight. King retorted that he would leave the *Bulletin* office at the usual time the following afternoon, May 14. This he did; he had proceeded only a short distance down Montgomery Street when Casey confronted him, ordered him to draw and defend himself, then raised his own weapon and fired. The bullet struck King in the chest and passed through a lung.

The wounded editor staggered into a near-by store and collapsed. The entire city had been following the feud between the two men, and its violent conclusion aroused the citizens to a high pitch of excitement. While doctors attended the injured man, Casey's supporters hurried him to the city jail to protect him from the wrath of his victim's friends. Within an hour a large crowd had gathered before the jail, loudly demanding that the prisoner be turned over to them.

The sheriff appeared and addressed the gathering, assuring them that Casey would be given a prompt and impartial trial. His remarks were greeted with shouts of derision. Threats to lynch the prisoner were made, and for a time an assault on the building seemed imminent. But cooler heads prevailed, and most of the demonstrators eventually left. However, a few remained overnight to thwart any attempt to spirit the prisoner out of the city.

Among the groups that had gathered on the downtown sidewalks on the evening of the shooting were many who recalled a similar situation five years earlier when the townspeople, aware that their elected officials were too weak or too corrupt to enforce the law, had taken matters into their own hands. Demands for a revival of the Vigilance Committee of 1851 were heard on every side. A circular was hastily printed, summoning the citizens to a mass meeting to be held in a vacant warehouse on Battery Street. Several hundred answered the call, but although there was much heated discussion, no decision was reached. Next morning another meeting was held, this time on the second floor of a building on Sacramento Street — a building that was later fortified with sacks of sand and became known as Fort Gunnybags. William T. Coleman, a merchant who had played a leading part in the earlier committee, was named chairman of the new organization; an oath pledging "their lives, fortunes and sacred honor" to the cause was drawn up, and the membership roll was opened to volunteers. Some years later Coleman wrote:

> The organization was to be entirely impersonal, and each man was to be known only by his number. An organization into military companies, well officered, was perfected the first evening. Within two days after the first meeting twenty-five hundred men were enrolled and equipped with arms, while drilling was carried on

Badges worn by the Vigilantes of 1856. Strict discipline was maintained among members of this organization. While on duty they were required to wear badges identifying the companies to which they belonged.

constantly day and night. . . . While the work of organization and preparation was progressing we were informed of numerous counter movements by opponents of the committee. Word was brought that the roughs were organizing in large numbers, arming, and threatening with determined energy to defend Casey, Cora [who was waiting trial for the murder of a United States marshal] and their friends. . . . The next day it developed that a strong effort was being made by the mayor and others to organize and bring into action all the militia of the state that were available. The large and better part of the militia of the city had, however, already joined the committee.

On May 16, two days after the shooting of King, California's governor, J. Neely Johnson, arrived from Sacramento (which had become the capital of the state two years earlier) and urged the Vigilantes to disband and allow the prisoner to be tried in the local court. Coleman and his fellow Vigilantes refused, pointing out that the city government was controlled by Casey and his friends and that there was no possibility of their giving him a fair and impartial trial. Then, on Saturday, May 18, the committee, its preparations complete, ordered Casey and Cora to be taken from the city jail and brought to Fort Gunnybags.

At 9 o'clock the following morning twenty-four companies of armed men converged on Portsmouth Square from various parts of the city. Each company took up a designated position before the jail and stood at attention while a demand was made on the sheriff that he surrender his prisoners. In the face of this massive show of strength no resistance was offered, and Casey and Cora were loaded into a carriage and driven to the committee headquarters. Immediately on arriving they were brought to trial, the organization's Executive Committee sitting as a court. "No outside counsel was permitted, wrote Coleman, "but all witnesses desired by the prisoners were summoned and gave their testimony in full. Both were convicted of murder in the first degree and sentenced to be hanged."

A short time before the trial began word reached the committee that King had died of his wounds. Three days later, on May 22, the editor was given an impressive funeral. As the mile-long procession moved through the downtown streets, the condemned men were hanged from a gallows set up in front of Fort Gunnybags.

In San Francisco many believed that the Vigilance Committee of 1851 had failed to accomplish its purpose because it had disbanded before its work was fully done, and those in charge of the 1856 organization were determined not to make the same mistake. They accordingly set about the task of ridding the city of lawless elements. This proved a difficult plan to carry out, for although the identity of the ringleaders was known, the much-debated question was how best to deal with them. In most instances the nature of their crimes did not warrant the punishment meted out to Casey and Cora. Imprisonment for a brief period would have accomplished no lasting good, and the committee had no means of holding them longer. "It was therefore suggested," Coleman wrote, "that if, after a fair trial, the charges against them were proved, no course would be so satisfactory and safe as banishment, with a warning never again to return under pain of death."

The committee proceeded on that basis. A list of several score of law-breakers was compiled, and armed squads were dispatched to round them up and bring them to headquarters for trial. Some were dismissed for lack of evidence, others were found guilty and held until an outbound ship was about to sail, then were hustled aboard. Whenever possible, the prisoners were placed on ships bound for their native countries.

That program was carried out in orderly fashion. The arresting squads brought in their daily quota of suspects to be tried by the Executive Committee, which held sessions each afternoon and evening. So rapidly was this work accomplished that by mid-June — only a month after the committee was organized — plans to wind up its affairs and disband got under way. July 4 was chosen as the day when the members, in military formation, would march through the downtown streets to Portsmouth Square and, after appropriate ceremonies, be mustered out.

As far as anyone could foresee, the committee's work was almost done. As it turned out, however, it had only just begun.

This two-story building, the former Post Office, stood at the corner of Kearny and Clay streets. In 1856 it was the rallying point for members of the "Law and Order" party, which opposed the Second Vigilance Committee. A portion of Portsmouth Square appears in the foreground.

5. MR. COLEMAN'S "WHITE ELEPHANT"

One of the most vehement of the committee's critics was David S. Terry, a Justice of the State Supreme Court and a close friend and political associate of Governor Johnson. One day the fiery former Texan came from Sacramento to rally support for the Law and Order Party, as the anti-Vigilante forces termed themselves. On the afternoon of his arrival, he was in the office of a politician, Reuben Maloney, when three committee members appeared with orders to arrest Maloney and bring him to headquarters for questioning. Terry identified himself to the men and forbade them to make the arrest. The Vigilantes withdrew and returned to Fort Gunnybags for further instructions. On orders of the Executive Committee, the party was reinforced and dispatched to make the arrest — peaceably if possible, but by force if necessary. Meanwhile Terry and several companions had set off with Maloney, intending to place him under guard in the state armory where he presumably would be out of reach of his would-be captors.

As the two groups were hurrying through the streets — the Vigilante squad heading for Maloney's office, and Terry's group on their way to the armory — they chanced to meet on Clay Street, near Portsmouth Square. As the leader of the Vigilante party, S. A. Hopkins, approached Maloney, Terry stepped forward, attempting to bar his way. Hopkins brushed past, and as he did so Terry drew a bowie knife and plunged it into the other's neck, inflicting what at the time was believed to be a fatal wound.

The committee's response to that challenge was both prompt and decisive. At once orders were issued for the arrest of Terry and those who had been with him at the time of the stabbing. The tolling of the bell atop Fort Gunnybags sounded a general alarm, and when the members assembled they were ordered to round up the committee's enemies wherever found and bring them to headquarters. So speedily was this accomplished that by nightfall not only were Terry and his companions in custody, but more than two hundred others had been brought in.

Most of those arrested were released the next day. Judge Terry and several of his companions, however, were held under close guard. No charges were filed against the Justice pending the outcome of his victim's wound. Several days passed while the issue remained in doubt, during which hourly bulletins from the patient's bedside were anxiously read throughout the city. Few doubted that should the wound prove fatal, Terry's own life would be in jeopardy. When it became evident that the wounded man would recover, the community breathed a collective sigh of relief.

Nonetheless, the prisoner was brought to trial, though on the lesser charge of assault. The hearings, which lasted the better part of a month, were marked by frequent bitter exchanges between the prisoner and those prosecuting him, exchanges that served to intensify the already deep animosities dividing the city. The unenviable position in which the Vigilantes found themselves was thus summarized by Josiah Royce:

If Hopkins should die, one could only with great difficulty avoid hanging Judge Terry, unless, indeed, one was willing to abdicate, and leave the mob to hang him itself. But to hang by popular judgment a supreme court judge is an act involving certain obviously embarrassing responsibilities. And if, as later actually proved to be the case, Hopkins did not die, then a supreme judge whom one could not effectually banish nor yet imprison long, whom one must not hang, and whom one could not gracefully release without any punishment, would indeed be a "white elephant."

The means the committee chose to get out of its dilemma proved satisfactory to no one. For after holding their prisoner for seven weeks he was given his unconditional release, his captors contenting themselves with passing a resolution stating that "the interests of the state imperatively demand that he resign his position as judge of the Supreme Court." Terry's release disappointed numerous San Franciscans, including many members of the committee itself, who deeply resented the prisoner's unrepentant

---

This banner is evidence of the widespread support given members of the Vigilance Committees of 1851 and 1856 in their efforts to put down lawlessness and rid the city of its criminal element.

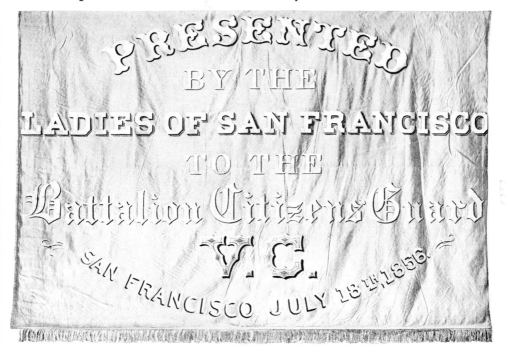

manner and truculent behavior throughout his trial. So strong was the feeling against him that on the day he was turned loose, friends hurried him to safety aboard a naval vessel in the harbor. A few nights later he slipped ashore, returned to Sacramento, and once more donned his judicial robes.

While Terry's long drawn-out trial was in progress, the committee's campaign to rid the city of objectionable characters continued. After three months of continuous activity, during which its members patrolled the city streets day and night, it was able to point to these accomplishments: twenty-five dangerous criminals had been deported; several times that number had obeyed orders to leave the city and state, while the number who voluntarily left in order to escape prosecution was estimated at between five hundred and eight hundred; four men were tried for murder, found guilty, and executed—James Casey for the shooting of James King of William, Charles Cora, the slayer of U. S. Marshal William H. Richardson, Philander Brace for a murder committed two years earlier (for which he had twice been acquitted by the local courts), and Joseph Hetherington for the fatal shooting of Dr. Randall, a San Francisco physician.

The hanging of Brace and Hetherington was the committee's final major act. Nine days later, on the afternoon of July 18, the members assembled for the last time, paraded through the downtown streets, then gathered before Fort Gunnybags, turned in their arms, and were mustered out.

Much has since been written about the Vigilante movement, both in praise and blame. But even the committee's critics grant that its members took matters into their own hands only after the regular law-enforcement agencies had failed of their duty, either through incompetence or dishonesty, that the committee broke the rule of the corrupt politicians and that it awakened the law-abiding citizens to a realization of their civic responsibilities. This last is borne out by the fact that at an election held a few weeks after the committee had disbanded, a slate of candidates pledged to a thorough overhauling of the city government was voted into office by a substantial majority.

V

Che Fifties

1. THE CHANGING SHORELINE

By the mid-1850s the former frontier village had taken on the appearance of a substantial, well-ordered city. Although many evidences of its helter-skelter beginnings still remained—some, indeed, have persisted to the present—rarely has a transformation so great been accomplished in so brief a time. The frequent early-day fires had taught a costly but valuable lesson; namely, that only by rebuilding the burned areas with fire-resistant materials could a repetition of such disasters be prevented. The consequence was that by 1855 the downtown streets were lined with scores of impressive-looking banks, hotels, theaters, shops, and other business houses, all built of brick or stone.

About the fringes of the central district the tents and board shacks of the Forty-niners had given way to acres of prim wooden cottages crowded together on their narrow lots, some built close to the board sidewalks, others with iron fences enclosing tiny front gardens. In the residential districts the streets themselves, which a year or two earlier had been mere rutted trails, dusty in summer and knee-deep in mud during the rainy season, had been graded and in some instances paved with wood planks.

South Park and Rincon Hill, both south of Market Street, were then considered the city's most desirable residential areas—mainly because of their milder climate and comparative freedom from wind and fog. There the city's bankers, merchants, and other prosperous citizens built their homes; many were handsome structures, elegantly furnished in the style of the day, and each with a stable and carriage house in the rear. It was not until the early 1870s when the new mining and railroad millionaires built their mansions on Nob Hill that South Park and Rincon Hill ceased to be centers of wealth and fashion. Today the district is given over to factories and warehouses.

As population grew, the city continued to expand. Streets and buildings ascended the slopes of Nob and Telegraph hills to the north and east

In the early days, as shown in the 1851 street scene *(above)*, storage space was so scarce that the hulls of abandoned ships were drawn up out of the mud and converted into warehouses. From Frank Marryat's *Mountains and Molehills.* This photograph *(below)*, also made in 1851, shows part of the "forest of masts" that covered the waters of the Cove. *(The Society of California Pioneers.)*

These curious "iron houses" *(above)* were built in 1851 of metal shipped around the Horn from Boston. They stood at the corner of Jackson and Battery streets for many years and were demolished a few months before the fire of 1906. Community celebrations *(below)* were popular during the 1850s. In 1851 the observance of Washington's Birthday drew this large crowd to Portsmouth Square.

This excellent lithograph, made in Paris in 1855, pictures the city
as it was during that year. California Street is shown on the right,

of the business district, and in the opposite direction spread over the present retail shopping district and out Market Street toward the mission.

The greatest changes, however, took place in the vicinity of the original village. From earliest times the residents had depended for a livelihood almost entirely on trade with the ships that visited the harbor, and as
the activity of the port increased, facilities for the more expeditious handling
of goods had to be provided. The first steps in that direction were taken,
as related earlier, before the gold discovery, when the work of filling in the
shallow cove began and the first piers were built. Once the rush got under
way, the existing facilities were quickly overwhelmed. Accordingly, a group
of merchants organized a "Wharf Association" and in May, 1849, began
building a new series of piers.

The earliest of these, which became known as the Long Wharf, followed the line of Commercial Street. By the end of 1849 it had attained a
length of eight hundred feet; later it was extended several hundred feet
farther. The total cost of this structure was $180,000; however, it proved
to be a lucrative investment, for the wharfage fees are said to have returned
the full amount to the builders in less than three months. So profitable a
venture naturally attracted other investors. Piers were soon being built

Goat (Yerba Buena) Island in the center right, and Telegraph Hill on the left.

from the ends of every street from Market Street on the south to the base of Telegraph Hill. One of the best known was Howison's Pier, a forty-foot-wide structure that extended one thousand feet into the bay and permitted the largest ships to tie up at its end. A second, the Clay Street Wharf, also forty feet wide, had a length of eighteen hundred feet, and a third, Cunningham's Wharf, which was built in the form of a T, could accommodate half a dozen vessels at one time. By the end of 1850 nearly two miles of piers, representing an investment of $1,500,000, were either completed or in process of building.

Meanwhile the city itself was encroaching on the cove. Several piers were solidly lined with houses built on piles, containing shops, restaurants, and other businesses—and so great was the need for storage space that many abandoned ships were drawn into the shallows and converted into warehouses. Throughout 1850 and 1851 the work of filling in the tidelands between the shore and the pier ends continued. By the end of 1851 the crescent-shaped cove had been reclaimed to the point where the piers had been replaced by streets over more than half their lengths.

This filling-in process was a major undertaking. For to raise an area of some forty square blocks several feet above high tide, and to protect

Old St. Mary's Church *(top)* was the city's first cathedral. This historic structure has stood at the corner of California Street and Dupont (now Grant Avenue) for well over a century. In 1856 its handsome clock tower and steeple were still unfinished.

The three-story Custom House *(left)* at Battery, Washington, and Jackson streets was built in 1854 and housed the Post Office and other federal departments until it was demolished in 1904 and replaced by the modern structure.

A view of Battery Street *(below)* in the mid-1850s. The ornamental façade of the Merchants Exchange Building, then newly completed, is seen in the center.

Russian Hill is seen *(above)* from the crest of Telegraph Hill in 1856. In the foreground are the closely-built houses of the North Beach district.

Looking toward Telegraph Hill *(below),* from the vicinity of California and Stockton streets, the upper story of the Montgomery Block at Montgomery and Washington streets is visible at the extreme right.

One of a revealing series of photographs made in 1856, this view looks down Stockton Street toward the bay, with Alcatraz and Angel islands visible in the background.

the fill with bulkheads on the water side, required the moving of huge amounts of earth and rock. A familiar sight during that period was the "steam paddy," a diminutive locomotive that shuttled on temporary tracks through the downtown streets, drawing carloads of sand from the near-by hills to be dumped in the cove.

By that means [wrote the authors of *The Annals of San Francisco*] Sansome, Battery and the intersecting streets to a considerable distance were gradually filled up, and firm foundations given for the substantial brick and stone houses that were beginning to be erected there. The town continued to move eastward, and new streets were formed upon piles further out into the bay . . . as house after house was reared on innumerable piles, while the steam paddy and railroad wagons, and horse-carts without number, were incessantly bearing hills of sand piecemeal to fill up the hollows, and drive the sea far away from the original beach. Where once ships of a thousand tons floated there now rose great tenements of brick and mortar securely founded on solid earth.

During the first several years the urgent need for docking facilities had justified the building of piers and the filling in of the cove. However, as the shoreline was pushed ever farther out into the bay, strong opposition developed. Shipowners protested that as the piers were extended beyond the sheltered cove, the vessels tied up to their ends were exposed to strong winds and tides. Also opposed were those who had purchased water-front lots only to find as more of the tidelands were reclaimed, their property no longer faced the water but was some distance inland.

The controversy came to a head in April, 1853, when a bill was introduced into the State Legislature authorizing the sale of additional water lots for a distance of six-hundred feet beyond the existing boundary line. During the weeks while hearings on the bill were being held the matter was hotly debated in the local press. The measure failed to pass, but by so narrow a margin that the proposal was several times renewed during the next few years. A compromise was eventually reached. In 1863, the Legislature passed a bill creating a Board of State Harbor Commissioners, giving that body permanent control over the harbor installations of the city.

2. BY STEAMER AND STAGECOACH

California's isolation from the rest of the country had long been regarded as the chief obstacle to its fullest development. Plans for speeding communications between the two coasts got under way soon after the Americans had taken over in 1846. Early the following year Congress passed an act granting a subsidy to two newly organized steamship companies for carrying the mails between New York and San Francisco, and in October, 1848, the 150-ton steamer *California* sailed from New York to inaugurate the run between San Francisco and Panama. Although gold had been found more than eight months earlier, the discovery had aroused so little interest in the East that the *California* sailed with most of her cabins empty. However, during the long voyage around the tip of South America the delayed rush began. When the little craft dropped anchor off Panama City on January 17, 1849, some 1,500 gold hunters were waiting there, all clamoring to board her for the final leg of the journey. The ship, which had been built to carry 210 passengers—60 in the cabins and 150 in the steerage—could not accommodate all who applied. However, close to 400 were taken aboard, crowding the little ship to her utmost capacity. She reached San Francisco on February 28, 1849.

During the first few months after the new service began there was much confusion. No attempt was made to observe regular sailing dates; instead, the steamers on both oceans made the round trips as rapidly as possible, never able to carry more than a small percentage of those who applied; many of those fortunate enough to obtain passage complained at the poor food and lack of proper accommodations. By the end of 1849, however, both companies—the United States Line on the Atlantic and the Pacific Mail on the Pacific side—were operating on schedule, with twice-monthly sailings from both coasts. Although the land crossing at Panama was dangerous because of yellow fever and other tropical diseases, the steamer route by then had become the favorite means of travel. Its chief advantage was that it reduced the time of passage from New York to San Francisco to less than half that of the around-the-Horn sailing ships or via the overland trails.

The side-wheel steamers of the early and middle 1850s offered three types of accommodations: First-class passengers occupied cabins, usually containing four berths, that opened either on the deck or into the dining salon; the second-class cabins were situated farther aft—these were large compartments containing at least twelve berths and on some ships as many as fifty. The greater number traveled third class, or steerage.

The steerage was deep in the ship, well forward [wrote one early-day passenger]. Here, in dark, crowded quarters, filled from floor to ceiling with tiers of berths, passengers lived in noise and confusion, with no hope of privacy. In the earlier steamers there was no segregation of the sexes; men, women and children were crowded indiscriminately into a single large compartment where the only open spaces were narrow aisles between long lines of berths. They were usually built in groups of three both vertically and horizontally, so that the person occupying that farthest from the aisle was obliged to climb over the other two . . .

The space allotted to each steerage passenger was small indeed. The berths were mere pieces of canvas attached on wooden frames six feet long and eighteen inches wide, and the distance

In 1854 the *Flying Cloud*, most famous of the early clipper ships, made the run from New York to San Francisco in 89 days, an all-time record for the around-the-Horn passage. (*Gleason's Pictorial.*)

(*At right*) Throughout the 1850s most of the merchandise arriving from East Coast ports was carried in the fleet and graceful clippers. Ship owners used colorful "Clipper cards" to attract trade.

THE CLIPPER SHIP *FLYING CLOUD*, 1851

between one and its neighbor above was a scant two feet. Passengers were obliged to furnish their own bedding and eating utensils. Their food was served them direct from the galley, outside which they lined up at mealtime to have their plates and cups filled. They ate lying down in their berths or standing in the passageways.

As time passed, travel by water became less of an ordeal. Larger ships replaced the original steamers on both oceans, and the completion of the Panama Railroad in 1855 eliminated most of the delays and hazards to health during the crossing of the Isthmus. Moreover, the companies first in the field did not long maintain their monopoly on this lucrative coast-to-coast trade. By the middle of 1851 a competing line, owned by the New York shipping magnate Cornelius Vanderbilt, began operations. The Vanderbilt Line made the crossing at Nicaragua rather than Panama—a shorter and healthier route—and therefore enjoyed a considerable popularity during the next several years. Competition between the rival companies, plus a falling off in the amount of traffic as interest in the gold discovery subsided, brought a sharp drop in passenger fares together with improved accommodations. By 1855 the only discomforts of the coast-to-coast trip were tropical heat and a plenitude of mosquitos during the land crossing. Two ever-present hazards, however, remained: the frequent wrecks on the uncharted West Coast, where lighthouses and other navigational aids were few, and fires aboard the wooden ships.

The activity of the port was not confined to servicing the ships engaged in the coast-to-coast trade. The California of the period had few roads, and those that existed were often impassable in winter because of a lack of bridges spanning the rain-swollen streams. Passengers and freight bound for interior points were therefore carried by water wherever feasible. During the gold rush, goods needed to supply the mining towns were shipped

aboard light-draft vessels to Sacramento, Stockton, and other points on the upper bay and its tributaries, and there transferred to wagons or pack animals and transported over improvised roads into the foothills. By the early 1850s, however, a fleet of river steamers, some of them elaborately fitted up, were plying between San Francisco and the interior towns, some making regular trips up the Sacramento River for a distance of more than two-hundred miles. With the rise of agriculture, traffic on the inland waterways increased as the products of the farms and ranches were brought down to deep water to supply local needs to be transshipped to foreign markets.

Ships engaged in trade with trans-Pacific ports, and with those up and down the coast, added to the growing activity of the harbor. Tall clipper ships were usually to be seen tied up to the wharves unloading goods from the East Coast or the Orient, and taking on wheat, flour, and other produce raised in the interior valleys. To supply the local need for building materials, steam schooners brought lumber from mills on the Mendocino and Humboldt coasts, and other ships made regular trips north to Puget Sound and Alaska carrying miscellaneous cargoes.

Meanwhile the establishment of overland stage lines had made the coast-to-coast journey by land less of an ordeal, though here the rate of progress was slower. To be sure, by the mid-1850s the trails were no longer crowded with long trains of heavily loaded wagons; roadways had been cleared over the mountain passes, and way stations established where men and animals could pause and refresh themselves. Yet as late as 1855 the trip from the Missouri River to Sacramento still brought hardships that taxed the strength of all but the most hearty.

Of the two most traveled routes, San Franciscans favored the central, or California, trail, which crossed the Sierra, followed the Humboldt River across present-day Nevada, and reached Independence, Missouri, by way of Fort Hall, South Pass, and Laramie. This was much shorter than the more southerly trail by way of Santa Fe, and avoided its extreme summer heat. During the winter months, however, deep snow often blocked the Sierra passes, forcing the transcontinental stages to take the southern route.

Until well into the 1860s the bulk of the freight and passenger traffic between the two coasts continued to be carried by sea. For the most part it was those traveling to or from points west of the Alleghenies who made the trip by land. Although the services offered by the pioneer stage lines improved gradually, it was not until 1857, when Congress passed a bill granting a liberal subsidy for carrying the mails between St. Louis and San Francisco, that reasonably fast and dependable service was inaugurated. The contract was awarded the Butterfield Overland Stage Company, a far-flung transportation system that at its height had close to a thousand employees, several times that many horses and mules, and more than a hundred Concord coaches.

This arrangement proved unsatisfactory to San Franciscans, for the Butterfield stages followed the roundabout southern route, and consequently the service they offered was no faster than that provided by the Panama steamers. Local residents joined those in Sacramento, Salt Lake City, and other northern communities in urging the federal government to subsidize a second transcontinental stage line, this one to follow the central route. This demand for faster service led to what has come to be regarded as one of the most romantic phases of early Western transportation, the Pony Express.

The service was inaugurated on April 3, 1860, when a rider left St. Joseph, Missouri, on the first leg of the two-thousand-mile trip to Sacramento. Riding day and night, and changing mounts every twenty-five miles, the messengers covered the distance in approximately ten and a half days. Two round trips were made each week, the riders carrying letters—for which a charge of $5 per half-ounce was made—in pouches attached to

---

Cunningham's Wharf, a T-shaped, 300-foot-long structure, was one of many such facilities built out into the bay during the 1850s and later. Tied up to its end are two light-draft river steamers, the *Senator* and the *New World*.

the pommels of their saddles, each rider covering up to seventy-five miles before being relieved. The riders were unarmed and depended on the fleetness of their mounts to elude attack by hostile Indians.

The service continued nineteen months, during which San Franciscans were able to exchange letters with correspondents in New York and other cities in less than two weeks—a privilege they were not to enjoy again until after the completion of the transcontinental railroad nearly a decade later. In the meantime the wires of the overland telegraph were being strung across the western third of the continent. When, on October 26, 1861, that project was completed, the Pony Express passed out of existence.

3. FRONTIER JOURNALISM

The building of the overland telegraph marked the end of the pioneer era of San Francisco journalism. Until that time, news of the outer world had arrived at irregular intervals, either by overland stage or aboard the twice-monthly steamers, and word of important events was posted on bulletin boards in front of the steamship or express offices. The local papers were therefore for the most part journals of opinion and were read mainly for their editorial comment on local issues. The news columns were largely given over to accounts of domestic happenings or to news from elsewhere in California.

As mentioned earlier, San Francisco's first newspaper was Sam Brannan's *California Star*, whose first number appeared on January 9, 1847. Five and a half months later, a second weekly, the *Californian*, which had been founded at Monterey on August 15 of the previous year, was moved to San Francisco. The two papers continued to serve the little town until the late spring of 1848, when the exodus to the gold fields caused both to suspend publication. The *Californian* was revived in July, and its rival soon thereafter; a few months later the two were combined, becoming the *Star and Californian*. Less than a year later the paper was sold and rechristened the *Alta California*, under which name it long remained an influential West Coast journal. During its early period it was edited by Frank Soulé, one of the authors of *The Annals of San Francisco*.

The *Alta California*—which became a daily in January, 1850—did not long have the field to itself. On August 25, 1849, appeared the first number of the *Pacific News*, a four-page tri-weekly owned and edited by William Faulkner and Warren Leland. In January, 1850, a second daily, the *Journal of Commerce*, was launched; its editor was Washington Bartlett.

These pioneer journals were all printed on hand presses, most of them from type that had been worn and battered from much use. The advertisements which covered their entire front pages and much of the inner pages, accurately reflected conditions prevailing at the time: the cards of buyers and sellers of gold dust, of commission houses and auction rooms, announcements of the sale of merchandise on newly arrived ships, of the sailings of river boats to Sacramento and other interior points, plus the schedules of stage lines and Panama steamers, and much else.

In a community where goods of every sort were often in short supply, the publishers were sometimes hard put to find adequate quantities of paper. During times of scarcity the limited amount on hand was conserved by reducing the page size and by printing fewer copies. There were occasions when the owners were forced to use whatever type of paper could be had. This had some curious results. One early issue of the *Pacific News* was printed on sheets of Chinese tea paper that was bought from a physician who had been using it to wrap drugs. Another appeared on brown manila paper, and a third on a page formed by four sheets of foolscap glued together.

One feature of the early journals was their special numbers called "Steamer Editions." These were issued on the Saturdays preceding the fortnightly sailings of the Panama steamers; on the day they appeared long lines formed before the newspaper offices to buy copies—at $1 each—to send to friends and relatives in the East.

Early in 1851 appeared the first issue of a fourth local paper, the *Daily Herald.* Others followed in such numbers that by the end of 1853 twelve dailies were being published, as well as six weeklies and two tri-weeklies. Among the newcomers were one German and two French weeklies, the first of the many foreign-language newspapers that attested, as they do now, to the city's cosmopolitan population.

Few of the early-day journals lasted more than a year or two. Some were founded to support a particular cause, or to further the political ambition of the owner; having served the purpose they dropped from sight. Of the original group only the *Alta California* went on to a long and distinguished career. In the mid-1850s, however, two competing papers were founded that were to survive in one form or another for well over a century. These were James King of William's *Evening Bulletin,* established in 1856, and *The Call,* the first number of which appeared on December 1 of that year.

While the staffs of the daily journals included a number of writers who later became prominent in the literary life of the city, the local weeklies were their chief training ground. The earliest and most influential of the weeklies was the *Golden Era.* Founded in 1852, it quickly attracted a group of contributors of such talent that it has since been termed "the cradle of California literature." For more than a decade the *Era's* office on lower Clay Street was a favorite gathering place for the local literati. One of its employees was a young compositor, Francis Bret Harte, whose *M'liss, Condensed Novels,* and other early works appeared in the weekly. Another frequent contributor in the beginning 1860s was Mark Twain, both during the period when he was a reporter on the *Virginia City Enterprise* and later. Members of the *Golden Era* group, too, were Charles Warren Stoddard, who wrote under the name of "Pip Pepperpod," Prentice Mulford, Stephen Massett, and "Old Block" (Alonzo Delano). The paper, a brightly written potpourri of fiction, poems, news, and editorial comment, was a success from the beginning. Within a month after the first number appeared its city circulation had reached two thousand.

The city's first monthly magazine, the *Pioneer*, was founded in 1854 by Ferdinand C. Ewer, a scholarly cleric who later became rector of Grace Episcopal Church. The *Pioneer's* announced purpose was "to avoid heavy twaddle and to seek to entertain." It lived up to that motto for two years, then fell victim to the depression of 1856. During its brief career the *Pioneer* published the humorous sketches of Lieutenant George H. Derby, U.S.A., and that classic of mining-town life, the letters of Louise A. K. S. Clappe, who wrote under the name of "Dame Shirley."

The city's isolation from the rest of the country was mainly responsible for the profuse flowering of literary and artistic talent during the 1850s. Separated as they were by several thousand miles from the old established cities of the eastern seaboard, San Franciscans were obliged either to provide for their own cultural needs or else to go without. There was never any question as to which course they would choose. The city's rapid rise from crude frontier outpost had not yet been completed before the citizens began launching enterprises appropriate to its proud position as the West Coast metropolis. One evidence of this was the establishment of two important libraries, that of the Mercantile Library Association in 1852, and of the Mechanics' Institute two years later. (The two were merged in the early 1900s and became the present Mechanics' Institute and Library).

Two organizations designed to preserve the record of the beginnings of the city and state were launched during that period, the Society of California Pioneers in 1850, and the California Historical Society in 1852. The following year the California Academy of Sciences, the first scientific society on the Pacific Coast, was founded in a Montgomery Street office in 1853, and, like the Mechanics' Library and the two historical societies, has continued down to the present. In the early 1850s, too, there were several halls where concerts and lectures were regularly held, and at least one art gallery.

4. THEATERS AND BEER GARDENS

Most Forty-niners were not, as they have sometimes been pictured, true frontiersmen, with a natural preference for life on the far fringes of civilization. Their letters and diaries make clear that the hardships and

Not all the hardships of the period were borne by those in the crude foothill mining camps. This street scene *(above)* in the winter of 1849 shows the muddy streets of the city.

During the early part of the gold rush the saloons *(left)* and gambling houses were the town's only centers of conviviality. Both scenes are from Marryat's *Mountains and Molehills.*

crudities of the mining camps held small attraction for them, and that after a few weeks or months at the diggings the all but universal wish was to return to the familiar environment of home.

Even among those who, either by choice or from necessity, cast their lot permanently with the new land, were many who missed the material comforts and divertissements they had left behind. These, however, wasted little time deploring the lack of such amenities; instead, they set about improvising them. In entertainment a beginning had already been made. For long before the American conquest the fun-loving Spanish-Californians had no lack of means by which to relieve the monotony of frontier life. Among them were the celebration of religious festivals at the missions, feasts and fandangos at the *haciendas* of the *rancheros*, bull-and-bear fights, rodeos and other feats of horsemanship.

During the early stages of the gold rush the miners were too much occupied at their pans, rockers, and sluices to be diverted from the serious business at hand. Soon, however, the gambler made his appearance, set up his gaming tables in the camps and supply towns, and offered the miner an evening of excitement and sociability in return for whatever dust he had in his poke.

Throughout 1849 and much of 1850 San Francisco's gambling casinos and their attendant bars were the residents' chief, and indeed virtually their only, centers of conviviality. Because gold dust was plentiful and profits large, owners of such establishments spared no expense in fitting them up. Descriptions of the more elaborate resorts tell of scores of candles set in crystal chandeliers, of carpeted floors and upholstered chairs, and of six-piece orchestras playing day and night. In a community that was still half city and half camp, where most of the population lived in tents or other crude shelters and the streets were often seas of mud, such establishments held an attraction that few resisted.

The lure of the faro tables and roulette wheels remained strong as long as the mines continued to produce heavily. But as gold dust became less plentiful, fewer of the miners frequented the gaming rooms, and other forms of recreation became popular. In San Francisco the early-day circuses drew large crowds. By the end of 1850, three were competing for patronage: one on Kearny Street between Clay and Washington streets, a second on Montgomery near California, and a third on the western side of Portsmouth Square. Of them, the authors of *The Annals of San Francisco* wrote:

> They were mere tent structures, where, on rude benches, con-
> gregated crowds of easily satisfied and deeply interested spectators,
> and where spring-boards bounced men of various sizes successively
> over one, two, and three horses; and daring riders, on broad

wooden saddles, jumped through hoops and over ropes. . . . Nowhere else were to be had the materials for more legitimate displays, and the little-exacting populace were forced to content themselves with what they could get—paying without a murmur, their $3 for pit seats, $5 for box places, and $55 for the princely luxury of a private stall.

Preceding the earliest of the circuses by several weeks was what might well have been the town's first formal entertainment. This was a "concert of vocal music" held in the schoolhouse on Portsmouth Square on the evening of June 22, 1849. The artist, who conducted the entire program, was Stephen C. Massett, a native of New York and the composer of "The Moon on the Lake is Beaming," "List' While I Sing," and other once-popular ballads. The lengthy program ended with what was described as Massett's celebrated "Yankee Town Meeting" during which he "gave imitations of seven different persons." Tickets were $3 each, the little schoolroom was packed to the doors, and the artist realized a profit of more than $500. Two other aspects of this pioneer entertainment have been preserved: The front row of seats was reserved for ladies, and four were present; and, in order to accompany himself while he sang, Massett had borrowed the town's only piano, which belonged to the Collector of the Port. To move the instrument across the Square from the Custom House to the schoolhouse cost $16. Nearly three years later, on February 23, 1852, Massett gave a farewell performance before returning East. This time he appeared in a spacious concert hall before an audience of elegantly dressed men and their ladies, and when he sang "The Moon on the Lake is Beaming" he was accompanied, not by a borrowed piano, but by an orchestra of well-trained musicians.

By the time Massett departed, concerts, plays, and similar types of entertainment were no longer a novelty. The town's first plays were produced by two actor-managers named Atwater and Anderson. In January, 1850, they rented the second floor of a building in the rear of the *Alta California* office on Washington Street and staged a melodrama called *The Wife* and Shakespeare's *Richard III*. Encouraged by the success of that venture, the owner of one of the circuses converted his Kearny Street tent into a theater, and again the amusement-starved populace filled every seat at every performance.

Other playhouses followed in rapid succession. In April, 1850, the town's first theater built expressly for that purpose opened its doors, the initial attraction being a troupe of French vaudeville artistes. On July 4 Messrs. Robinson and Evrard opened their Dramatic Museum on California Street just off Montgomery. A month later the Jenny Lind, the first of several theaters of that name, was opened. There a stock company headed by a Mr. Stark and a Mrs. Kirby enjoyed great popularity until the theater, along with the entire center of the city, was destroyed in the fire of May 3, 1851.

In a period of less than two years the Jenny Lind was three times reduced to ashes. After the third blaze, its owner, Tom Maguire, put up facing the Square, a handsome stone building that became one of the architectural ornaments of the early city. It did not long serve its original purpose, however, for less than a year after its gala opening it was bought by the city and thereafter served as the city hall. Maguire then put up Maguire's Opera House on Washington Street. There for nearly two decades appeared a succession of attractions ranging from vaudeville shows and melodramas to grand opera and Shakespeare, the latter interpreted by some of the most eminent Shakespearean actors of the day.

By the mid-1850s San Francisco's reputation as "a good theater town" was well established, and troupes of players were regularly arriving on the steamers from the East Coast. Their usual procedure was to play a few weeks at one of the local houses, then tour the interior, making one-night stands at Sacramento, Stockton, and the foothill mining towns, and, after a second engagement in San Francisco, either return East or continue on to the Hawaiian Islands and Australia. Such traveling companies enabled San Franciscans to see most leading actors and actresses of the period. The list includes Junius and Edwin Booth, Mrs. Judah, the husband-and-wife team of James and Sarah Stark, Caroline Chapman, and a host of others.

San Franciscans also had their local favorites. One was the versatile David "Yankee" Robinson, co-owner of the Dramatic Museum. Robinson was not only an actor and manager, but a playwright as well, who delighted audiences by adapting well-known plays and filling them with local references. One of his original productions was a melodrama called *The Reformed Drunkard*, which as *Ten Nights in a Barroom,* was for many years a stand-by of stock companies all over the country.

One name that loomed large in the theatrical annals of the day was Lola Montez. When Dublin-born Lola arrived in the spring of 1853, word of her sensational career as a Spanish danseuse and favorite of the elderly former King Ludwig of Bavaria had preceded her. So many wished to see that much publicized young woman that tickets to her opening performance at the American Theater were eagerly bought for as much as $65 each. Lola proved to be an indifferent actress, but her "spider dance"—a spirited pantomime during which she shook whalebone spiders from her abbreviated dress and stamped on them—made the expected sensation, and she played to packed houses. She further endeared herself to her audiences by marrying Pat Hull, a local newspaper editor whom she had met on the steamer coming from Panama. At the end of her San Francisco engagement Lola announced her retirement from the stage, and she and Hull moved to the

The American Theater, built in 1854, stood at the corner of Sansome and Halleck streets. Many of the most renowned actors and actresses of the day appeared in one or another of the local playhouses.

foothill town of Grass Valley. But life in that mining town soon palled; her brief marriage ended, and she returned to the San Francisco stage. Then she set off on a tour to Australia, and California saw her no more. During her brief stay at Grass Valley, she met a talented child named Lotta Crabtree and helped her embark on a successful career as actress and singer.

Not until the 1860s did another visiting actress cause so great a furor as had Lola. Like her, Adah Isaacs Menken had a degree of charm and beauty that more than made up for her shortcomings as an actress, and, like her, too, whenever her audiences began to drop off, she had an unfailing means of reviving public interest. Just as the announcement that Montez would dance her spider dance had assured a full house, so word that Menken would appear in *Mazeppa* caused long lines to form before the box office of Maguire's Opera House. "In scant attire," wrote one local reviewer, "she lay strapped to the back of a white horse which raced across the stage and up a zigzag mountain path against the backdrop. Her gorgeous hair swept out behind her, and she was a magnificent picture. The audiences went wild over her."

Although the theater was first in popularity among San Franciscans of the day, they did not lack other forms of entertainment. In 1851 the "plank road," which connected the center of the city with the Mission Dolores, made that district more accessible, and the following year a race track was built there. The Mission track remained a popular attraction for many years. In 1853 the opening of a resort called Russ Gardens drew other pleasure seekers to that area. Built by a German emigrant named Christian Russ and patterned after the beer gardens of his homeland, the Gardens was a favorite spot where family groups gathered to hear band concerts, to stroll about the landscaped grounds, to eat, or to drink beer at tables beneath the trees. On Sundays and holidays troupes of acrobats, tightrope walkers, and trained animal acts performed on an open-air stage.

The Mission District shortly had a second amusement park. This was The Willows, named for a clump of trees that grew near the present intersection of 18th and Valencia streets. The atmosphere of The Willows was Gallic rather than Teutonic, and it was patronized mainly by the city's large French colony. One of its attractions was San Francisco's first zoo, among whose prize exhibits was an ostrichlike bird, an emu. The emu inspired young Bret Harte to one of his earliest ventures in verse:

O say, have you seen at The Willows so great,
    So charming and rurally true,
A singular bird, with the manner absurd,
    Which they call the Australian emu?

By the early 1860s several other resorts of the same general character had been established about the fringes of the city. One was Hayes Park, situated in Hayes Valley, a few blocks southwest of today's Civic Center. These, along with Russ Gardens and The Willows, continued to flourish until the middle of that decade when a new and more elaborate park, called Woodward's Gardens, was opened on Valencia Street. Built by Samuel Woodward, whose What Cheer House at Sacramento and Leidesdorff streets was then a popular downtown hotel, the new resort far surpassed its rivals in the number and variety of its attractions. The resort, which had originally been its owner's home, occupied two city blocks. Woodward converted his residence into a museum, and on the wooded grounds built a dance hall, theater, restaurant, conservatory, and a number of other attractions. Woodward's Gardens became the most popular of the city's outdoor resorts and remained so for several decades.

In 1852 the Jenny Lind Theater, on Kearny Street opposite Portsmouth Square, was bought by the city and, after being extensively remodeled, became the City Hall. On the left was the El Dorado, a famous gambling house.

The rapid expansion of the city is indicated by this map, which appeared in Lecount & Strong's *San Francisco Directory* for 1850. The shaded area in the foreground shows that by then most of Yerba Buena Cove had been filled in. Yerba Buena Cemetery, on outer Market Street, was near the site of the present Civic Center.

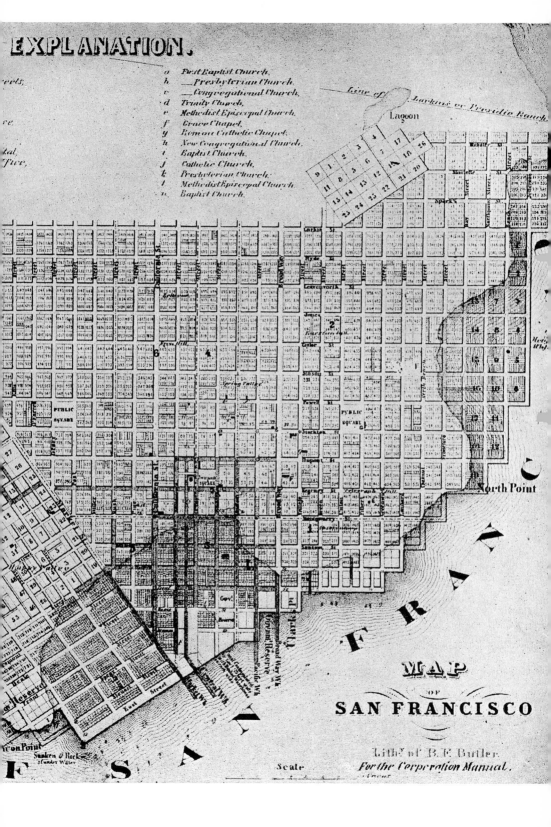

EXPLANATION.

MAP
OF
SAN FRANCISCO

Lith. of B. F. Butler.
For the Corporation Manual.

Scale

5. THE "LIMANTOUR TAX"

San Franciscans of the day had need of their theaters, amusement parks, and other places of recreation. For throughout the 1850s they were obliged to cope with many pressing problems. Not the least of these was the necessity of establishing legal title to the land on which their homes and places of business stood.

This had come about because much of the land on which the city was built had earlier been parceled out to individuals by the Mexican authorities. Such grants, the majority of which had been given in return for service in the Mexican army, were of various sizes. Some—including those adjacent to Yerba Buena Cove—had an area of less than half an acre; others covered several square miles. After the pueblo was established, the *alcaldes* had raised funds for administrative expenses by the sale of town lots, and their successors had done likewise. The first such sale under American rule was an auction of tideland lots, which as stated earlier, took place in July, 1847. Later that year, following the completion of the O'Farrell Survey, a second and larger auction of city-owned land was held.

At the time these sales were made no one doubted the city's title to the property it was selling. Soon, however, they were being seriously questioned. By the beginning of 1848 a number of claimants had appeared before the U. S. Land Commission—which had been appointed to adjudicate such matters—and presented documents that appeared to establish their ownership of large areas of land within the city limits. The problem faced by the commission was involved, for the records inherited from the Mexican officials were far from complete, and there was strong evidence that some claims were fraudulent. Of those, John S. Hittell wrote:

> No records pertaining to them were found in the archives. Among these was a grant to Goat [now Yerba Buena] Island, purporting to have been made to Juan Castro in 1838; a grant for a square league west of Yerba Buena, purporting to have been made to Fernando Marchena on August 14, 1844; the Santillan and the Limantour grants. The Santillan, based on a paper dated on February 10, 1846, conveyed to Prudencio Santillan, at that time a parish priest at the Mission, all the vacant lands that formerly belonged to the Mission, south of Yerba Buena and the Presidio. . . . J. Y. Limantour presented to the United States Land Commission two papers purporting to grant lands within the present limits of the City of San Francisco. One, dated on the twenty-seventh of February, 1843, gave him the tract of land between California Street and Mission Creek, extending out to the westward till it made two leagues, and, also, a second tract of two leagues, west of

Yerba Buena. . . . It is worthy of remark that the fraudulent claims of Santillan and Limantour covered about twelve thousand acres of the same land, and, within the limits of both claims Peter Sherreback wanted two thousand two hundred acres. The invalid Mexican grants were three deep over a considerable area.

Of numerous lawsuits growing out of such claims, that filed by Limantour was by far the most celebrated. Limantour, who claimed to have been a captain in the French navy, had arrived in California in 1841, where he quickly made himself a figure of importance. One means by which he gained the friendship of the Mexican officials was by providing them with badly needed supplies during the frequent periods when public funds were low. He made himself particularly useful in that respect during the years when José Micheltorena occupied the governor's chair, and when, in 1845, the governor was deposed he accompanied Micheltorena back to Mexico. Limantour paid another visit to California in 1847, then dropped from sight. For six years nothing was heard of him.

Then, early in 1853, he appeared before the Land Commission at San Francisco, filed documents that purported to give him title to land in and about the city, and asked that they be confirmed. The amount of land included in the so-called grants was very large. One conferred on the petitioner four square leagues within the city itself; a second awarded him the two bay islands, Alcatraz and Yerba Buena, the Farallone Islands offshore, and part of the Tiburon peninsula.

When the claims were first filed they aroused little attention. Newspapers pronounced the documents forgeries and denounced Limantour as a swindler, pointing out that he had delayed producing them until less than a month before the deadline set for presenting such claims. It was

Typical of the substantial buildings put up in the financial district in the 1850s is this office of the Pacific Accumulation Bank on the northwest corner of California and Montgomery streets.

assumed that his real purpose was to force landowners to pay him whatever sums he could extort in order to clear the title to their property.

During hearings before the commission, however, the matter took on a more serious aspect. Limantour and his attorneys produced numerous witnesses who testified to the authenticity of the documents and the circumstances under which they had been granted. So convincing was their testimony that after protracted hearings the commissioners, on January 22, 1856, pronounced the grants genuine and confirmed the applicant's claims so far as the San Francisco property was concerned. As might be expected, their ruling caused consternation throughout the city. A meeting of property holders was hastily called and steps were taken to appeal the ruling to the Federal District Court. Several years passed, however, before the case came to trial. Meanwhile Limantour enjoyed a profitable trade in the sale of quitclaim deeds to property in the disputed area, his fee being 10 percent of the assessed value of the land. How much he profited by that device is not known, but during the years while the issue remained in doubt it was customary for buyers of land to insist on evidence that the "Limantour tax" had been paid before the deal was consummated. Most estimates placed his total gains at between $200,000 and $250,000.

The long-drawn-out Limantour trial was, of course, followed with the closest interest by San Franciscans, thousands of whom had a financial stake in its outcome. Because much government-owned land—the bay islands, some parts of the north bay, and virtually all the presidio—were included in the supposed grants, the attorney general sent a lawyer to San Francisco to aid the local property owners to prepare and try the case. The man chosen for that mission was Edwin M. Stanton, then in private practice at Washington, who was to become President Lincoln's Secretary of War.

The trial opened in August, 1858, more than five years after the disputed documents had been filed. It soon became apparent that the attorneys for the landowners had prepared their case well. Evidence was presented proving conclusively that the purported grants were forgeries, that the paper on which they were written was not to be had in California at the time they were supposed to have been issued, and that the seals affixed to them did not come into use until a later date. It was established too that several of Limantour's key witnesses had given perjured testimony.

The court's decision, rendered on November 19, 1858, upheld the contention of the property owners on every point and dismissed the action on the ground of fraud. Limantour, who was indicted for perjury, avoided prosecution by fleeing to Mexico, where he lived until his death in 1885. By then, the Limantour case, which had been one of the sensations of the 1850s, had been all but forgotten.

VI

The Sixties

1. THE DECADE OPENS

In 1850 San Francisco had a population of less than 35,000; by 1860 the number had grown to 56,800. Population figures, however, fail to tell the full story. When the decade began, the place was still half city and half camp. The residents lacked most of the material comforts—and many of the necessities—of older communities. The unpaved streets were lined with hastily thrown-up wooden buildings. Heaps of merchandise were piled on the shore of the cove, and the cove itself was crowded with abandoned ships lying side by side and slowly sinking into the mud. Means of maintaining order and protecting life and property were almost entirely lacking, and fires frequently reduced the business district to rubble.

In the summer of 1859 Richard Henry Dana returned to San Francisco for the first time since his famous visit twenty-four years earlier. This time he arrived aboard the Pacific Mail steamer *Golden Gate* after a comfortable voyage up from Panama. He put up at the newly completed Oriental Hotel—which, he stated, "as well as I could learn, stood on the filled-in cove, not far from the spot where we used to beach our boats from the *Alert*"—and thus recorded his impressions on awakening the next morning:

> When I . . . looked from my windows over the city of San Francisco, with its storehouses, towers, and steeples; its courthouses, theaters, and hospitals; its daily journals; its well-filled learned professions; its fortresses and lighthouses; its wharves and harbor, with their thousand-ton clipper ships, more in number than London or Liverpool sheltered that day, itself one of the capitals of the American Republic, and the sole emporium of the new world, the awakened Pacific . . . and when I saw all these things, and reflected on what I once saw there, and what now surrounded me, I could scarcely keep my hold on reality.

The changes that so impressed this visitor had all taken place since the beginning of the gold rush ten years earlier. Along the bay front from Rincon Point to the base of Telegraph Hill the shallows of the cove had been filled in for a distance of close to half a mile from the original shore-

107

This animated scene, with plank-paved streets, horse-drawn wagons and carts, and merchandise displayed on the sidewalks, was characteristic of the downtown streets during the 1860s.

line. The land thus reclaimed had been solidly built up with warehouses, industrial plants, wholesale and retail establishments of many sorts and, on the water side, with piers and docks to which the largest vessels of the day could tie up.

The business district that had once been confined to the vicinity of Portsmouth Square had spread to the south and east. Montgomery Street had become the main thoroughfare. The part of Montgomery between California and Washington streets was the financial and commercial center of the city and, indeed, of the entire West Coast. There, and on the intersecting streets, were the leading banks and brokerage houses, the offices of steamship and stage lines, of express companies, and, of other business enterprises. The opposite end of Montgomery, from California Street to Market Street, was lined with substantial two- and three-story buildings, the street floors of which were occupied by a wide variety of shops, and the floors above by hotel rooms or offices.

By then, however, Kearny Street had become the city's chief shopping center. The largest retail stores were there, and near by were the best-known theaters, restaurants, bars, and other gathering places. It was the street along which the wealth and fashion of the city daily took afternoon promenades. But the center of the shopping district was already spreading toward the southwest. Along Sutter, Post, and Geary streets the small wooden cottages put up during the 1850s were giving way to the shops of the retail merchants. As churches, schools, and theaters outgrew their original quarters, they, too, followed the trend in that direction. The city park bounded by Geary, Stockton, Post, and Powell streets was built up on all four sides. The park itself, a favorite meeting place for those who supported the North on the slavery question, had come to be called Union Square.

The 1850s had been an uncommonly eventful period. Within a single decade the citizens had twice taken over control of civic affairs, and later, surrendered their authority to the regularly elected officials. What had been an unprepossessing collection of houses spread in haphazard fashion over the sandhills had been transformed into what by the standards of the time was a modern, convenient, well-governed city. San Francisco had seen, too, a marked change in the economics of the region it served and

The Montgomery Street building of the Miners Exchange Bank is featured in this photograph, with Telegraph Hill in the background.

Looking across Portsmouth Square toward the intersection of Kearny and Washington streets, the City Hall and El Dorado gambling house are on the right, and, on the Washington Street side, the Bella Union, one of the city's many theaters.

on which its own prosperity depended. By the mid-1850s the decline in the yield of the placer mines had brought on the city's first major depression—yet before the decade ended, the rise of agriculture and industry and the continued development of world trade had placed its economy on a firmer, more lasting foundation.

2. SILVER REBUILDS A CITY

Three major events—the Civil War, the development of rich silver mines in Nevada Territory, and the building of the transcontinental railroad—were among the high points of the 1860s. Each had an important bearing on San Francisco's evolution.

First in order of time was the uncovering in the spring of 1859 of huge deposits of silver-nitrate ore on the slope of Sun Mountain on the far side of the Sierra. The discovery and development of this new bonanza took place at a time when California mining was on the decline. In San Francisco it set off a movement comparable to that of 1848-1849 as thousands hurried across the mountains and staked out claims or established businesses in Virginia City, Gold Hill, and other Comstock towns. For, unlike other mines discovered in the middle and late 1850s, this one came up to expectations—it was destined to be the richest in the history of the Far West. It has been estimated that during the next twenty years the Comstock mines produced well over $300,000,000.

By far the greater part of this treasure found its way to San Francisco. The most valuable mines and mills were controlled by San Franciscans, their development was financed with San Francisco capital, and their enormous profits sent energizing new currents through every phase of the life of the city. As in 1849, when San Francisco had been the chief source of supply for the Sierra gold camps, the city furnished not only the machinery needed to take out and reduce the ore, but most of the necessities—and all the luxuries—demanded by residents of the prosperous silver towns.

Profits from the Comstock produced the city's first crop of multimillion-aires, including the four "silver kings," John W. Mackay, James C. Fair, James L. Flood, and William S. O'Brien. Mackay had been an itinerant prospector, Fair a mechanic, and Flood and O'Brien the owners of a Washington Street bar and restaurant called the Auction Lunch. The four con-

One of the horse-drawn cars of the Market Street Railroad Company. This line, called the Hayes Valley route, operated from the Ferry Building to Golden Gate Park and the cemeteries adjacent to Lone Mountain. The photograph was made about 1880. (*Roy D. Graves Collection.*)

trolled the Consolidated Virginia and California mines whose profits for several years averaged $500,000 per month. Others reaped profits almost as large. William C. Ralston and William Sharon—whose Bank of California had financed many of the properties—both made large fortunes which they spent in different ways: Ralston by building the Palace Hotel, the Metropolitan Theater, and other imposing local buildings, and Sharon by having himself elected to the U. S. Senate. Scores of other San Franciscans became wealthy, either by lucky investments in the richer mines or by supplying goods or services to the populous Comstock towns.

It has been said that during the next fifteen years San Francisco was "rebuilt" with Nevada silver. That is hardly an exaggeration. By the mid-1860s a building boom such as the city had not known since gold rush days was under way. In the financial district about California and Montgomery streets new banks and brokerage houses and multi-story office buildings replaced the more modest earlier buildings. Elsewhere in the downtown area existing hotels and retail stores were enlarged and new ones built. The growing number of theaters, restaurants, bars, and clubrooms — many of the latter handsomely fitted up — was further evidence of the new prosperity. So, too, was the increased activity in the industrial district south of Market Street. There numerous new foundries, machine shops, and metal-working

Much of the machinery used to operate the West's pioneer rail-roads, mines, and sawmills was produced locally. Here the first locomotive manufactured in California leaves the Vulcan Iron Works on First Street.

The Hunter's Point Drydock was built in 1868. This 465-foot drydock, chipped out of solid rock and faced with granite, could accommodate the largest ships then plying the Pacific.

plants were built, some of which operated around the clock to supply the Comstock mines and mills with hoisting engines, wire cables, and mechanical equipment of many sorts.

In 1864 — when the yield of the mines first topped $16,000,000 — more than a thousand new buildings were put up in downtown San Francisco. Among them were the Donahue, Kelly Bank on Sacramento and Montgomery streets, McGuire's Academy of Music on Pine Street, and the city's first professional school, the Toland Medical College, on Stockton Street near Chestnut. The following year additions were made to the three leading hotels, the Occidental, Lick, and Cosmopolitan, which increased their combined capacity by six hundred rooms. Of the new annex to the Cosmopolitan, on Bush Street between Montgomery and Sansome, Langley's *City Directory* for 1864-65 stated: "The second story, which is reached by a spacious stairway from the Bush Street entrance, is occupied for the meetings of the Washoe Club, an association of individuals who have realized largely from the silver drifts of Nevada." According to that same source, the number of buildings in the city on August 1, 1865, was 15,518, of which 12,268 were of wood and 3,250 of brick or stone. In 1866 the Bank of California moved into new quarters on the corner of California and Sansome streets, a site it has occupied ever since. The establishment of this bank, together with the completion of the Merchants Exchange Building near by, firmly established California Street as the financial center of the West Coast. By 1866 the value of land on California and Montgomery streets had risen to an unprecedented $3,000 per front foot.

This substantial brick building on Market Street opposite Kearny housed St. Patrick's Orphan Asylum. The board sidewalks shown here were long a characteristic feature of the city.

Civic improvements kept pace with those financed by private capital. During 1864 and 1865 an extensive program of street repair and sidewalk building was carried out. At that time many of the downtown streets were still paved with wooden planks or cobblestones. Both these materials had serious drawbacks — the first were expensive to keep in repair, and the second were noisy when horse-drawn vehicles passed over them. During the mid-1860s the use of what was called "Nicholson pavement" was tried — wooden blocks on a base of asphalt. It was claimed that it could withstand the wear and tear of traffic better than planks, prevent horses from slipping on the cobbles — a frequent source of accidents during wet weather — and deaden the sound. However, "Nicholson pavement" must have developed other faults, for its use was eventually abandoned.

Other public projects of the early and middle 1860s were the grading of Broadway between Kearny and Montgomery streets which at one point required cutting through solid rock to a depth of sixty feet, the building of a bridge across Mission Cove to provide a direct route to Potrero Point, and the widening of Kearny Street by setting back all buildings on its west side from Market Street to Broadway. Another evidence of rapid growth was the building in 1864-65 of the Lincoln School on Market Street at Fifth.

A census taken by the Board of Education showed that in June, 1867, there were then 34,710 children under fifteen years of age in the city, as compared to 12,116 in 1860, an increase of almost 300 per cent. During the fiscal year 1866-67 eight new public schools were built, bringing the total to thirty-eight. In addition, there were several private schools, with a total enrollment of 4,200 students. Among them were St. Ignatius College, which had been founded in 1855, on the south side of Market Street between Fourth and Fifth, St. Mary's College, "near the county road to San Jose," and the City College, at the corner of Stockton and Geary streets. Among the religious, benevolent, and protective societies were two orphan asylums, a Young Man's Christian Association, a home for the deaf, dumb and blind, an industrial school for underprivileged boys and girls, and an old people's home. The city's hospitals included the four-story United States Marine Hospital at Rincon Point, the City and County Hospital, on the corner of Stockton and Francisco streets, and three privately owned institutions — the Maison de Santé, founded in 1858 by the French Mutual Benevolent Society, St. Mary's, operated by the Sisters of Mercy, and the German Hospital.

The cultural interests of the residents kept pace with the city's material progress, as indicated by the number and variety of its musical organizations, literary societies, and libraries. Largest of the libraries was that of the Mercantile Library Association, founded in 1853. In 1867 it had a collection of twenty thousand books, housed in its own building at the corner of Montgomery and Bush streets. Next in size was the library of the Mechanics' Institute in the Institute's new building on Post Street. As mentioned earlier these two collections were combined, and have continued to serve the reading public for close to a century.

The prosperity of the early and middle 1860s also resulted in a rapid increase in the number and size of the city's industrial plants and in the diversity of their products. Each year local factories produced a greater variety of manufactured goods which formerly had to be imported from the East.

3. HORSE CARS AND STEAM DUMMIES

The city's many steep hills and intervening valleys had long posed a difficult transportation problem. This was further aggravated by the fact that, as mentioned earlier, the first streets were laid out in a rigid checkerboard pattern without regard to the contour of the land, with the result that many ascended the hillsides at angles so steep that horse-drawn vehicles could not climb them. Moreover, much of the site was covered with sand dunes which were constantly shifting under the action of the strong winds blowing in from the ocean. The consequence was that travel from one part of the city to another was likely to be a slow and tedious process.

The first recorded public transportation was an omnibus line that ran on a half-hourly schedule between Portsmouth Plaza and the Mission. It began operating in 1852, the fare being fifty cents on week days and one dollar on Sundays. Then, on July 4, 1860, service was commenced on the city's first street railway. This was the San Francisco Market Street Railroad Company, the tracks of which began at the corner of Market and Battery streets, extended out Market to Valencia, and ended at Seventeenth Street. Of the

Hayes Valley looked like this in the 1860s. The steam train in the foreground operated on upper Market Street. The Protestant Orphanage occupied the hilltop on the left.

problems encountered by that pioneer venture, one of its owners later recalled that:

> The entire line of Market Street from Hayes Valley to Third Street was a succession of sand hills. . . . After they were cut through and the railroad started, we had much trouble keeping the sand off the track. The cutting, for economy's sake, was narrow, and, as the sand dried in the embankments, it slid down and covered the tracks. This difficulty was finally overcome by the use of brush or scrub oak, which was used as a sort of thatch that covered and held the sand.

Keeping the tracks clear of sand was only one of the problems faced by this company. Its cars were not drawn by horses — as was usual with street railways of the time — but by small locomotives called steam dummies. These caused so many runaways that they became a hazard to the public. In an effort to minimize the danger of accidents, the management had each car preceded by a horseman who rang a bell and waved a flag to warn of its approach.

The original company did not long survive. A few years later it was forced into receivership and sold to a newly completed railroad which connected San Francisco with San Jose. For a time the trains operated down Market Street to the railroad's terminus at Front Street. In 1867 the steam dummies were discontinued over the Market Street portion of the line, and horse-drawn cars substituted; meanwhile the narrow cuts had been widened and many of the sand hills leveled.

Several of the early streetcar lines were built by the owners of tracts of land in outlying parts of the city to make their property more accessible from the downtown area. One such concern was the Omnibus Railroad Company, whose tracks extended from North Beach to Portsmouth Square, then continued on beyond Market Street to South Park. Another was the Central Railroad Company. The tiny red cars of this line crossed Market at Second Street, and proceeded out Post Street to Lone Mountain, where several of the city cemeteries were situated. From the Lone Mountain terminus horse-drawn stages carried passengers over four miles of intervening sand hills to the ocean front where on the cliffs overlooking Seal Rocks Sam Brannan had built the first of a series of Cliff Houses. A third streetcar line, the Potrero and Bay View Company, began operations in 1866. The building of this five-mile-long line, which opened up the Potrero Hill, Mission Bay, and Hunters Point industrial districts, made necessary the bridging of Mission Bay and Islais Creek and the cutting through the shoulder of Potrero Hill.

By the late 1860s the street railway system had expanded to a point where by paying a five-cent fare and using one's transfer privileges one could ride to or from virtually any part of the city. Franchises authorizing the building of new lines were freely granted by the Board of Supervisors — often in the face of strong opposition by existing companies. The cars of each line were painted a distinctive color. Originally all were drawn by two horses and were manned by both driver and conductor. Later, as an economy measure, the City Railroad introduced smaller one-horse cars which made it possible to dispense with the conductor. A lever on the front platform of the new cars permitted the driver, who collected fares and issued transfers, to open the rear door for passengers to disembark. The horses of all lines had bells attached to their harnesses, and their tinkling as the animals jogged through the streets was a characteristic sound of the early city.

Another novelty in the way of rolling stock, introduced in 1868, was the "balloon car," which was circular in shape and so built that on reaching the end of the line the upper portion could be swung about for the return trip, thus eliminating the need of turntables.

The "palace car," still another innovation, was an elegantly appointed vehicle introduced by Samuel Woodward to promote travel to his Valencia Street amusement park. When the "palace car" was first put into service, it was greeted with this enthusiastic paragraph in a local weekly:

> This car is elegant in design, luxuriously fitted up with velvet carpet, and sofas extending the length of the car, upholstered in embroidered tapestry costing sixteen dollars per yard. The fresco paint work was done by a San Francisco artist, at a cost of two hundred dollars. The object of the car is to supply a want long felt by the ladies desiring to visit Woodward Gardens at hours when gentlemen are engaged and cannot accompany them. It being strictly a ladies' car, no gentlemen will be admitted unless with ladies.

Steamer Day, so named for the twice-monthly sailings of the
Panama steamers, was long a San Francisco tradition. It was the
day when letters were written, bills were presented and paid,
and gold dust collected for shipment "back East." This humorous
cartoon by a local artist was published in 1866.

There will be no disgusting pipe or cigar smoking on the platform,
nor the usual standing crowds to be squeezed inside, but every
passenger will be seated. The fare will be ten cents, and it is worth
the extra five cents to enjoy such luxury.

While the streetcar system was being developed, the facilities linking
the city with the rest of the country were also expanded. By 1860 larger and
faster steamers on both oceans had substantially reduced the time of passage
to the East Coast, and competition between rival lines had brought about
lower passenger fares and freight rates. Frequent sailings of the speedy
clipper ships by way of Cape Horn had assured adequate supplies of goods
not produced locally, and so had helped end recurring shortages of essential
materials.

Trade with the fast-developing communities in the Central Valley had
likewise been stimulated by the introduction of new and larger steamers.
Numerous light-draft side-wheelers regularly plied the waters of the bay and
the rivers and estuaries that empty into it. One firm, the California Steam
Navigation Company, operated a fleet of eight vessels on the run to Sacramento, with sailings from the Pacific Street wharf at 4 o'clock each after-

This view up the California Street hill from Montgomery Street
shows St. Mary's Church at the corner of Dupont (now Grant
Avenue) and, higher on the hill to the left, Grace Cathedral,
founded in 1863 by the Episcopal bishop, William Ingraham Kip.

noon. At Sacramento these vessels connected with smaller craft that continued up the river to the head of navigation at Red Bluff. Other lines offered regular service to Stockton, with stops at Vallejo, Benicia, and other towns on San Pablo and Suisun bays. Still others served the port of Alviso at the southern end of the bay, or followed winding channels through the marshes to Petaluma and Napa. Meanwhile traffic to and from Oakland and Alameda in the East Bay and to Tiburon on the Marin shore had been facilitated by larger ferries and more frequent service. Until 1873 the Davis Street wharf was the San Francisco terminus of the transbay passenger ferries. During that year the first of the ferry buildings, a long, shedlike structure surmounted by a wooden clock tower was built at the foot of Market Street.

4. RAILS SPAN THE CONTINENT

The 1860s, which marked the high point in the development of water transportation in California, also marked its decline. For by then the railroad age had arrived, and all over the country rails were being laid in the confident expectation that the iron horse would cure every economic ill.

In San Francisco that feeling was particularly strong. The city's isolation from the rest of the nation, and the slowness, discomfort, and high cost of travel between the two coasts, had long been a trial to the residents. All looked forward to the day when it would be possible to ride from the Pacific to the Atlantic, not on the uncomfortable overland stages or aboard the time-consuming steamers, but by that new miracle of transportation, the railroad train.

The plan to lay rails across the western half of the continent and connect them with existing lines east of the Mississippi had been advocated since the early 1850s. Bills granting subsidies to help build a transcontinental railroad were regularly introduced into each session of Congress and just as regularly defeated. The reason for their failure to pass was that the issue of the Pacific railroad, like virtually every other issue of the day, had become linked with the slavery question. Both North and South were eager to establish the line; but there was a difference of opinion where it should be built. As early as 1853 Congress had appropriated $150,000 to finance a survey to find a practicable route. The survey was conducted by a party of Army engineers, and took three years. The chief result of their lengthy report — it was published in twelve volumes between 1855 and 1861 — was to add fuel to the controversy. For the report made clear that the road could be built by any of three routes: the northern, the central, or the southern. During long-drawn-out debates in Congress partisans of the North would consider only the first two, while those from slave-holding states held out for a southern crossing.

The controversy ended with the outbreak of war. Once the fighting began, the question was no longer where the road should be built, but how to speed its building. For by then it was recognized that a transcontinental railroad was a military as well as an economic necessity. Although Californians in general favored the Union cause, there were so many ardent supporters of the Confederacy in the state as to constitute a threat of divided loyalties that could not prudently be ignored. Moreover, gold and silver — two highly useful commodities in wartime — were then being produced in quantity in California and Nevada. Most of this treasure was shipped by water, and there was always danger of the Panama steamers falling into the hands of Confederate privateers.

Californians did not fail to make use of these arguments when the Pacific Railroad bill came up for consideration at the next session of Congress. The act, which was passed early in 1862, was all its sponsors could have wished. It authorized the building of a railroad between Sacramento and the Missouri River — the so-called central route — and granted its builders a 400-foot-wide right of way, together with alternate sections of public land for a distance of ten miles on both sides of the tracks. To finance the project the builders were to receive government bonds maturing in thirty years and bearing 6 per cent interest; the amount advanced ranged from $16,000 per mile in the level sections to $48,000 in the mountains.

The contract to build the western half of the road was awarded the Central Pacific Railroad Company. The company's chief sponsor was a young

The original Ferry Building at the foot of Market Street was this shed-like structure, built by the Central Pacific Railroad as the western terminus of its transcontinental line. It continued to serve as the city's "front door" until 1898 when it was replaced by the present building.

engineer named Theodore D. Judah; associated with him were four Sacramento merchants: Collis P. Huntington, Charles Crocker, Leland Stanford, and Mark Hopkins. Judah withdrew, leaving the four in control. They amassed large fortunes by the building of the railroad, and added to them by the way they operated it after it was completed. The Central Pacific and its successor, the Southern Pacific, soon became potent factors in the political and economic life of the state and remained so until after the turn of the century.

The acquisitiveness of the Big Four, as they came to be called, early won them the enmity of San Franciscans. In 1863 the State Legislature passed an act authorizing the city to exchange $600,000 in municipal bonds for an equal amount of Central Pacific stock. The measure was submitted to the voters, and during the campaign that followed charges of bribery and other irregularities on the part of agents of the Big Four were freely made. The enabling act carried, but by so narrow a margin that the Board of Supervisors refused to issue the bonds. A compromise was eventually reached by which the city, instead of accepting the railroad stock — which was believed to be worthless — made the company an outright gift of $450,-000. This proved to be a bad bargain on the part of the city fathers — less than a decade later the value of the rejected stock had increased fourfold.

In the beginning San Francisco's hostility toward the railroad and its owners came about because of the company's policy during the construction period of importing boatloads of Chinese coolies to make the cuts, tunnels, and fills of the Sierra crossing. The competition of "cheap Chinese labor" was already a lively political issue in California, and this action by the railroad added fuel to the fire. But Charles Crocker, the partner in charge of construction, ignored the protests of the labor organizations and continued to add the industrious, cheap, and docile coolies to his force. At the end of 1865 some 6,000 of "Crocker's pets" were at work on the line. That number was gradually increased; by the time the rails were joined at Promontory Point in May, 1869, their total had reached 15,000.

On the day the railroad was completed San Franciscans forgot their grievances and joined the rest of the nation in celebrating the event. Buildings were decorated with flags, volunteer firemen and other uniformed groups paraded through the downtown streets, and from a platform in Portsmouth Square a succession of speakers announced that the city was entering an era of unparalleled growth and prosperity. That feeling, which was general, sprang from a belief that the railroad would bring a great wave of emigrants from the East and Middle West. Estimates were freely made that the city's population, which then was about 150,000, would reach one million by the end of the next decade. In preparation for the expected newcomers, plans for a wholesale expansion of facilities had for some time been under way. The speculative fever, already at a high point because of trading in Nevada silver stocks, now came to include real estate. This brought about a sharp rise in the value of downtown property and the opening of numerous new residential districts at the city's perimeter.

But it soon became clear that the new railroad was not going to perform the expected miracles. The daily long trainloads of emigrants failed to materialize; the rows of new houses in the recently opened subdivisions attracted few buyers, and the city's merchants learned that instead of bringing them additional business the new road was having the opposite effect: the goods of eastern manufacturers that had formerly been shipped by water and so had passed through the city, were now routed directly to the inland markets. Hence, trade with the interior, long a mainstay of the city's economy, declined sharply.

Of the period that followed, John S. Hittell, writing in 1878, stated:

> Everybody had wanted to sell, and nobody to buy; and a general and severe panic ensued. Many of the losers gave vent to their vexation by complaints that the Pacific Railroad was a damage to San Francisco; that the peninsula position of the city did not permit her to profit by railroads; that she had been built up by steamboat traffic and could not prosper after it was destroyed; that the cars from the Atlantic states could not be expected to come around the southern arm of San Francisco Bay, and that therefore some town on the eastern or northern shore of the bay . . . must

be the main terminus of the railroads to the Pacific slope; and that
as the network of tracks would extend every year, so would the
relative importance of San Francisco decline. For thirteen years the
prices of real estate and the amount of sales had risen rapidly; and
now so soon as the great road for which California had prayed as
necessary to the proper development of her natural wealth, and for
the foundation of a new era of prosperity to surpass that of the
gold discovery, was completed, there was a panic more severe than
that which accompanied the decline of the placers after 1853.

            ✓   ✓   ✓

Sacramento became the western terminus of the new road and remained
so for several years. Meanwhile plans were being laid to extend the rails to
deep water, and the question arose which bay community would enjoy the
distinction and the economic benefits of being chosen as the new terminus.
The railroad's owners were well aware of this rivalry and turned it to their
own advantage by announcing that the road would end at whatever town
offered the most substantial inducements.

San Franciscans were told that the trains would be brought into the
city provided the voters approved a $3,000,000 bond issue to build a bridge
across the lower bay at Ravenswood. When that measure was defeated at
the polls, a new proposal — that of a bridge from Alameda to Hunters Point
— was put forward, only to be withdrawn when surveys indicated that the
cost would be prohibitive. The company's next move was to petition Congress to grant it the use of Goat (now Yerba Buena) Island as its western
terminus. This was vigorously opposed by San Francisco businessmen, who
foresaw that much of the commerce of the port would thereby be diverted to
the mid-bay island.

While the controversial Goat Island bill was pending in Congress, promoters of a second transcontinental line, the Atlantic and Pacific Railroad,
arrived in the city. They were warmly received, particularly when it became
known that they planned to make San Francisco its western terminus. Much
of the support of this project vanished, however, when it was learned that
the city was expected to vote the road a $10,000,000 subsidy.

The long struggle for a direct connection by rail with the interior ended
when the Central Pacific owners eventually agreed to extend its tracks to
the southern end of the bay, and there connect with a newly completed
peninsula railroad, the San Francisco & San Jose. This roundabout route
continued in use until 1871 when the Oakland Mole, a two-mile-long combination earth fill and trestle, was built over the shallows of the east shore.
From that date until the opening of the San Francisco-Oakland Bay Bridge
sixty-five years later, most of those entering and leaving the city did so
aboard the picturesque transbay ferries.

5. THE SANITARY FUND

News of the firing on Fort Sumter reached the city, via Pony Express, on April 24, 1861, twelve days after the event, and was greeted with an upsurge of patriotism on the part of nearly everyone. On the afternoon of the following day a great crowd assembled in Portsmouth Square, applauded speakers who pledged the city's support of the North, and denounced those of their townsmen who favored the cause of the rebels.

At a second mass meeting a day or two later steps were taken to reactivate the Republican political clubs that had been formed during the Presidential campaign of the previous autumn. Members organized into military companies patterned after those of the earlier Vigilance committees, their purpose to thwart rumored plots on the part of Southern sympathizers to take over control of California and swing its support to the Confederacy. Their uneasiness was heightened by the fact that the regular Army troops stationed at the Presidio and elsewhere throughout the state were being withdrawn and sent to the eastern fighting fronts. Because their departure left the city virtually defenseless, the Home Guard, as it was called, prepared to take over until volunteer units could be recruited to replace the regulars.

Fears that Southerners in the state might attempt a coup were not altogether groundless. Some of their leaders were, in fact, planning such a venture: a series of bold moves by which they hoped to capture San Francisco, Sacramento, and other key points and set up a California Republic which, though nominally independent, would throw its support to the South. In retrospect the likelihood of such a plot succeeding appears small, but a number of factors, in the opinion of its leaders, made the plan seem feasible. One of their arguments was that many Californians believed that the state had no vital stake in the war, and hence that they should remain aloof from it. Among those supposed to hold that view were most Spanish-Californians, and many foreign-born emigrants who had arrived during the gold rush and later. A number of newspapers in the state held that view. The *Los Angeles Star,* commented:

> It is not for California to take sides. By preserving a strict neutrality, and affording shelter to all who may flee to her from the storm, she will render more effectual aid to the preservation of the Union than by mixing in the deadly strife and transferring to our peaceful shores the horrors of civil war. Peace is unquestionably our policy, and if any are indisposed to abide thereby, they had better transport themselves to the scenes of war and blood.

Another circumstance strengthening the position of those who planned to keep California out of the war was the fact that several high state offices were occupied by men who shared their views. This had come about because in the statewide election of 1860 the Southern sympathizers had voted as a unit, whereas the opposition had divided its vote between several candidates and so had elected none of them. Hence, when the fighting began, several important state officials were either avowed Secessionists or firm advocates of a policy of nonintervention.

In the Presidential election of that year San Franciscans cast 14,360 votes, of which the electors pledged to Lincoln received 6,825 votes, and those of rival candidates, 7,535. The fact that Lincoln had received less than half of the city's vote aroused uneasiness among supporters of the Union. Soon after the war started a group of their leaders wrote Secretary of War Cameron expressing their deep concern. Their letter begins:

> A majority of our present state officers are undisguised and avowed Secessionists, and the balance, being utterly hostile to the administration, are advocates of a peace policy at any sacrifice. . . . Every appointment made by our Governor [John C. Downey, who had assumed office in January, 1860] unmistakably indicates his entire sympathy and cooperation with those plotting to sever California from her allegiance to the Union, and that, too, at the hazard of civil war.

> About three-eighths of our citizens are from slaveholding states, and almost as a unit in this crisis. . . . These men are never without arms, have wholly laid aside their business, and are devoting their time to plotting, scheming, and organizing. Our advices, obtained with great prudence and care, show us that there are upwards of sixteen thousand "Knights of the Golden Circle" [a secret society of Southern sympathizers] in the state, and that they are still organizing, even in our most loyal districts.

The letter goes on to state that in addition to the avowed Secessionists there were many Californians who, although "hailing from the free states and styling themselves Union men," are opposed to the war, and others who "had affiliated with the disunionists to avoid paying a pittance toward maintaining the integrity of the government in its hour of trial." The final paragraph reads:

> We need not remind you of the vast importance of preserving California to the Union. Its great geographical extent, its mineral and agricultural wealth, the fact that it is our chief seat of empire upon the Pacific, and that its political action will exercise a powerful, if not controlling, influence upon its neighbors to the north, imperatively demand that no precaution should be neglected to insure its fidelity.

Evidently the concern of this group of San Franciscans was shared to some extent by the authorities at Washington, for early in 1861 they dispatched Brigadier General E. V. Sumner to San Francisco to take over the command of the Department of the Pacific. Sumner's orders were to replace Brigadier General Albert Sidney Johnston, a native of Kentucky, whose loyalty to the Union cause was being widely questioned in California. Sumner arrived on April 24. On assuming his command the following morning, Sumner learned that Johnston had already sent his resignation to Washington. Sumner also learned that the charges of disloyalty against his predecessor were groundless. "It gives me great pleasure," he wrote to Secretary Cameron, "to state that the command was turned over to me in good order. General Johnston had forwarded his resignation before I arrived, but he continued to hold the command, and was carrying out the orders of the Government." Johnston made his way to Richmond, was commissioned a general in the Confederate army, and less than a year later was killed leading his troops at Shiloh.

San Franciscans of the day were not immune to a wartime hysteria that exaggerated the danger of subversion and saw disloyalty when none existed. Yet their contributions to the war effort were many and varied. Throughout the conflict the city met each call for volunteers, promptly furnishing its assigned quotas of the 17,000 men who enlisted in California. In addition to those who joined the locally organized units, many made their way to the eastern fighting fronts, some to join the Union Army and others that of the Confederacy.

California was too far from the main theater of the war to play a significant part in the actual fighting. Its chief military function, therefore, was to man the frontier outposts after the regular Army troops were withdrawn, and so to keep lines of communication open and put down Indian uprisings between the Rockies and the Sierra.

The state's real contribution, however, and that of the Far West in general, was in the field of economics. Gold from California and silver from Nevada and Arizona played a decisive role in bolstering the credit of the Union at home and abroad. It permitted the North to buy badly needed war materials from England, France, and other European countries, whereas the Confederacy, shut off from access to that treasure, saw the value of its currency decline to the point where it was eventually forced into bankruptcy. The claim has been made that had it not been for the flow of the West's precious metals into the federal treasury the war might have ended in a stalemate or perhaps even in a Confederate victory.

San Francisco, through which port the bulk of the gold and silver passed on its way East, was also a liberal contributor to the Sanitary Fund, a movement that did much to ease the lot of sick and wounded Union soldiers. The fund was founded in Boston early in 1862, and a San Francisco branch was established later that year. The success of the local chapter was mainly due to the efforts of Thomas Starr King, pastor of the First Unitarian Church. King organized a fund-raising campaign which proved so effectual that by the end of 1862 close to $500,000 in gold was raised for the fund, more than half of which was contributed by San Franciscans. This permitted the fund greatly to broaden the scope of its activities, and thereafter its managers looked to the West Coast for a major part of its revenues. In the fall of 1863 King received this appeal from the Boston headquarters:

> The sanitary funds are low. Our expenses are fifty thousand dollars per month. We can live three months, and that only, without large support from the Pacific. Twenty-five thousand dollars a month, paid regularly while the war lasts, from California, would make our continuance . . . a certainty. We would make up the other twenty-five thousand dollars here. We have already contributed sanitary stores, of a value of seven million dollars, to all parts of the army. . . . California has been our main support in money, and if she fails us we are lost.

In his reply King promised that San Franciscans would undertake to contribute $200,000 to the fund during the coming year, and expressed his belief that an additional $100,000 would be raised elsewhere in California.

> A monthly subscription was organized [wrote John S. Hittell], and the sum of $25,000 a month—nearly $1,000 for every business day—was sent by San Francisco, which then had not more than 110,000 inhabitants. The final report of the commission, published after the close of the war, showed that of $4,800,000 cash received, California supplied more than $1,200,000 in currency. The gold value of the latter amount was about $940,000, and of this sum San Francisco supplied about half.

6. CIVIL WAR DAYS

But the city also had its ardent Southern sympathizers, and although they were comparatively few, their activities aroused uneasiness among both the civil and military authorities.

One member of this group was William A. Scott, pastor of the Calvary Presbyterian Church, then one of the city's largest. Scott was a native of Tennessee, and, like King, an eloquent speaker as well as a classical scholar. He had taken over his pastorate in 1854 and speedily made himself a leader in the religious and cultural life of the city. One commentator wrote of him:

> His refusal to concern himself exclusively with the spiritual welfare of his parishioners served to alienate many of his former admirers, and presently earned for him the title of "preacher-politician." . . . His habit of speaking his mind first got him into serious trouble some two years after his arrival when he launched a violent attack on the San Francisco Vigilance Committee of 1856.

View of the harbor from Rincon Hill. The building in the foreground, known as "the house of many corners," was one of a
number of such eight-sided residences put up in various parts of
the city during the 1850s and 1860s; two are still standing.

He next came into disfavor when it was noticed that during his ser-
mons he asked divine guidance to the country's "Presidents"—which was
taken to mean that he was referring not only to Lincoln but to Jefferson
Davis as well. His loyalty having been brought into question, his subsequent behavior was closely watched. When, in September, 1862, the local
synod of the Presbyterian Church passed a resolution expressing sympathy
with, and support of, the Union cause, it became known that the vote on
the resolution was eight to one, the lone dissenter being Scott. On being
asked why he had opposed the measure, Scott is said to have replied,
"Jefferson Davis is no more a traitor than George Washington."

Many were shocked at the pastor's open espousal of the Confederate
cause. He was denounced in the local pro-Union papers, and crowds gathered in the open space opposite his church while speakers demanded his
arrest as a traitor. Scott continued to preach for several weeks longer, then
resigned his pastorate, sold his Rincon Hill home, and took the next steamer
to New York. On behalf of the congregation, most of whom had remained
loyal to their truculent pastor, the trustees of the church presented him
with a parting gift of $8,000 in gold. From New York, he and his family
continued on to England, where they remained until after the war. In the
early 1870s he accepted a call to another San Francisco church from a
group of his former parishioners. There he remained until his death in
1885.

Another wartime episode that attracted wide attention was the so-called *Chapman* incident. In the summer of 1862 a group of Southerners conceived a bold plan—that of buying a swift sailing ship, loading her with guns and provisions, and slipping her out of the harbor. Once at sea, they planned to intercept an outbound Panama steamer, capture her and her cargo of gold and silver, deposit the passengers and crew on one of the islands off the Southern California coast, and then make their way around Cape Horn to a Confederate port, meanwhile keeping a lookout for other treasure-bearing Union ships.

For a time preparations for that picturesque exploit went well. A suitable ship, the schooner *Chapman,* was found and purchased; a crew was assembled, and guns and ammunition were smuggled aboard—all seemingly without arousing the suspicion of the port officials. On the night of her scheduled departure the *Chapman* was towed from the dock and dropped anchor in the bay, awaiting the ship's navigator who had unaccountably failed to show up at the appointed time. The wait lasted through the night, and with the coming of daylight the conspirators realized that they had been duped: sunrise revealed the U. S. gunboat *Cyane* anchored near by, her guns trained on their ship, and several boatloads of marines approaching. The leaders had time only to destroy some incriminating documents—including a letter of marque and a commission as captain in the Confederate navy, which had been issued to one of them by Jefferson Davis. The boarding party climbed on deck and placed the entire group under arrest. It developed that the federal authorities had all along known of the plot, the missing navigator having kept them informed, and that they had waited until the ship was about to sail before springing the trap.

The three ringleaders, Ridgley Greathouse, Asbury Harpending, and Alfred Rubery (the last-named a nephew of the English publicist John Bright) were tried for high treason; each was found guilty and sentenced to ten years' imprisonment and a fine of $10,000. Later, however, the fines were remitted and the trio released upon their promise not to attempt further acts of piracy.

❦   ❦   ❦

Another source of uneasiness during the war years was the inadequacy of San Francisco's harbor defenses, and the realization that the city could not be defended from an attack in force either by land or sea. Even before the fighting began, the city's vulnerability had been widely recognized, and steps had been taken to strengthen its defenses. Fort Point (now Fort Winfield Scott) at the southern entrance to the Golden Gate—its forty-foot-thick brick walls had been building since the mid-1850s—was rushed to completion; also, additional guns were mounted on the heights above, and on Alcatraz Island. By 1863 the Army post at Alcatraz—then the headquarters of the Department of the Pacific—had been converted into "a prime fortress, garrisoned by 120 soldiers . . . with a belt of encircling batteries, a massive brick guardhouse, and a barracks, three stories high, with accommodations for 600."

The original purpose of these preparations was better to repel attack by Confederate privateers that might make their way into North Pacific waters to prey on Union shipping. Soon, however, San Franciscans were confronted by what appeared to be a more serious threat. This was the possibility that one or another of the European nations that had once laid claim to West Coast territory might take advantage of the country's involvement in civil war to seize control of California and Oregon.

In a letter to Governor Stanford, Brigadier General George Wright, who had recently assumed command of the Department of the Pacific, thus outlined what steps should be taken in the event of such an attack:

> In case of war with a maritime power, the immediate attention of the enemy would most certainly be directed to this city, the great entrepôt . . . of the Pacific Coast. To prevent the egress of ships of war, we have the forts at Fort Point and Alcatraz Island. Additional batteries could easily be thrown up, and with such naval forces as could be concentrated in the harbor, it is believed the city would be safe. The General Government has but a small amount of funds available for defensive works on the coast, but I apprehend no embarrassment on that account, not for a moment doubting that the loyal and Union-loving people of California will most cheerfully respond to any call which may be made on them, whether of men or money to defend their state from foes without and traitors within.

General Wright detailed a member of his staff, Colonel Rene De Russy, to make a survey of the harbor defenses and suggest means of strengthening them. De Russy recommended doubling the number of guns on Alcatraz and Fort Point, and building new batteries at the north portal of the Golden Gate, on Angel Island, and at Rincon Point. The last-named was near the center of the city; guns placed there would command parts of the bay that were out of range of the existing defenses. During 1862 and 1863, however, little could be done to carry out these recommendations. No facilities for manufacturing cannon existed on the coast, and the arsenals of the East were fully occupied supplying needs closer to home. On March 12, 1862, General Wright wrote to the chief of ordnance at the Benicia Arsenal: "We must establish a foundry, cast our own guns, projectiles, etc., and be prepared to meet any emergency."

No guns were cast at Benicia or elsewhere on the coast until after the war was over. However, a San Francisco shipyard and iron works shared the distinction of assembling and launching a highly welcome defensive weapon. This was the ironclad monitor *Comanche,* which had been built in a New England yard, then dismantled and shipped around the Horn in the clipper ship *Aquila.* The *Aquila* arrived in mid-July, 1862, whereupon the work of reassembling the craft began. All went well until September 15 when a storm caused the *Aquila* to sink beside the dock, carrying most of the *Comanche's* machinery to the bottom. However, divers recovered the missing parts. The monitor was eventually completed and began patrolling the waters outside the Golden Gate.

Three European nations—England, France, and Russia—all had naval squadrons in the Pacific. During the war years the ships of all three were occasional visitors in the bay. This was yet another source of uneasiness to those charged with the city's safety. There was always the possibility that foreign warships might enter the harbor on ostensibly friendly missions and, once inside, train their guns on the city and demand its capitulation. In the summer of 1864 Brigadier General Irvin McDowell, General Wright's successor as commander of the Department of the Pacific, wrote his superiors in Washington stating that "there are now lying English, French, and Russian men-of-war covering the shipping and town completely," and adding that "we have not a single gun, either ashore or afloat, bearing or that can be brought to bear on them, to require them to leave should we want them to go."

The War Department's reply was the same as that given earlier: no weapons could be spared to arm the proposed batteries. Instead, it was suggested to McDowell that foreign warships "be required to anchor at points where they would be within range of existing batteries." This was done, and although the weakness of the city's defenses continued to be discussed by several local newspapers for some time longer, the subject was eventually dropped and San Franciscans seem to have spent the final months of the war feeling relatively secure.

In the Presidential election of 1864, Abraham Lincoln, who four years earlier had carried California by the narrowest margin, received the endorsement of an overwhelming majority of the voters. In San Francisco 21,024 votes were cast, a figure that exceeded that of Boston, a city twice its size. How the election results were received in San Francisco was thus described by H. H. Bancroft:

> Late in the day the indications of California's 30,000 majority for Lincoln over McClellan began to come in from such portions of the state as could be heard from by telegraph. . . . The city waited breathless, far into the night, for the first news from east of the Mississippi, and while it waited windows were illuminated and few households thought of sleep. Toward midnight there began to move through the principal streets a solid column of 4,000 . . . while women crowded the balconies and windows waving

handkerchiefs and flags, laughing and weeping together in a contagion of exultant emotion; for then it was known that the President whom all trusted was to remain in his place.

At the time of Lincoln's second inauguration the fortunes of the Union armies, which had been at a low ebb during much of the previous year, had taken a turn for the better. The Confederate armies were being pushed back all along the line, and the knowledge that victory was close at hand made San Francisco's observance of the inaugural a gala event.

Lee's surrender on April 9 set off a second citywide celebration. This time, however, the jubilation was short-lived. Five days later, while many of the downtown buildings were still decorated in celebration of peace, news of Lincoln's assassination stirred wartime animosities to renewed life.

> Soon hot blood began to stir [wrote Bancroft]. Terrible denunciation and threats of retribution passed from lip to lip. Nothing more fitting could be thought of than that the newspapers which had encouraged treason should be destroyed, and to this work the people lent themselves with a will. Four years of patient tolerance of too great freedom of speech was revenged by demolishing a number of newspaper offices. . . . As soon as possible the military was called out to assist the police in suppressing the riot, but only a few arrests were made. . . . By the next morning order was restored.

On April 20, to the accompaniment of muffled drums and the tolling of church bells, 14,000 marched through the downtown streets, the buildings of which had been draped in black, and at Union Square listened to a memorial address delivered by Horatio Stebbins, who had succeeded Thomas Starr King as pastor of the First Unitarian Church.

VII

The Seventies

1. THE DISCONTENTED DECADE

As the 1870s opened, San Francisco was completing its first quarter-century under American rule. They had been uncommonly active years. Few cities had witnessed so many dramatic events in so brief a period of time: its transfer to the sovereignty of the United States; the struggle for order that culminated in the Vigilance committees; the decline of the California placers and the rise of the Comstock's silver mines; finally, the changes brought about by the Civil War and the accelerated development of northern California's natural resources.

It might be expected that a period so crowded with events would have been followed by one of comparative tranquillity. Yet the ten years immediately ahead were to see changes hardly less far-reaching. They brought with them a variety of new problems which aroused contention so bitter that the 1870s have sometimes been called "the discontented decade."

The prime source of discord in that period was the competition offered white workers by "cheap Chinese labor." Although the beginning of anti-Chinese sentiment in California dates back to gold-rush days, it was not until the mid-1860s when the Central Pacific's owners began importing Cantonese construction workers that the slogan "The Chinese Must Go!" began to be heard.

The Chinese who arrived in 1849 and 1850 were made welcome by the San Franciscans. They were industrious and unassuming, and willing to serve as household servants, or to perform other humble tasks that few of the others would do except under the spur of necessity. In the diggings, too, the first Chinese were looked on, if not with approval, at least with tolerance. For there they kept to themselves and were content to stake out the less promising claims or to rework those that had been abandoned by the whites. Moreover, the first wave of Argonauts had included few Chinese. During 1850, when the first count was made, only 787 had reached San Francisco—a tiny percentage of the thousands who arrived that year. By 1853, however, their number had increased to 4,000, and proposals to restrict their further immigration began to be heard. Two years later, in

135

1855, the first of a series of Chinese exclusion acts was passed by the State Legislature, only to be declared unconstitutional by the federal courts. Meanwhile, as the yield of the placers declined and gold became less plentiful hostility to the Chinese increased. At some Sierra towns the miners sought to rid themselves of what they regarded as unfair competition by passing laws requiring the Chinese to pay a substantial head tax for the privilege of working their claims. At others, mobs attacked the camps of the Chinese, wrecking and burning their cabins, and forcing the occupants to flee.

Many of those driven from the mining country joined their countrymen at San Francisco, Sacramento, Stockton, and other coast and interior towns, all of which soon had "Chinatowns"—clusters of board shacks where they lived apart, having only limited contact with the rest of the community. Because they worked for wages far below what other laborers, with their higher standards of living, needed to sustain themselves, they came to be looked on as a threat to the white man's security and were treated accordingly.

Curiously enough, in San Francisco—which eventually became a hotbed of anti-Chinese sentiment—such hostility developed slowly. During the years when thousands of "Crocker's pets" were being brought into the country, few local residents protested. For San Franciscans were anxious to see the railroad completed as soon as possible, and, in addition, were enjoying a wartime prosperity. As long as jobs were plentiful and wages high, no one feared the competition of the Chinese. However, the slack times that followed the war's end changed that attitude. The Eastern factories were again making civilian goods, and the local plants, which no longer had a monopoly on the production of such articles, were forced to curtail their operations or in some cases, to shut down. The number of unemployed mounted month by month. In casting about for someone to blame for their unhappy lot, the jobless, urged on by their leaders, joined a state-wide outcry against cheap Chinese labor.

It was not long until labor's feelings came to be shared by the merchant class. For many local Chinese were not content to remain lowly wage earners, and soon were launching businesses: laundries, restaurants, grocery stores, and shops of various sorts. Others hired themselves out as apprentices in local factories until they had learned the trade, then set up businesses of their own. Two local industries—cigar-making and the manufacture of clothing—they entered in such numbers that by the early 1870s they had gained an almost complete monopoly. In 1873 San Francisco had 115 cigar-making plants, employing 3,480 workers, and doing an annual business of $4,000,000; almost all were owned and staffed by Chinese. Much the same situation existed in the garment industry, where scores of crowded workrooms in the Chinese quarter turned out work clothes, hats, caps, and

For well over a century San Francisco's Chinatown has been the largest concentration of Chinese outside the Orient. With its picturesque temples, colorful shops and markets, and restaurants serving exotic foods, it has long been a favorite attraction to residents and visitors alike. This famous Genthe photograph is of pre-earthquake Chinatown when queues were worn.

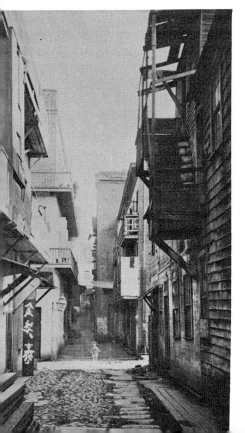

During the 1870s, '80s and '90s the houses fronting on the narrow alleys on both sides of Grant Avenue sheltered not only numerous clothing and cigar factories but gambling resorts, houses of prostitution, and opium dens. The entire quarter was destroyed in the 1906 fire.

dresses, which the owners were able to sell at prices well below those of their competitors.

Although before the end of the Civil War feeling against the Chinese had resulted in occasional acts of violence, these had been quickly brought under control. The situation first got out of hand in the summer of 1866, when a contractor who was filling in an area of tidelands in the industrial district sought to reduce expenses by discharging his white crews—whose wages were $1.25 per day—and replacing them with Chinese coolies, who reportedly were paid less than half that sum. A day or two later the displaced workers and their friends, some three hundred strong, suddenly appeared on the scene, swinging clubs and hurling rocks. When the brief assault was over, one Chinese was dead, fifteen had been injured, and the others had fled. The rioters then descended on the shacks where the Chinese workers had been housed and burned them to the ground. By then completely out of control, the mob converged on a second Chinese "shanty-town," this one at Hunters Point; it, too, was destroyed. As a result of that violent outbreak, several leaders were arrested, charged with disturbing the peace, and released on bail. Later the charges were dismissed, and the excitement simmered down.

In the San Francisco of the day, however, hostile feeling against the Chinese was not universal. Strongly opposed to them were the factory hands, owners and employees of laundries, restaurants, and other businesses with whom they were in direct competition, and wage earners in general. On the other hand, there were many who not only tolerated John Chinaman, but looked on him as a useful member of the community. Chinese "houseboys"—a generic word for cooks, gardeners, and other domestic servants—had long been a tradition in the homes of the city's more prosperous families. So also were the itinerant peddlers who, as they made their daily rounds, were a familiar feature of the residential streets. Amelia Ransome Neville thus recalled them in this passage from her *The Fantastic City*:

> Through residence neighborhoods of the old city passed the colorful figure of the Chinese vegetable vendor in blue cotton blouse and trousers, padded slippers, and a broad hat like an inverted tray of woven bamboo. Over his shoulder he carried a flexible pole and, slung on either end of it, a huge basket overflowing with fresh greens and glowing fruits that bobbed rhythmically to his swinging gait. On Fridays the Chinese fisherman followed him on his rounds and stopped at the curb to weigh silver fish in his scales. Chinese peddlers of silks and brocades, carved ivory and jade, carried their wares from house to house packed in cases that were tied in great squares of yellow cotton. It was an adventure to have one brought in with his pack. He would step softly into a

room with many little bows and kneel on the floor to untie the knotted cloth; and presently the carpet would be covered with a fascinating confusion of bright silks, ivory fans, lacquer boxes, pale green tea-cups of "Canton Medallion," and carved sandalwood that scented everything.

But the street peddlers and unobtrusive household servants did little to counteract the hostility against their countrymen on the part of many San Franciscans. For as the postwar depression deepened and the number of jobless continued to rise, demands that something be done to end the competition of Chinese labor became more frequent. As the municipal election of 1875 approached, leaders of the anti-Chinese forces organized a Workingman's party, put a slate of candidates in the field—and succeeded in electing virtually the entire ticket.

When the new mayor, Andrew J. Bryant, took office on December 4, 1875, he and the other officials proceeded to make good their campaign promises by passing a series of highly restrictive measures aimed at the Chinese. One ordinance sharply increased the license fees charged Chinese businessmen. Another prohibited Chinese laundries from operating in any except fireproof buildings; a third barred them from appearing on the streets after 2 a.m.; and yet others prohibited the pack-carrying Chinese peddlers from walking on the sidewalks, revised the rules governing housing and health in their native quarter, and imposed heavy fines on those convicted of gambling or smoking opium.

Few of these measures accomplished the hoped-for results. Some were invalidated by the state and federal courts; others were laxly enforced, and still others—including the prohibition against gambling and opium-smoking —proved impossible to enforce. By then the city's economy, which had shown some improvement, was again in difficulties.

The opening of the year 1878 [states Langley's *City Directory* for 1878-79] was marked with an extraordinary depression in almost all branches of labor; the city was thronged with a multitude of men out of employ such as had never before been known, and, for the first time in her history, organized methods of relief, and free dispensation of charity, were absolutely necessary in providing food and shelter for many of her people. As an aggravation to this fact . . . the character of the new labor movement then in progress of development in the city was not fully established, which deterred capitalists, speculators and builders from any but the most conservative course.

For some time large groups of jobless workers had been congregating each afternoon on a sand lot on outer Market Street and applauding speakers who denounced the Chinese and those who employed them. In late July, 1877, one of the sand-lot orators, James d'Arcy, so aroused his listeners that at the end of his harangue they set off in a body toward Chinatown, bent on destroying it. The rioting that followed lasted most of the night. The mob roved unchecked through the narrow streets and alleys of the quarter, smashing windows, kicking down doors of laundries and other places of business, and setting fire to their interiors, then cutting the hoses of firemen when they arrived to put out the blazes.

The rioters eventually dispersed, and the next day was comparatively quiet. But the speeches of d'Arcy and the other leaders kept the emotions of their followers at so high a pitch that new outbreaks seemed inevitable. Mayor Bryant, himself a staunch friend of labor, issued a proclamation warning that the police had been ordered to take any measures that might be needed to suppress further violence. Meanwhile the city press, the clergy, and others joined in urging on the workers a respect for law and order. But the spokesmen of the workers replied that years of effort to solve their problems by legal means had failed; this time they were determined to take matters into their own hands.

On the evening of July 25 a call was issued for the jobless workers to assemble at a protest meeting at Fifth and Mission streets. An estimated five thousand responded, listened to another of d'Arcy's fiery speeches, and, despite a strong force of police who were present to preserve order, again got beyond control. This time only part of the mob headed for Chinatown. Others broke up into smaller groups and spread throughout the city. Again laundries were raided and burned; rocks were thrown through the windows of shops and factories where Chinese were employed, and a number of those encountered on the streets were stoned or beaten.

In the face of this emergency, the law-abiding citizens responded much as they had under similar conditions in the past. When it became obvious that the police was unable to suppress the rioting, a meeting of prominent business and professional men was called, and an organization patterned after the committees of 1851 and 1856 was hastily formed and given the title of the Committee of Safety. William T. Coleman, who had headed the second Vigilance Committee, was put in charge; volunteers were recruited, armed with pick handles, and began patrolling the streets in threatened areas. These preparations were still under way when the committee's leaders received a call for help from the hard-pressed police. A waterfront warehouse containing goods imported from China had been set afire, and the rioters, by slashing the hoses, were preventing the firemen from playing water on the flames.

One hundred committeemen were dispatched to the scene. They arrived to find the rioters occupying a bluff near the burning warehouse, from which they were hurling rocks at the policemen and firemen below. On orders of their leader, the committeemen charged up the steep hillside and after a brief but sanguinary battle during which clubs were swung freely, succeeded in dislodging the rioters. During the melee a number of shots were fired, and one of the committee members received a wound from which he died the following day. Several leaders of the fleeing force were arrested, whereupon a group of their friends attempted to free them. This brought on an hour-long battle before the would-be rescuers were driven off.

That ended the fighting for the day. But the temper of both parties was such that more trouble was expected the next morning. Faced by that explosive situation, Mayor Bryant issued an order prohibiting public assemblages and banning unauthorized persons from the streets after 10 p.m. The Committee of Safety appealed for help to the local federal authorities, who responded by providing members with muskets from the government arsenal at Benicia, and by stationing two warships, the *Pensacola* and the *Lancaster,* off the waterfront, with detachments of sailors and marines ready to disembark on short notice. Meanwhile companies of armed committeemen had augmented the police in patrolling the streets and dispersing crowds, while others remained at the state armory ready to hasten to any trouble spot.

This impressive show of force had the desired effect. No further rioting took place; the Committee of Safety soon disbanded, and an uneasy peace was restored.

2. DENNIS KEARNEY'S SAND-LOTTERS

These, however, were but preliminary skirmishes in a campaign that was to be waged almost continuously for well over a decade. During most of that period the labor forces were led by Dennis Kearney, the most eloquent of the "sand-lot orators." Kearney was a former teamster whose drayage business had failed during the depression of the mid-1870s. He had been a member of the Committee of Safety—which was known to the workers as "Coleman's pick-axe brigade"—and so had had a hand in putting down the disorders of July, 1877. After he lost his business he joined the Draymen's and Teamsters' Union, and began taking an active part in the meetings on the sand lots.

There he quickly made his influence felt. A forceful speaker, he attracted a following by the vehemence of his attacks not only on the Chinese and their employers but on politicians, financiers, stockbrokers, and businessmen in general. Among his favorite targets were the mining and railroad magnates. During one of his tirades he shouted: "The monopolists who make their money by employing cheap labor . . . have built themselves fine mansions on Nob Hill and erected flagpoles on their roofs; let them take care they have not erected their own gallows." On another occasion he threatened to provide each of his followers with "a musket and one hundred rounds of ammunition," to lead them on a march to Sacramento,

The old City Hall and Hall of Records, about 1875. It was from
the wooden platform in the right foreground that Dennis Kearney
and other sand-lot orators addressed their followers.

and should the legislators fail to pass a pending Chinese exclusion bill, to
"string them to the nearest lamppost."

Extravagant pronouncements of that sort, however, attracted scant
attention from the residents in general, most of whom put them down to
the boastings of a harmless demagogue. But when Kearney took to leading
large groups of sand-lotters into the middle of the city and holding meetings on downtown street corners, the public became apprehensive. One day
he led three thousand followers to the top of Nob Hill, and there staged a
mass protest against Crocker's "spite fence." This was a thirty-foot-high
board fence Crocker had built about the cottage of a neighbor, an undertaker named Yung, who had refused to sell his property to the railroad
man. Crocker owned the rest of the block and was building an elaborate
residence there. In his speeches Kearney had been making much of the
"spite fence," terming it a further example of the arrogance of great wealth.
On arriving in front of the millionaire's mansion he mounted its steps and
delivered another of his fiery speeches in the course of which he shouted,
"If I give an order to hang Crocker, it will be done!"

Threats of that sort, together with the knowledge that some of his
followers had armed themselves and were daily holding drills, increased
the public's uneasiness. The local newspapers, most of which until then
had been sympathetic to the cause of the jobless workers, joined in demanding that means be found to curb the agitator's growing influence. In response
to their urging, Kearney and two of his lieutenants were arrested. They
were charged with having violated a city ordinance prohibiting unauthorized assemblages, and sentenced to two weeks in the county jail. This was
the first of several jail terms served by Kearney, from each of which he

emerged more popular than ever with his followers, who looked on him as a martyr.

By then San Francisco's "workingmen's revolt" had attracted national attention, and Kearney was called on to help organize similar movements elsewhere in the depression-ridden country. When, in the fall of 1877, he returned from a speech-making tour of Eastern cities five thousand of his adherents welcomed him back by a parade through the downtown streets.

Stirred to action by that massive show of strength, the State Legislature passed a measure called the Murphy Riot Act. Under its provisions, Kearney was again arrested. His subsequent trial occupied several weeks and ended in his acquittal. Thereupon he invited members of the Legislature to a forthcoming meeting of the Workingmen's party so that they might, in his words, judge for themselves whether the policies he advocated endangered the public safety. His offer was accepted; a committee composed of members from both houses attended, was given places of honor on the platform, and listened to a Kearney speech that was "as free of slander as a minister's sermon." The lawmakers returned to Sacramento and recommended that the Murphy Act be repealed.

Kearney's successes were made easier by the economic situation, which had been steadily worsening. Four years of crop failures caused by abnormally light rainfall, plus an already severe business recession, had reduced whole communities to the verge of want. In such localities Kearney's promise to raise wages and create jobs by driving out the Chinese and forcing employers to disgorge a larger share of their profits, fell on fertile soil.

At an election held in June, 1877, to choose delegates to frame a new state constitution, four slates of candidates were put up: by the Republicans, the Democrats, the Workingmen, and a group without party affiliations. Of the 152 candidates elected, more than one-third were pledged to the Workingmen's party, which gave them control of the convention. In the end, however, this proved an empty victory. For dissension developed between the radical and moderate wings of Kearney's party, and he was ousted from the presidency. He was able to regain the office a month later only to lose it once more, this time on charges that he had misappropriated party funds. Kearney vehemently denied the charges and was eventually cleared of wrongdoing. But the episode ended his influence in the party, and a short time later he withdrew permanently from the political arena. His later career has elements of irony. He reassumed the role of businessman, amassed a considerable fortune by speculating in wheat, sugar, and other commodities, and again became a pillar of the city's conservative element. He died in 1907.

Dennis Kearney's influence on the political thought of his day persisted long after he had retired to private life. For it came to be recognized that despite his rabble-rousing tactics, many of his strictures against the existing order were valid. The 1870s were a materialistic age; both in business and politics standards of ethics were low, and the workingman had ample grounds for believing he was being denied a fair share of the wealth he helped produce. While Kearney's more ardent followers accepted his belief that only by force could labor achieve its just ends, most workers rejected violence in favor of electing to office men pledged to bring about needed reforms by peaceful means. It was this wing of the party that eventually repudiated Kearney and other radical leaders. For several decades thereafter it played an influential and, on the whole, beneficial role in the political life of the city and state.

3. FREE LUNCHES AND OTHER AMENITIES

By the 1870s the city had developed several characteristics that have ever since been referred to as "typically San Franciscan." One of these was a novel feature of its architecture — its omnipresent bay windows. From the late 1860s until the turn of the century virtually every residence, as well as numerous hotels and office buildings, followed the prevailing trend. The theory behind the bay window, and the reason for its continued popularity, was that it admitted a maximum of sunshine and light and so in a measure compensated for the city's frequent fogs and chill winds. Their all but universal use made the local architecture conspicuously ornate even by the no means austere standards of the day. Ranged in rows, one above the other, and covering their entire exteriors, the protruding windows gave such important downtown buildings as the Palace, Grand, and Baldwin hotels, the Phelan Building, and scores of others a complexity of outline that rarely failed to attract the attention of visitors. The bay-window theme was repeated, with variations, in the newer residential districts beyond Van Ness Avenue, in the outer Mission district, and on the slopes of Russian and Nob hills. There block after block was solidly built with narrow two-story dwellings, the facade ornamented with bay windows projecting from the front parlor and the master bedroom above.

Another feature characteristic of San Francisco life during the 1870s was the unusually large number of residents who lived in hotels or lodginghouses and ate all their meals in restaurants. This custom was a carry-over from gold-rush days when the population was predominantly male and family life was the exception. Two decades later the proportion of women to men was approaching an equilibrium; the federal census for 1870 listed 75,842 males and 61,577 females. But the habits of pioneer days were deeply ingrained, and San Franciscans of the older generation were slow to adopt the ways of domesticity. Many preferred to live as permanent guests in downtown hotels or in "housekeeping rooms" close to the central area. Even those who had become householders patronized the city's restaurants more often than was customary elsewhere.

THE SEVENTIES

From the 1870s until the end of the century the most striking feature of local architecture was the omnipresent bay window. The device owned its popularity to the fact that it admitted a maximum of sunlight into the rooms — an advantage in a city where fogs are frequent and the sky often overcast. *(Roy D. Graves)*

A type of residence once extremely popular and still frequently encountered in older parts of the city—is pictured below: two-story "flats" with their facades ornamented with a profusion of "millwork" and, of course, the inevitable bay windows. *(Roy D. Graves)*

The variety and quality of the food served in the city's restaurants was likewise a heritage from pioneer times. For San Francisco had been settled by natives of many countries, and although with the passage of time few such groups continued to live in separate "foreign colonies" (which had been the case in the 1850s) all preserved some of the customs of their home-lands — including a preference for their native cookery.

Thus during the 1870s and later the San Francisco diner-out could choose from a wide variety of eating places. These ranged from those serving the exotic dishes of China, India, and other Oriental countries, to the numerous "two-bit houses." These were unpretentious establishments with long "family style" tables and sawdust-covered floors where plain but substantial meals were offered at a fixed price of twenty-five cents. In between these two extremes were restaurants, bars, and hotel dining rooms catering to virtually every taste and every pocketbook. Then as now, those in the North Beach area specialized in the pastas of Italy, the price of meals including a bottle of California wine. The highly seasoned dishes of Mexico had been the staple food of the Californians since the coming of the first white men, and cafés featuring tamales, enchiladas, frijoles, and chile con carne were both numerous and well patronized.

Half a dozen long-established French restaurants catered to the local gourmets. Earliest of these was the *Poulet d'Or*, which dated from 1850 and originally occupied a board shack on Dupont Street near Clay. The miners, who had difficulty pronouncing the name, took to calling it the Poodle Dog, and it and its successors and imitators have used that name down to the present. There were also restaurants serving the foods of Germany, Switzerland, Russia, and England. In the mid-1870s one visitor wrote: "It is possible in San Francisco to dine or lunch in any language; to eat the especial dishes of any civilized country."

The restaurants of the period also offered a variety of California foods that impressed world travelers, who singled out for special praise such distinctly local delicacies as crab, shrimp, and abalone. Duck, quail, and other wild game frequently appeared on local menus, as well as roast venison and, on occasion, grizzly steak.

Another gastronomic novelty that frequently elicited comment from strangers in the city was the bountiful free lunches served in all San Francisco bars, where the purchase of a schooner of beer or other drink entitled the patron to what was described as the equivalent to a seven-course meal.

The bars were even more numerous than the restaurants and as heavily patronized. A writer in the *City Directory* for 1875-76 commented:

Nowhere on earth is the temptation to drink as strong as here. Business is brisk, competition sharp, and the climate the most constantly stimulating anywhere to be found. Rivalry spurs them on every hand, and scores stand waiting to take their places the moment they step aside. So they drive 'til nature falters or weakens and calls for rest. But nature's rest they cannot or will not afford; an artificial stimulant is quicker; it is everywhere close at hand; it seems to save time; companions press; everybody does it and they follow the fashion.

4. SPECULATION

The comments quoted above sprang in part from a weakness shared by virtually every segment of the population — speculation in mining stocks. That practice, too, was part of the city's heritage. The gold rush itself had been a gamble in which the miner wagered time, money, health, and often life itself, against the chance of washing a fortune from the foothill stream-beds. Since success or failure at the diggings was largely a matter of luck, and since the excitement of the gaming tables often the only recreation of his leisure hours, it is not surprising that the miner adopted the gambler's philosophy as a way of life. Or that, in later years, he preferred to risk his savings in highly speculative ventures that promised large and fast returns rather than in more conservative enterprises where the profits, though surer, were likely to be small.

Speculation in the stocks of the Nevada silver mines was all but universal during the 1870s. This drawing, from *Frank Leslie's Illustrated Newspaper*, pictures a run on a local bank during one of the frequent breaks in the market.

Sidewalk trading in bonanza stocks, 1877. The faces are those of prominent local brokers. The Nevada Bank, owned by the Comstock Silver Kings, Mackay, Fair, Flood and O'Brien, appears in the background. *(The Bancroft Library.)*

This gambling spirit, which had persisted all through the 1850s and 1860s, reached its high point in the 1870s. In his *History of the San Francisco Stock and Exchange Board,* Joseph L. King, who was one of the city's leading stockbrokers, tells how at the height of the gambling craze so many would-be investors daily gathered before the California Street office of the exchange that they completely blocked the street. "A policeman was stationed every morning to make a passageway between us, so that citizens having business in that locality could get through," King recalled. His account continues:

> And from whence came our orders? Imprimis — from San Francisco, and, literally, from the kitchen to the pulpit; from every shade of life, and every nationality. . . . Chinamen were large gamblers in mining stocks. Sacramento, Virginia City, and Carson City were large traders; Virginia City in particular. Wherever the telegraph line extended, orders would roll in on us.

Part of the fascination of the game was the rapid rise and fall in the value of the stocks. Rumors of a new strike at one of the better known properties might cause the price of shares to increase tenfold overnight — and a week later to fall far below the former selling price. In the spring of

1871 the opening of a new ore body in the Crown Point mine at Gold Hill sent its stock skyward. By June the price of shares, which eight months before had sold for $3, reached $6,000. This and other spectacular rises spurred the mining fever to new heights. Between January and May, 1872, the market value of the stocks traded on the San Francisco Exchange rose from $17,000,000 to $81,000,000, nearly a fivefold increase in as many months. Then in June came the crash. In ten days $60,000,000 in paper profits were wiped out, and thousands of San Franciscans, their brief period of affluence at an end, found themselves penniless. A small group, however, including the brokers — those who were themselves not speculating — and some insiders who had foreknowledge of the impending crash, profited enormously.

Although the panic of 1872 had made clear the methods by which the value of the stocks had been manipulated, the confidence of the public was only temporarily shaken. The extraordinary richness of some of the mines, plus the announcement of new discoveries at Virginia City, Gold Hill, and other Nevada silver towns, brought on a new era of speculation. By 1874 the city again was riding—precariously as it proved—on the crest of another wave of prosperity.

> The Gold Hill bonanza [wrote John S. Hittell] had now
> [1874] reached the height of its splendor, and the Crown Point
> and Belcher were paying immense dividends. In three years and a
> half the two mines had taken out more than forty million dollars,
> a result previously unapproached in the experience of the Washoe.
> While they were still at the flood tide of their prosperity, the still
> greater bonanza of the Consolidated Virginia was found near the
> northern end of the lode, and in May it began monthly dividends
> of three hundred thousand dollars. Every week brought news from
> the advancing drifts, cross-cuts and winzes, and proved the ore
> body to be larger and richer. Experienced miners, who were rep-
> resented as trustworthy experts, expressed the belief that the ore
> in sight would yield fifteen hundred millions. The excitement was
> intense; the aggregate value of the Comstock shares, as indicated
> by the quotations of the market, rose at the rate of a million dollars
> a day for nearly two months, and the year closed when the fever
> or frenzy of speculation was near its culmination.

San Franciscans, however, eventually became aware that the millions in Comstock profits pouring into the city were not an unmixed blessing. Trading in mining stock had become so heavy that an ever-larger share of money needed for the development of local industries was being diverted to finance mining properties in the Washoe district, at Austin, Hamilton, White Pine, and other Nevada boom towns. Of the millions invested in such stock, only a tiny percentage was returned in the form of dividends.

The Nevada Bank, built in 1875 and long the headquarters of the bonanza firm, stood on the northwest corner of Montgomery and Pine streets. In this photograph it is decorated for the Centennial Fourth of July celebration of 1876. *(California State Library.)*

Huge sums were expended developing claims that never produced a ton of millable ore, yet the search continued from year to year. Buyers of such stocks held on as long as their funds lasted, paid frequent assessments, and in the end were lucky to salvage a fraction of their investments. More conservative gamblers, who traded only in stocks of the producing mines, seldom fared much better. Such shares were forced so high that even their large and regular dividends usually yielded less than their owners might have received had they invested in less speculative enterprises.

In the end, San Franciscans came to realize that while the mines were enriching a few — notably the promoters, stockbrokers, and suppliers of mining equipment — the effect on the city as a whole was calamitous. In 1879 the *Alta California* commented: "These five years have brought disaster and money famine to the masses, notwithstanding the enormous yield of the precious metals." The writer's account concluded: "Capital, no longer generally distributed, is concentrated in colossal fortunes, which may be counted upon the fingers. Manufactures have lessened in number, and those that still exist struggle for life."

Some idea of the extent of San Francisco's stake in the Comstock mines may be gained from the fact that when it was learned that the ore bodies of the lode's richest properties, the Consolidated Virginia and the California, were nearing exhaustion, the market value of their stocks declined $140,000,-000. That sum, according to Hittell, represented "an average of $1,000 for every white adult in the city, and though a large majority had never owned any of these shares, all were affected indirectly, if not directly, by the decline."

The most dramatic event of that period of reckless speculation was the failure of the Bank of California, which closed its doors on the afternoon of August 26, 1875. Long the leading financial house on the West Coast, the bank, through its Virginia City branch, had played a leading part in the development of the Comstock mines. Its president, William C. Ralston, was a man of sanguine temperament who could see naught but uninterrupted prosperity for San Francisco and the rich region it served. For years he had been extending liberal support, both on the bank's account and personally, to local enterprises — hotels, theaters, office buildings, manufacturing plants, steamship and railroad companies, land settlement projects, and irrigation developments. Hence, when the depression of the mid-1870s struck, a dangerously large part of the bank's resources was tied up in these undertakings. As always during times of impaired confidence, the free flow of capital was halted, and hoarding became widespread. Money was drained off the market as individual investors as well as business and financial houses sought to safeguard their positions by calling in outstanding obligations.

The situation in the summer of 1875 was thus pictured by the *Evening Bulletin* in its issue of August 27:

> The upward movement in mining stocks, which began last October and continued until January, was the most extensive and protracted that had ever occurred in the city; and the collapse in February was the most terrible. The market has not since recovered from the setback it then received, though some of the lost ground has since been partially regained and values have been relatively higher. There have been no serious breaks since February

Norton I, self-styled "Emperor of North America and Protector of Mexico," paraded the streets in his bedraggled uniform accompanied by his faithful dogs. His fifty-cent "bonds" were accepted by the local merchants. *(Society of California Pioneers.)*

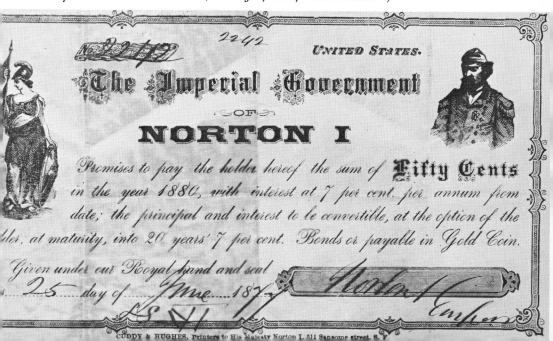

until within the past week. At the beginning of the month it was
thought that the market was going to take another upward turn,
but a reaction set in and the subsequent dropping condition has
been further accelerated this week.

During the third week of August matters reached a climax. On the
morning of the 26th all local banks opened as usual. At the Stock and
Exchange Board, Comstock shares continued to fall under the pressure of
heavy selling. At 11 o'clock a broker for William Sharon — who was manager
of the Bank of California's Virginia City office and one of the institution's
principal owners — came on the floor with what was presently recognized as
an unlimited selling order. Soon a rumor arose that the purpose of the
broker's action was to raise funds for the bank, and suspicion that it was in
difficulty spread through the financial district. By 2 o'clock long lines had
formed before the counters of the bank's paying tellers; a run was in progress. Forty minutes later Ralston stopped further payments and ordered
the doors closed.

On the afternoon of the following day the bank's trustees met to consider plans for its rehabilitation. Their efforts were successful, and a little
more than a month later, on October 3, it resumed business. A writer for
the *Alta California* gave this description of the reopening:

> Within the bank, as the hour . . . approached, every officer
> and attache was at his post. The paying tellers stood ready . . .
> and the first thing that attracted the attention . . . was a solid
> pile of twenty-dollar gold pieces, arranged at their station, and
> representing, as has been usual, a half-million, as the advance
> guard of two millions more that lay in the vaults.

The result of the first day's business was summarized thus: deposits
$1,020,000; withdrawals $254,000. The *Alta's* account concluded: "The out-
look of the bank is indeed very encouraging. No one will lose a dollar . . .
notwithstanding all the adverse reports that have been circulated."

On the evening of the day the bank reopened, the city celebrated
another event — the completion of the Palace Hotel. This great structure,
seven stories high and containing eight hundred rooms, was the largest and
most impressive of the city's buildings, and it remained so until its destruction in the 1906 fire more than three decades later. The Palace was the most

Wanted for stage robbery! Announcements of cash rewards—
plus a percentage of the treasure
recovered—were regularly
posted throughout California
during the 1870s and earlier.
The notice reproduced here is
dated July 27, 1875. (*Wells
Fargo Bank History Room.*)

This view down Montgomery Street in the 1870s shows the newly completed Palace Hotel at the far end. Another leading hotel, the Lick House, at the corner of Montgomery and Sutter streets, is visible through the row of ornate street lamps. (*California State Library.*)

The main entrance to the Palace, through which carriages were driven into the huge Grand Court, was on the New Montgomery Street side of the block-square hotel. This drawing (*below*) appeared in the *California Spirit of the Times* in 1875, the year the hotel was opened. (*California State Library.*)

grandiose of William C. Ralston's contributions toward the rebuilding of the city; however, he did not live to see the completion of his great hotel. On the day following the closing of the bank he met with the trustees, tendered his resignation as president, then went to North Beach for his customary afternoon swim in the bay. On this occasion he swam farther out than usual and was soon seen to be in difficulties. A boat was dispatched to pick him up; he was unconscious when brought ashore and died on the beach a few moment later — whether by accident or design was never definitely known.

5. ANDREW HALLIDIE'S INVENTION

The city's system of public transportation — the beginnings of which were described in Chapter VI — was greatly extended during the 1870s. By mid-decade half a dozen companies were operating horse-drawn street-cars between the business center and the outlying industrial and residential districts.

One of the longest and most heavily patronized of the new lines was that of the Sutter Street Railway. Its downtown terminus was at Broadway and Davis streets; from there its tracks ran up Broadway to Battery, along Battery to Market, then out Sutter to Polk, along Polk to Vallejo, out Vallejo to Octavia, and so to the bay at Harbor View. At Polk and Vallejo streets a branch line extended out Pacific Avenue to Fillmore, along Fillmore to California, and from there to Point Lobos Road, now Geary Boulevard. Over the company's fifteen and a half miles of track it operated 51 cars and 10 "dummies." (The "dummies" were small open cars with transverse seats, that were attached to the regular cars, and were general favorites during fine weather.) The company's financial statement for 1877 states that it maintained a stable of 181 horses; that the cars operated from 5:20 a.m. until midnight; that the period of usefulness of its horses averaged four years, and that to replace the animals cost the company approximately $5,000 annually.

Competition between the rival streetcar companies was keen, and each strove to gain and hold the patronage of the public. The length to which one pioneer line went to provide cars that were both convenient and elegant was thus described by a writer in 1877:

The Omnibus Railway Company

It now has running thirty of the most elegant, best constructed, excellently lighted, convenient and comfortable one-horse cars that the skill and taste of that veteran car builder, John Stephenson, could construct. Among several modern improvements in the new cars, the most notable, and the one likely to prove the most generally acceptable, especially to ladies without escorts, is the new

Service on Andrew Hallidie's Clay Street Hill Railroad Company, first of the city's cable car lines, began in 1873. During the first several years only the section from Kearny Street to the top of the hill at Jones was operated by cable; over the balance of the line horses furnished the motive power.

arrangement of the check-strap connecting with the driver's bell. Just inside the car it divides in two, one of which runs along the upper corner, on each side, from end to end. From these, at convenient intervals, short, connecting straps hang sufficiently low to be conveniently grasped and pulled without rising. Thus a lady can readily give the stopping signal without leaving her seat or asking anyone to do it for her.

When these words were written, however, an even greater advance in the local street transportation system was already under way. This had come about because many city streets were too steep to be scaled by horse-drawn vehicles. The question of how to provide service for those who lived on the hilltops had long been debated.

The man credited with having solved that problem was Andrew S. Hallidie. He had reached San Francisco from his native London in 1852, and by 1870 was operating a factory that manufactured wire rope, a product widely used in quartz mines throughout the West. It has been said that his invention of the cable car — which has ever since been a novel feature of the city's public transportation system — came about because he had one day witnessed an accident during which a team of horses was injured while trying to pull a heavily loaded car up one of the hills.

The basis of Hallidie's plan was a moving cable buried in a slot beneath the tracks, to which the cars were attached by a device called a "gripping clamp." Once the practicality of his invention had been demonstrated, Hallidie and his backers organized the Clay Street Hill Railroad Company and were given a franchise to operate the new cars from Clay and Kearny streets to Chestnut and Larkin, a distance of about two and a half miles. In the beginning, only the section of Clay Street that lay between Kearny and Leavenworth streets was operated by cable; over the balance of the line the cars were drawn by horses.

These, the first of the city's cable cars, began operating in October, 1873. The venture was a success from its inception, and during the next few years a number of the older companies converted their stables into power-houses and adopted the new method. One of the first was the Sutter Street Railroad Company; its change-over from horses to cables was made in 1877. The following year saw the completion of the California Street line, which connected the financial district with the crest of Nob Hill, then continued to First Avenue, an over-all distance of about three miles.

This company's powerhouse was at the intersection of California and Hyde streets. There two steam-driven engines, each developing five hundred horsepower, supplied the power that kept two cables — each nine thousand feet long and weighing twenty-two tons — moving at approximately ten miles per hour. This company's rolling stock consisted of twenty-five com-

This 1884 view, showing numerous cable cars lined up in front of the Ferry Building, is evidence of how rapidly the city adopted that new method of street transportation.

The bayside turntable of the Powell-Hyde Cable Car Line is at the foot of Hyde Street near three popular attractions: the Maritime Museum, Ghirardelli Square, and Fisherman's Wharf. (*S. F. Convention & Visitors Bureau.*)

bination cars and dummies, the first seating sixteen passengers, and the second eighteen. The round trip was made in twenty-five minutes, and the fare each way was twenty-five cents.

The cable cars supplemented the horse-drawn vehicles but did not supplant them entirely for many years. As late as 1888 horsecars still operated over more miles of track than those drawn by cables. In that year the city's six cable companies had twenty miles of double tracks and carried an estimated thirty million passengers.

The introduction of electric carlines, which could be built and maintained at less cost than the cables, hastened the end of the cable car era. The change to trolleys was already under way by the turn of the century, and the fire of 1906 speeded the process. But by then riding the slow-moving cables had become a favorite local custom, and San Franciscans have ever since refused to dispense entirely with these relics of an earlier and more leisurely age.

6. GROWTH

An economic survey published in 1877 and covering the previous year throws light on the city's progress since the first buildings were put up beside the cove, an even century earlier.

In 1876 San Francisco had 27,000 buildings, of which 4,500 were of brick or stone and the remainder of wood. Taxable property had an assessed value of $269,000,000; and of $182,000,000 in California savings accounts, all but $32,000,000 was on deposit in San Francisco banks.

This bird's-eye view of the city in 1878 is from a drawing by C. P. Parsons. The Golden Gate is at the far right, the animated harbor is in the foreground, and in the distance are the barren sandhills of what are now the solidly built up Richmond, Sunset, and south-of-Twin Peaks districts.

In domestic and overseas commerce, the number of ships arriving from United States ports was 1,019, and from foreign countries, 612. Wheat, flour, and wool were the leading foreign exports, most of which were sent— in sailing ships—to China, India, and Europe. During the same twelve months the amount of freight reaching the city from beyond the Mississippi over the new railroad averaged approximately 10,000 tons per month, while slightly more than half that amount was shipped East. Included in the latter was a considerable amount of merchandise brought from the Orient aboard the trans-Pacific steamers and forwarded by rail to the East Coast.

Before 1869 most passengers and virtually all freight passing between the two coasts went by sea. During the first year after its opening, the railroad carried 32,000 westbound and 23,000 eastbound passengers; by 1876 these figures had increased to 65,000 and 47,000. The Chinese continued to arrive in considerable numbers despite determined efforts to exclude them, but by then many were returning to their homeland. In 1876 approximately 10,000 arrived and 8,000 left.

The year 1877 had been comparatively prosperous. In 1878, however, slack times returned, bringing another sharp decline in business activity and a consequent rise in the number of unemployed. With private business stagnating and the future uncertain, it became almost impossible to launch new enterprises or to extend those already in existence. The consequence was that land values declined, new construction tapered off, and real estate sales dropped from $24,000,000 the previous year to less than $15,000,000.

As a means of compensating for the slacking off of private construction, the city speeded up its own building program. During the middle and late 1870s much work was done on the city's streets. The original cobblestone pavements on many of the main thoroughfares were torn up and replaced with basalt blocks. At the same time granite crosswalks were installed at the street intersections. The construction program included, too, the building of schools, firehouses, and other facilities.

By far the largest and most costly of such projects was the new City Hall. Work on that ambitious project had begun in 1871; according to the 1878-79 edition of Langley's *City Directory* it was destined to be "not only the largest and most durable structure in the city, but . . . the largest edifice of this description in the United States." Occupying the site of the pioneer Yerba Buena Cemetery—a triangular plot of land bounded by Market, Larkin, and McAllister streets—this new civic monument was expected to be completed in four years and to cost $1,500,000. Both estimates were far wide of the mark. Seven years later only one wing of the eight-hundred-foot-long main building (there was to be a separate Hall of Records) had been completed, and its slow progress and mounting costs had become a public scandal. Charges of corruption, including collusion between the builders and city officials, were freely made; meanwhile the public, impatient at the slow progress, took to referring to it as the "new City Hall ruin."

The main building, the City Hall itself, was a complex structure in what was referred to as the French Renaissance style of architecture. One contemporary writer described it as "a series of pavilions . . . adorned with Corinthian pilasters and columns forty-eight feet in height, the whole of which was to be surmounted by a lofty clock-tower, a mansard roof and several lesser towers." Later, as an economy move, the main tower was abandoned and replaced by a dome that was criticized by artistic-minded residents as out of scale with the rest of the building. To the east of the main building and connected with it by a covered arcade was the Hall of Records, a circular building 95 feet in diameter, surmounted by a dome rising to a height of 134 feet.

The fact that work on both structures proceeded at so slow a pace was blamed in part on the city's policy of financing the project on a "pay as you go" basis; that is, only such funds could be spent each year as were raised by an annual tax of fifteen cents per hundred dollars' assessed value of real and personal property.

Well over a quarter-century elapsed between the ground-breaking ceremonies in 1871 and the day when the building was fully completed and occupied. It remained in service only a few years longer, then was reduced to rubble by the earthquake of 1906.

✔   ✔   ✔

Another civic project that was as long in the making as the "new City Hall ruin," but that, unlike the other, was to be a source of pride and pleasure to San Franciscans for many years to come, was the Golden Gate Park.

This project also dates from the 1870s, for although the city had acquired title to the 1,017-acre site—which at the time was described as "a dreary waste of shifting sand hills"—several years earlier, it was not until 1871 that the work of transforming it into one of the world's largest and most beautiful parks actively began.

That formidable task was undertaken because San Francisco had long needed parks and other open spaces. For the city's growth during gold-rush days had been so rapid that little thought had been given to providing recreational facilities. As early as 1855 Frank Soulé, one of the authors of *The Annals of San Francisco,* had commented:

> Over all these square miles of contemplated thoroughfares there seems no provision made by the projectors for a public park —the true "lungs" of a large city. The existing plaza, or Portsmouth Square, and other two or three diminutive squares, delineated in the plan, seem the only breathing-holes intended for the future population of hundreds of thousands. This is a strange mistake,

One of the oldest buildings in Golden Gate Park, this handsome glass Conservatory, a gift of the Crocker family, has been standing since 1877. A more recent innovation is the colorful flower clock in the foreground. (*S. F. Convention & Visitors Bureau.*)

One of several entrances to the Japanese Tea Garden in Golden Gate Park is the Torii Gate, pictured at left. It was erected in 1917. (*Redwood Empire Association.*)

and can only be attributed to the jealous avarice of the city pro-
jectors in turning every square vara of the site to an available
building lot. . . . Not only is there no public park or garden, but
there is not even a circus, oval, open terrace, broad avenue, or any
ornamental line of street or building or verdant space of any kind,
other than the three or four small squares alluded to; and which
every resident knows are by no means verdant, except in patches
where stagnant water collects and ditch weeds grow.

The three earliest town maps, those of Vioget, O'Farrell, and Eddy,
added only two open spaces to the original Spanish plaza; namely, Union
Square—a gift to the city from Mayor John W. Geary—in the present-day
retail shopping center, and Washington Square in the North Beach area
at the base of Telegraph Hill.

As time passed the lack of open spaces to relieve the monotony of the
long rows of closely built houses became more evident. But although the
need of more and larger parks was pointed out from time to time, the matter
was so long delayed that when action was finally taken the only land available for a park of any size lay several miles beyond the built-up section
of the city.

The manner in which San Francisco acquired the unprepossessing tract
of brush-covered sandhills on which the park was later built can be briefly
told. In 1868 a federal district court rendered a decision upholding San
Francisco's claim to certain lands in the western and southwestern part of
the city that had earlier been settled by a group of squatters and who had
since resisted all attempts to oust them. Following the court's decision, the
squatters had made known their intention to appeal the case to a higher
court. Rather than resort to further lengthy litigation, the Board of Supervisors agreed to a compromise by which the city received clear title to a
half-mile-wide tract of land that fronted on the ocean and extended three
miles inland.

When the plan to convert its newly acquired property into a park was
first announced, many greeted it with ridicule. Few believed that the area
could be made habitable, much less transformed into a place of beauty.
For a time their doubts seemed justified, for during the first several years
progress was painfully slow. However, William H. Hall, the park's first
superintendent, persevered, and signs of progress became evident. His first
step was to set out many varieties of grasses and shrubs in order to bind
down the shifting sands. When these had taken root, thousands of small,
wind-resistant trees—mostly pines, Monterey cypress, and flowering euca-
lypti from Australia—were planted. Toward the eastern end of the property,
growing in spots where they had a measure of protection from the winds,
were groves of stunted oaks, and there the first paths, driveways, and flower
beds were laid out.

By the late 1870s so much had been accomplished that a Sunday drive out Point Lobos Road and a stroll through "the park" had become a local tradition. Langley's *Directory* for 1877-78 reflects the pride San Franciscans took in their new showplace. Among its attractions were "seven lakelets; also arbours, grottos, mounds and rustic benches." By then two miles of roads and paths had been completed, and an additional half-mile was being built; more than 135,000 trees and shrubs had been set out, and another 32,000 were being raised in the park nursery, to be planted the following spring.

Hall served as superintendent until he retired in 1887. He was succeeded by a young Scot, John McLaren, who was to hold the post continuously for fifty-six years; today's park is very largely the result of his industry, skill, and persistence. The new superintendent had strong opinions—some called them prejudices—as to the uses to which the new park should be put. One of his favorite theories was that it must become and remain a sylvan retreat where the city dweller could enjoy the beauties of nature without having his attention distracted by the works of man. The two objects he opposed most strongly were statues and "Keep off the Grass" signs. As for the latter he was permitted to have his way; no such signs were allowed in the park as long as he remained in charge. And although he failed in his effort to bar statues, he saw to it that trees and shrubbery were so planted as to screen from the view of passers-by most of the Civil War generals and other dignitaries for whose cast-iron replicas he was obliged to find places.

McLaren's hope of preserving the natural beauty of his park received a severe, though temporary, setback in the early 1890s. Following the close of the World's Columbian Exposition at Chicago in 1893, a group of San Franciscans organized the California Midwinter Fair as a means of publicizing the city's salubrious winter climate. Against the vigorous opposition of the superintendent and others, a two-hundred-acre area near the eastern end of the park was chosen as its site. During the next year the spot was cleared of trees, roads were built, and more than a hundred buildings put up. Among the latter were several large pavilions that housed exhibits which had earlier been shown in Chicago.

The fair opened on January 1, 1894, and closed on July 9. It attracted 2,500,000 visitors and was credited with having first made known to the world California's attractions as a year-around vacation land. Immediately after its close McLaren and his staff set about restoring the grounds as closely as possible to their former condition. Most of the buildings were razed and their sites replanted with trees and shrubs. Among the buildings permitted to remain were the Art Museum, a large wooden structure built in the form of an Egyptian temple. Another is the Japanese Tea Garden,

First of the city's three world's fairs, the California Midwinter
Exposition of 1894 was built near the eastern end of Golden Gate
Park. The Japanese Tea Garden, only remaining relic of the fair,
is at the lower left.

which with its exotic paths, bridges and pools has ever since been one of
the park's most popular attractions; and a third is the large stone bandstand
facing the Music Concourse. The Concourse is a sunken garden shaded by
plane trees, beneath which each summer crowds up to 20,000 often gathered
on Sunday afternoons to listen to concerts.

During the 1870s and later, gifts designed to enhance the beauty and
usefulness of the park were made by wealthy San Franciscans. Among
these were an artificial waterfall donated by the railroad magnate Collis
P. Huntington, and an ornate glass conservatory, which was a gift of the
Crocker family, is still in use. Other gifts include Stow Lake, Prayer Book
Cross, which commemorates the first religious service in the English language held on the Pacific Coast, and more recently, the M. H. de Young
Memorial Museum, the Steinhart Aquarium, the Morrison Planetarium, and
the Simson African Hall.

The prime purpose has always been to make the park a place to which
visitors could come to refresh themselves in a setting of natural beauty,
but its large size has permitted numerous other recreational uses. Hidden
among its wooded hills and gardens and lakes are baseball diamonds, tennis
and basketball courts and bowling greens, a race track, a golf course, an
athletic field, and a municipal stadium with a capacity of 60,000.

VIII
Turn of the Century

1. RAILROADS AND POLITICS

From the time the city was founded, San Franciscans realized that its future growth and prosperity depended more than anything else on its foreign and domestic trade. That fact had, indeed, been recognized long before the first houses were built on the shore of Yerba Buena Cove. Soon after Mission Dolores was established in 1776 it became obvious that the San Francisco Peninsula was unsuited to large-scale agriculture or cattle-raising, then the padres' only sources of revenue. Thereafter the Santa Clara and Sonoma missions and the ranches of the interior were the chief sources of hides, grain, and other agricultural products, and such trade as the local mission and the later village carried on was confined almost entirely to bartering these products for merchandise brought on the early-day trading ships.

Thus San Francisco from the beginning was primarily a trading post, a center for the purchase and sale of goods produced elsewhere. Accordingly, the importance of improving means of communication between the town and its markets both at home and abroad had long been acknowledged. In the earlier period this attitude was evidenced by the liberal support given whatever promised to link the port more closely with the rest of the world—the trans-Pacific, coast-to-coast, bay and river steamers, and the pioneer stage and express companies.

From the 1850s on, San Franciscans had looked on the steamship and stage lines as stopgaps that must be made to serve until the arrival of the iron horse. Along with the settlers of the entire West Coast, they looked forward to the coming of the railroad with a faith that as yet had been unshaken by experience. The following forecast, written in the mid-1860s, is typical of that viewpoint:

> The roads promise to stimulate the occupancy of our farming lands in hitherto neglected sections of the state by giving cheap and speedy transportation for their products to nearer and more profitable markets. This will be more especially the case . . . in lands which, though universally productive, have hitherto been

166

considered almost valueless on account of the high cost of freighting. Another valuable feature in connection with the extension of railroads is the disposition of owners to bring large tracts of land into cultivation by selling the same in small subdivisions to actual settlers. . . . [Such lands] only require the extension of the railroad system projected to exhibit a productiveness and wealth that will surprise all who have not studied the capabilities of their soil and climate.

The first railroad to enter the city was that of the San Francisco & San Jose Railroad Company, which was organized in 1860 and three years later had been completed as far as Big Tree Station, on the site of present-day Palo Alto. By January, 1864, its rails had been laid to San Jose. In 1870 five local lines were being built and several others were in the planning stages. By then the San Francisco & San Jose road had been extended as far south as Gilroy, and a second company was building a line down the west side of the San Francisco Peninsula close to the ocean shore.

To serve the fast-growing communities in Marin, Sonoma, and Mendocino counties, two railroads, the San Francisco & North Pacific and the North Pacific Coast—the latter a narrow-gauge line—were being built. By 1870 both had been completed as far as the Russian River. The San Francisco & North Pacific was later extended to Eureka; its rival never got beyond the town of Cazadero in northern Sonoma County. To the south, both lines terminated on the Marin shore—the San Francisco & North Pacific at Tiburon, and the other at Sausalito. From there the passengers, like those crossing from the east side of the bay, boarded ferryboats for the final leg of the journey to San Francisco. Thus a further addition was made to the fleet of small sidewheel ferries that were to remain a distinctive feature of the harbor for many years.

However, the benefits the city had hoped to derive from the new railroads fell short of expectations. One reason was that, as stated earlier, persistent efforts to make San Francisco the western terminus of the transcontinental line had proved unavailing. Blame for that failure was laid to the machinations of the railroad's owners, who by 1880 had achieved an almost complete monopoly of transportation throughout the Far West. This they had accomplished not only by buying competing lines and extending those they already owned, but also by gaining control of law-making bodies in California and elsewhere on the coast.

In the early 1880s [wrote John P. Young, editor of the San Francisco *Chronicle*] the political power of the railroad became absolute. It controlled both political parties in California. Its power superseded all law, all government, and all authority that has hitherto been exercised by the people. The real capital of the state was moved from Sacramento to the railroad building at Fourth

and Townsend streets. There . . . were dictated public policies and
appointments not only in this state but through the entire West.
The stupendous organization became an over-shadowing influence
in all walks of life.

This sweeping estimate of the influence of the railroad group was
hardly an exaggeration. Efforts to break the company's power over the
economic life of the state continued for many years. It was not until after
the turn of the century when a San Francisco attorney named Hiram Johnson was elected governor and proceeded to make good his campaign
promise to "Kick the Southern Pacific out of Politics" that the rule of the
well-entrenched corporation finally ended.

2. STRIFE ON THE WATERFRONT

The growth of the labor movement and the long-drawn-out struggle
to improve the lot of the workers was another source of contention that
persisted well into the 1900s. The agitation of the middle and late 1870s—
mainly directed against "cheap Chinese labor," and led by Dennis Kearney
and his sand lotters—was described in Chapter VII.

By 1880 the troublesome Chinese problem was nearing a solution. In
1882, after long negotiations between Washington and Peking, an agreement was reached which resulted in a drastic reduction of the quota of
Chinese immigrants permitted to enter the country each year. Although
labor's hostility to competition by the Chinese continued for some time
longer, it manifested itself mainly by such devices as the boycotting of
businesses owned or staffed by them. As a result of the reduced immigration
attacks on Chinese laundries, restaurants and shops, and on individuals,
declined and eventually ceased entirely.

But the workingmen had other grievances, and there was never a lack
of leaders eager to right their real or imagined wrongs. One of several labor
organizations that attracted attention during the early and middle 1880s
was the California Internationalists, whose leader was Burnett Haskell,
editor of one of the city's truculent weeklies. At a meeting in the spring
of 1885 Haskell sought to consolidate the city's workers into a single union;
however, several strong unions refused to surrender their identities, and
the attempt failed.

Haskell's next venture was the launching of a state-wide organization
called the Federated Trades, and this time he was more successful. Under
his aggressive leadership the Federated Trades rapidly grew in influence
and power. It became the main bargaining agency of the allied unions in
negotiations with employer groups. The result was a new series of strikes.
The most far-reaching of these began in the summer of 1885 when 1,200
members of the Iron Trades Council walked out following the rejection
of the usual demand for higher wages, shorter hours, and better working

FERRY BUILDINGS.

CABLE CARS.

The upper view shows part of the fleet of ships that carried wheat grown in the Sacramento and San Joaquin valleys to markets in Europe and the Orient. The cars of the Sutter Street Railroad Company *(lower right)* operated from the Ferries to Golden Gate Park.

---

conditions. Negotiations dragged on for several months; then, as both sides continued to stand firm, the employers made good their threat to reopen their idle plants by hiring nonunion workers. This brought on a series of clashes between union men and strikebreakers, with numerous casualties on both sides. Eventually the contending parties tired of the conflict, the broken-off negotiations were resumed, both sides made concessions, and the strikers returned to work.

However, the chief battleground on which the industrial wars of the period were fought was the waterfront. For then as now, San Francisco's prosperity depended on its maritime trade. Anything that impeded the free flow of its water-borne commerce was reflected in all branches of business, and if long continued caused widespread distress. Both labor and management were aware of this; accordingly, whenever a strike of sailors, dock workers, or teamsters threatened to tie up the waterfront, both sides prepared for an all-out contest.

Several earlier attempts had been made to organize the seamen on the West Coast, but it was not until 1885 that the first effective union was formed. This was the Coast Seamen's Union, which was made up primarily of the crews of sailing ships engaged in the coastwise and inland trade. A year later another seamen's organization, the Steamshipmen's Union, was formed, and in 1891 the two were combined. At the time of the merger the new organization was the strongest maritime union in the country, with a membership of more than 4,000 and with $50,000 in its treasury. Soon thereafter the union presented shipowners with a demand for higher wages—which then averaged $25 per month—and for a number of other concessions, including better food and quarters. These were rejected by the operators, who maintained that the added expense would make it impossible for them to compete with foreign carriers or with ships manned by nonunion crews.

The walkout, which began in the summer of 1891, brought on what until then was the most bitterly contested labor-management struggle in the city's history. For many months East Street—the present Embarcadero, then a broad cobble-paved thoroughfare fronting on the docks—was the scene of almost daily clashes between the strikers and the nonunion sailors whom the owners had brought in to keep their ships operating. Both sides fought with clubs, stones, knives and, on occasion, firearms. The police found it impossible to maintain order, for while they were attempting to suppress one riot, others would break out elsewhere on the water front. Nonunion crewmen were waylaid and beaten, lines mooring ships to their docks were cut, lifeboats were smashed, and rocks thrown through the windows of restaurants, bars, and rooming houses harboring strikebreakers. The disorders reached a climax in the fall of 1891 when a waterfront boarding house and bar was dynamited; five persons were killed and a dozen injured.

As the strike dragged on, the public grew weary of the continued violence and increased its demand for a prompt settlement. But despite strong pressure, both sides remained adamant, and repeated attempts to work out a satisfactory compromise failed. Two full years passed before an uneasy peace was restored. Neither side benefited by the protracted struggle; the owners gained nothing to compensate for their heavy losses, and the sailors returned to find wages and working conditions no better than they had been before. The old antagonisms remained.

3. "BLIND BOSS" BUCKLEY

During much of the 1880s and 1890s other phases of the life of the city were only slightly less turbulent than that which marked the relations between management and labor. It was a materialistic age, and in business and government alike the standards of ethics left much to be desired. In nearly every major city of the land corrupt alliances existed between office-holders and those seeking favors at their hands, and bribery, rigged elections, and boss rule were the order of the day.

In San Francisco the early 1880s saw the rise of Chris Buckley, the so-called "Blind Boss," who from his Bush Street saloon built up a political

machine that permitted him to fill key posts at the City Hall with men of
his own choosing. As a youth Buckley (whose eyesight was so poor that he
could see neither to read nor write) had migrated to this country from
Ireland. Then, having received his training in practical politics at New
York's Tammany Hall, he moved to the West Coast in the mid-1870s and
for several years operated a combination bar and gambling house at Vallejo.

In 1880 he arrived in San Francisco and, with a partner named Fallon,
opened a Bush Street resort. There he catered to a clientele of small-time
gamblers who made a precarious livelihood trading in stocks at the Mining
Exchange. A resourceful politician, Buckley set about building his machine.
His immediate goal was to gain enough influence at the City Hall to permit
him to sell police protection to gamblers, prostitutes, and other underworld
characters. Despite his handicap, the Blind Boss made such rapid progress
that in the municipal election of 1885 virtually the entire slate of Buckley-
sponsored candidates were swept into office. That success made him "the
man to see" by all who had business, ligitimate or otherwise, with the city.

The fact that Buckley was able to get control of the city government
and to hold it for the better part of a decade was a tribute to his native
shrewdness and his cynicism. As long as he remained in power he was
careful at each election to place men of known integrity at the head of the
ticket, for he realized that nearly all the work of the various departments
was performed by lesser officials who could be depended on to follow his
orders. He is said to have welcomed attacks on himself and his methods in
the local press, his theory being that their only practical effect was to remind
those who had favors to ask at the City Hall that he alone could grant them.

Charges against Buckley and his cronies ranged from ballot-stuffing
and petty extortion to the sale of street-railroad franchises and the award
of fraudulent contracts for building streets, schools, firehouses, and other
public works.

*   *   *

Meanwhile statewide efforts to break the political power of the Southern Pacific Railroad had been making progress. In the hotly contested election of 1883 George Stoneman, a strong antirailroad man, was elected
governor, along with other state officials. San Francisco voters, however,
failed to follow the antirailroad trend, and Buckley-sponsored candidates
for city offices continued to be elected by substantial majorities. Defeated
on that front, the local reform group, which had the support of three of
the four San Francisco dailies, launched a campaign for the adoption of a
new city charter, one that its sponsors hoped would prevent the abuses
possible under the old. Buckley countered this challenge by pointing out
that under the new charter it would be possible to raise the existing tax
rate above the legal limit of $1 per $100, and by promising that the old

rate would be maintained as long as the incumbent officials remained in office. His campaign slogan, "Keep the $1 Limit," proved so attractive to the voters that at three successive elections the proposed new charter was rejected.

It was not until 1898 that the old charter, under which San Francisco had been governed since 1856, was replaced. Ironically, it was under this new instrument, which was supposed to eliminate wrongdoing on the part of city officials, that San Francisco fell under the domination of a boss even more adept at political corruption than Chris Buckley had been.

4. THE BURNHAM PLAN

As the final decade of the century opened, San Francisco had a population of 298,997. It was eighth in size among the cities of the nation, by far the largest on the West Coast, and second only to New York in the value of its foreign and domestic trade.

All this had been accomplished in a comparatively brief time and in the face of severe handicaps, the latter including San Francisco's lack of direct connection by rail with the rest of the country, its frequent and costly labor-management disputes, and its struggle to prevent inefficiency and corruption in the city government.

As the 1890s drew toward a close, by no means all these problems had been solved. Some continued to plague the city for another two decades, and others—notably the troublesome employer-employee relationship—remained a source of contention for an even longer period.

None of these, however, did the city irreparable harm; at worst they served to stay its progress only temporarily. During the 1880s and 1890s the rebuilding of the business district, which had begun in the late 1860s and got fully under way during the prosperous 1870s, continued, though at a less headlong pace. By then nearly all one- and two-story buildings on Kearny, Montgomery, Sansome, and the intersecting streets had been replaced by larger, more modern structures. Only in the area centering on Sacramento, Clay, and Washington streets did the austere, iron-shuttered buildings dating from the 1850s remain.

The banks, hotels, theaters, and office buildings of the 1870s and 1880s conformed to the ornate architectural standards of the day, their facades covered with elaborate decorations of stone or cast iron or with the ubiquitous bay windows. The new buildings of that type included the Palace, Grand and Baldwin hotels on Market Street, the Nevada Block, built by the Comstock mining firm, at Pine and Montgomery, the Bank of California at Sansome and California streets, the Phelan Building at Market and O'Farrell, and the California Hotel and Theater on Bush between Kearny and Dupont.

By the early 1890s, however, a new type of building had begun to appear: steel-frame structures that towered above their neighbors and added a striking new note to the downtown skyline. First in that category was the new home of the San Francisco *Chronicle* at the corner of Market and Kearny streets, ten stories high and surmounted by a clock tower; it was completed in 1891. This was followed by many others, among them the Mills, Kohl, and Merchants Exchange buildings in the financial district, the Flood Building on the site of the Baldwin Hotel—which had been destroyed by fire in the late 1890s—and, tallest of all, the nineteen-story Claus Spreckels Building at the corner of Market and Third streets; the last-named housed another of the city's newspapers, the *Morning Call*. Dating from the 1890s, too, is the structure that was destined to become an unofficial symbol of the city—the Ferry Building at the foot of Market Street, whose handsome 235-foot tower, modeled after the Giralda Tower at Seville, Spain, was completed in 1898.

Meanwhile, the residential districts continued to push outward from the site of the original village. To the west, lines of modest wooden houses spread over and about the intervening hills toward the ocean, while the homes of more prosperous citizens covered the sides and crests of Nob and Russian hills, lined both sides of Van Ness Avenue, and extended out Pacific, Washington, and other streets of the Pacific Heights area. At the same time square miles of narrow, two-story residences, each with bay windows and a profusion of "millwork," had fanned out over the sandy valleys and hillocks of the Western Addition, out Market Street to the base of Twin Peaks,

---

This photograph, taken from Alamo Square, shows a line of Victorian houses on Steiner Street between Fulton and Hayes. (*S. F. Convention & Visitors Bureau.*)

Looking north on Montgomery Street from the intersection of Market and Post, about 1880, the stone-paved streets and granite crosswalks are seen in the foreground.

and, completing the half-circle, covered the hillsides and sheltered valleys of the Mission District and on through the Potrero to the bay.

The domestic architecture of the period was frequently criticized by visitors who found both monotonous and depressing the many streets lined with houses of uniform design, and the absence of front gardens and sidewalk planting. Responsibility for this lack of variety was laid to the numerous building associations that flourished between the years 1870 and 1900. These organizations bought large tracts of land in outlying districts and on them built hundreds of houses of uniform design which were sold for modest down payments with the balance spread over a period of years.

Campaigns designed to give the city an appearance in keeping with the beauty of its site were launched from time to time. But to carry out the proposed plans would have necessitated an increase in the tax rate, and Boss Buckley's "Keep the $1 Limit" slogan proved so attractive to the voters that bond issues needed to finance such projects were consistently defeated. Meanwhile under the Buckley regime public facilities of all sorts fell into disrepair. The local newspapers in their editorial columns frequently deplored the badly paved streets, neglected parks, and outmoded schools, and compared them with the handsome hotels, theaters, and office buildings being put up with private capital. Conditions in the retail shop-

The brownstone Whittier house at Jackson and Laguna streets is one of many large residences that lined the streets of the Pacific Heights district during the final decades of the last century. The building is now occupied by the California Historical Society.

(*Below*) Union Square in the early 1880s. The Hopkins and Stanford mansions on the crest of Nob Hill are visible at the upper left.

ping district at length grew so bad that the merchants themselves hired crews to gather up the litter and repair the damaged streets and sidewalks.

Dissatisfaction with the conduct of municipal affairs eventually became so widespread, that as the local election of 1897 approached, a group of leading businessmen put up a slate of candidates pledged to "clean up the City Hall." After a spirited campaign, the incumbents were voted out of office and the rule of Boss Buckley came to an end. When the new mayor, James D. Phelan, took office he at once appointed a committee to consider plans for beautifying the city. Of a number of such proposals submitted to the committee, it recommended that of a local architect, B. J. S. Cahill. His plan called for enlarging the area about the City Hall and adding other public buildings, thereby creating an architecturally harmonious civic center set in handsomely landscaped grounds.

Although Cahill's project was considered too costly to be undertaken at the time, it gave impetus to a "city beautiful" movement that was to gain many adherents during the next few years. Modifications of the original plan were proposed from time to time; then, in January, 1904, at the behest of Phelan—whose term as mayor had expired—an organization called the Association for the Improvement and Adornment of San Francisco was formed. One of the association's first acts was to invite D. H. Burnham, a noted architect and civic planner, to make a new survey of the city. Burnham, who had performed similar services at Chicago, Cleveland, and other cities, accepted the assignment. On his arrival he established himself in a studio near the crest of Twin Peaks, from which the entire central part of the city could be seen.

The Colton and Crocker residences were at California and Taylor streets. See Crocker's "spite fence" which enclosed the cottage of a local undertaker named Yung.

The Nob Hill residence of James L. Flood was rebuilt and enlarged after the 1906 fire. It now houses the Pacific Union Club. (*California Historical Society.*)

In the 1870s Mark Hopkins and Leland Stanford, two members of the Central Pacific Railroad's Big Four, built these baroque wooden residences (*below*) on Nob Hill.

The James G. Fair home at 1120 Pine Street. The marriage there, in June 1890, of Tessie Fair and Herman Oelrichs was heralded as one of the most brilliant social events in the city's history. *(California Historical Society.)*

A Sunday crowd at the ocean beach, about 1900 *(below)*. Seal Rocks and the Cliff House are in the background. This, the second of three Cliff Houses to occupy the site, was built by Adolph Sutro in 1895; it was destroyed by a spectacular fire in 1907.

Burnham's recommendations, which were made public in the fall of 1905, were far more comprehensive than those of the Cahill plan. Like the latter, however, the City Hall was to be the focal point of the scheme. From it a series of broad, tree-lined boulevards were to extend outward like the spokes of a wheel, with an auditorium, museum, schools, and other public buildings occupying the triangular spaces about the hub. Other parts of the city were to be similarly treated, each with broad streets converging on circular areas that would serve as neighborhood service and cultural centers.

The Burnham plan was greeted with mixed feelings by San Franciscans. The proposed changes were so extensive that, as Burnham himself pointed out, several decades would be required to complete them. For they would necessitate the virtual rebuilding of large sections of the city—the widening of several heavily traveled streets, the cutting through of others to provide easier access to the downtown area, and the rerouting of some of the steeper hillside streets to conform to the contour of the land.

While the boldness of the conception was widely acclaimed, many felt that its great cost would prove an insuperable obstacle. The arguments continued through the winter of 1905-06. Some termed the plan the dream of an impractical idealist, others urged that it be officially adopted and carried out piecemeal over a period of years.

That was where the matter stood on the morning of April 18, 1906.

5. A GOLD RUSH AND A WAR

During the 1890s two events took place that, although they originated at points far distant from San Francisco, had an important bearing on its social and economic life. Toward the end of 1896 word of the discovery of rich gold fields at a remote spot on the Alaska peninsula reached the city. The news caused great excitement, and hundreds prepared to set off for the new bonanza. Later reports, however, minimized the importance of the finds, and interest subsided, only to be revived a few weeks later by the arrival of a steamer bearing $500,000 of Yukon gold consigned to the local mint. By the summer of 1897 the city was in the midst of another gold rush. Hundreds clamored for passage to the north, and every available ship was pressed into service. Many San Franciscans who themselves were unable to make the trip arranged to grubstake others in return for a half interest in their anticipated earnings. The picturesque garb of the gold hunter— flannel shirt, wool parka, and high leather boots—became a familiar sight on the downtown streets; merchants did a flourishing business outfitting the would-be miners, and for several months the interest remained high.

Throughout the winter of 1897-98 the local newspapers—all of which had correspondents on the scene—printed lengthy accounts of the hazards of the long trip, of life in the crude new camps that had sprung up in the Yukon country, and of the fortunes to be made when spring thaws permitted the frozen claims to be worked. But the excitement subsided even more quickly than it had begun. By midsummer of 1898 it became evident that the extent and richness of the gold fields had been grossly exaggerated. Only a few who reached the diggings profited in a material way from their long and difficult journey. By the end of the year most of the disillusioned San Franciscans had straggled back, and the city returned to normal.

But not for long. For scarcely had interest in the Klondike gold begun to fade when the city was stirred by a new sensation. In late April, 1898, war broke out between this country and Spain; the Atlantic fleet was dispatched to Cuban waters, Admiral Dewey's Pacific Squadron set out for the Philippines, and President McKinley issued a call for volunteers to occupy these and other Spanish possessions in both oceans.

With the opening of hostilities San Francisco became for the first time in its history a base for large-scale military operations. As the leading West Coast seaport it was the point where the men and material needed to conduct the Pacific campaign were assembled and shipped to the fighting fronts. Thousands of soldiers, newly recruited and hastily trained, poured into the city from all parts of the country. To house them while they received their equipment, completed their training, and waited to be sent overseas, a number of temporary camps were set up in and about the city. Several large "tent cities" were built on the Presidio reservation; another, occupying many acres, was on the sand dunes of the Richmond District, between the Presidio and Golden Gate Park.

The signing of the peace treaty on December 8, 1898, and its ratification by the Senate two months later, brought the war to an official close. Several years were to pass, though, before the city returned to a peacetime footing. For the terms of the treaty, which transferred the Philippines to the sovereignty of the United States, were bitterly opposed by the islanders, who had hoped for complete independence. Their revolt, under the leadership of Emilio Aguinaldo, brought on a continuation of the fighting, and peace was not fully restored until late in 1901.

In San Francisco the Spanish War and its aftermath were felt in many ways. The activity of the port was enormously stimulated. Not since gold-rush days had so many ships crowded the harbor. For more than three years many of the city's industries, particularly food-processing plants and shipyards, were busy exclusively with supplying wartime needs. War news monopolized the front pages of the newspapers, men in uniform crowded the downtown streets, and word of victories in the field set off city-wide celebrations. One exploit that San Franciscans followed with particular interest was the 10,000-mile cruise of the battleship *Oregon* — which had been built at the local Union Iron Works yard — from San Francisco around the Horn to join Admiral Sampson's fleet off Cuba. On the *Oregon's* return to her home port after the war ended she was given a tumultuous welcome.

Despite its jingoistic aspects, the Spanish-American War brought one lasting benefit to the city. The passing of the Philippines to the control of the United States greatly increased this country's stake in the Pacific, and that in turn caused a corresponding increase in the trans-Pacific trade that has ever since been a mainstay of San Francisco's economy.

6. THE RISE OF ABE RUEF

The wartime prosperity had brought about a temporary truce in the protracted struggle between management and labor, but peace had hardly returned before contention broke out again with all its former vehemence. In the spring of 1901 several thousand workers in the metal trades formed a new union, appointed a grievance committee, and presented their employers with demands for a closed shop, improved working conditions, and a workday shortened from ten to eight hours with no decrease in pay. When the demands were rejected, the workers went on strike. This walkout, the first of a new series, came to be looked on by both labor and management as a major test of strength. The employers, alarmed at the rapid progress being made in unionizing the various crafts, prepared to counteract that movement by forming their own organization, the Employers Alliance. As a means of dissuading the owners of struck plants from yielding to the workers' demands, the alliance members resorted to a new tactic — that of refusing to supply the shop owners with needed raw materials or to buy their finished products. Realizing that such a boycott would put them out of business, the shop owners stood firm in their refusal to negotiate with the strikers. The result was that the metal-trades strike was broken, and the men returned to work.

When, a few weeks later, the restaurant employees walked out, the same tactic was used, the wholesalers refusing to supply meat, groceries, or other products to owners who came to terms with the strikers. This time the unions countered with a boycott of their own, picketing non-union restaurants and calling out employees of the supply firms. Relations between the employer and employee groups, already badly strained, were further worsened by these moves. Next came a strike of the powerful Truckers' Union, a move that threatened to paralyze the business life of the city. The employers countered this by hiring non-union drivers, whereupon the strikers armed themselves with clubs and attacked the trucks whenever they appeared, beating the drivers and tossing the loads into the streets. After these disorders had continued for some time with neither side showing any disposition to yield, the union strategists called a strike of all dock workers. On July 30, 1901, some 13,000 longshoremen, warehouse workers, sailors, and shipbuilders walked out, bringing the activity of the port to an almost complete standstill.

Political boss Abe Ruef *(left)* and Eugene E. Schmitz, Mayor.

The resulting tie-up, with its attendant violence, lasted more than two months. Meanwhile San Franciscans in general, who were suffering heavy losses because of a quarrel in which they had no direct part, made persistent efforts to break the deadlock. When these failed, they appealed to the state authorities at Sacramento. In early October Governor Henry T. Gage called the leaders of the two factions together and announced that unless a voluntary settlement was reached within ten days he would order out the National Guard to patrol the streets and restore order. The governor's threat had the desired effect. New conferences were held, concessions were made by both sides, and, although the terms were satisfactory to neither, an uneasy peace was restored.

At a city election held a few weeks after the strike ended, the resentments built up during that long contest had an important bearing on its outcome. After the decline of Dennis Kearney's Workingmen's party, labor's interest in local politics had decreased, its leaders devoting their major efforts to organizing the workers and building strong unions. This time, however, dissatisfaction with the city administration — which the workers believed to be controlled by the Employers Alliance — led them to put up their own slate of candidates. The Union Labor party ticket was headed by Eugene E. Schmitz, a popular orchestra leader who was president of the Musicians Union; candidates for the other offices were all either union officials or strong partisans of labor. Their campaign was waged on a single issue: that of giving the workingman a larger voice in civic affairs. Schmitz, along with several other union candidates, was elected.

The new administration had not been long in office before it became evident that the man who wielded the real power at the City Hall was not

Mayor Schmitz but a little-known attorney named Abe Ruef. A skillful politician who preferred to operate through others while he himself remained in the background, Ruef had already gained considerable influence in local political affairs, working mainly on the precinct level. In the formation of the Union Labor party he had seen an opportunity to build a city-wide political machine. He had allied himself with the party's leaders, and it had largely been due to his shrewd advice that the party had scored its partial victory.

Although in the 1901 election the party had succeeded in electing a unionist mayor, most of the other officials, including a majority of the Board of Supervisors, belonged to the opposition. Hence, during Schmitz's first term Ruef remained in the background, patiently building up his machine. In 1903 and 1905 Schmitz was re-elected, each time by a larger majority, in the latter year carrying with him virtually the entire labor ticket. This was the goal toward which Ruef had been striving, for it put him in control of both the executive and legislative branches of the city government.

Until then Ruef had been content with the petty graft common to the political bosses of the day, that of extracting tribute from gamblers and prostitutes in return for police protection. But after the city boards and commissions had been filled with men of his own choosing, the scope of his operations widened. The word went out that anyone who had business with the city — whether it be a license to operate a bar, a contractor seeking a sewer contract, or a utility company that wanted an extension of a streetcar franchise — first had to come to terms with boss Ruef.

Ruef, however, handled these matters with discretion. Although such transactions always involved the transfer of money, he was too clever to lay himself open to the charge of accepting bribes. His customary procedure was to suggest that the applicant engage his services as attorney to present the client's request to the proper city board or commission. The size of his legal fee depended on the importance of the service rendered. He was not above accepting a modest $250 to take care of such routine matters as a violation of the building code or the dismissal of an indictment of a prisoner charged with assault and battery. When more important favors were sought, his fees rose sharply. When public-service companies asked permission to raise their rates, or discourage competition, or (as was the case with the company that operated the city street-railway system) to install overhead trolleys instead of placing them underground — Ruef demanded, and received, retainers that ranged from $25,000 to as much as $200,000.

Since only the regularly elected city officials could grant the favors Ruef sought on behalf of his clients, it was usually necessary for him to share his "legal fees" with the officials. The mayor and members of the Board of Supervisors were the chief beneficiaries. As the size and frequency of his handouts grew so did their greed. Although the conspirators went to great lengths to keep their transactions secret, bribery on so large a scale could not long be concealed. When it became clear that the city was being ruled not from the City Hall but from Ruef's modest office on North Beach, a concerted demand arose that the power of the boss be broken and Schmitz and his confederates forced from office.

But before that could be brought about, the city suffered a disaster so complete that this mattter, along with many others, had to be postponed.

The old City Hall and Hall of Records, about 1900. Work on these two structures, which stood on the site of the former Yerba Buena Cemetery, began in 1870, but so many delays ensued that several decades passed before they were eventually completed.

IX

Nineteen Six

1. APRIL 18TH

At 5:13 on the morning of April 18, 1906, San Franciscans were shaken from their beds by a shifting of the earth's surface of far greater violence than any the city had ever known.

On the campus of the University of California scientific instruments that registered the intensity of such movements on a scale ranging from a minimum of I to a maximum of X, fixed the degree of shock at IX. According to the Berkeley seismographs the initial movements lasted approximately forty seconds. They then diminished in force for ten seconds, resumed their original severity for another twenty-five seconds, then gradually subsided.

A board of seismologists, headed by Professor A. C. Lawson of the University of California, conducted an inquiry into the origin of the quake and made public their findings a few weeks later. The board's report stated that the disturbance was caused by a shifting of the earth along the San Andreas fault, an ancient rift in the earth's crust that parallels the central California coastline, lying partly on land and partly beneath the sea. The movement extended from the vicinity of Fort Bragg on the north to San Juan Bautista on the south, a distance of approximately 210 miles.

The temblor was severe enough to cause some degree of damage for thirty miles on both sides of the fault. Along the fault the earth shifted horizontally an average of ten feet. The vertical shift was much less, ranging from a few inches to four feet. The San Andreas fault passes out to sea at Bolinas Bay, about ten miles north of the Golden Gate, and curves back to land near Mussel Rock, a short distance south of the San Francisco County line; hence, the destruction would have been still worse had the city stood directly above the center of the disturbance.

Although San Francisco was badly shaken, the damage was not irreparable. Had there been no aftermath of fire, all traces of the disaster would probably have disappeared in a few months. Shattered windows, cracked plaster, and broken crockery were general in all parts of the city. There were a number of casualties, most of them caused by brick chimneys being shaken loose, crashing through roofs and falling on the sleeping occupants below.

The great majority of buildings sustained only superficial damage; those that suffered more severely were either badly constructed or stood on insecure foundations. The damage was greatest in those sections of the city that were built on "made ground." These included the district that had once been Yerba Buena Cove, some former swamplands, and areas in North Beach and elsewhere that had been reclaimed from the bay. At such places the earth movements were much more violent than where the foundations of the houses rested on solid rock.

Throughout the downtown area the sidewalks were littered with heaps of bricks or stone shaken from the cornices of buildings. The entire fronts of other buildings had collapsed and fallen into the street. Here and there the pavement had buckled and broken, and streetcar tracks had been twisted out of alignment. In general, however, the business district withstood the shock well. The two- and three-story brick or stone buildings dating from the 1850s and 1860s suffered little damage. The same was true of the city's first skyscrapers. The fact that in most cases the latter sustained only superficial damage vindicated the faith of their builders and confounded those who had maintained that such multistoried buildings should not be permitted in San Francisco, where earthquakes, while not frequent, were by no means unknown. The 1906 earthquake demonstrated that no properly designed and soundly constructed building was likely to be severely damaged by another earthquake of the same magnitude. It also made clear that shoddy workmanship and inferior materials, however well concealed, would fare badly in the event of a quake of even moderate intensity.

Because of the city's proximity to the San Andreas fault, San Franciscans had become accustomed to shiftings of the earth's surface. Few of the earlier quakes had serious consequences — not since 1868 had one caused extensive damage — and the residents had therefore come to look on them as posing no great hazard to the public safety. Thus, although it was at once evident that this was an earthquake of far more than average violence and that the injuries and damage to property were likely to be heavy, there was no disposition to regard it as a major catastrophe.

That feeling lasted only a few hours. By midmorning clouds of smoke were observed rising from many parts of the city. These, for the most part, had been caused by overturned wood stoves, damaged electrical connections, and leaks from broken gas pipes. The fire-alarm system had been put out of commission, and the fire chief, David Scannell, had been killed in the collapse of one of the station houses. Despite this, however, the crews of horse-drawn engines managed to make their way through the littered streets, and the blazes at first were being brought under control. But then the water supply failed and the fire-fighting equipment became useless. Although ample water remained in the city reservoirs, the earth movements had

The City Hall, April, 1906. Because its building had taken so many years, San Franciscans had come to refer to it ironically as "the new City Hall ruin." The 1906 earthquake made the name a singularly appropriate one. The building was so badly damaged that it had to be razed. *(Wells Fargo History Room.)*

broken the mains in so many places as to wreck the entire distribution system.

Only then did the full seriousness of the situation become evident. By noon huge columns of smoke were rising from unattended fires in the industrial district south of Market Street and several other points in the city. Although there was little wind, the flames spread so rapidly that by mid-afternoon the fire south of Market Street had eaten its way through the wooden hotels, shops, and rooming houses on Howard and Mission streets and was fast approaching Market Street.

For a time it was hoped that the flames could be prevented from crossing that broad thoroughfare and that the central business district could be saved. Efforts to halt its progress were concentrated on the block-square Palace Hotel at Market and New Montgomery streets. The Palace had its own water supply derived from artesian wells and stored in a reservoir beneath its grand court. Water from that source held the flames in check for several hours; however, the reservoir was eventually pumped dry, and the fight had to be abandoned. By late afternoon the south side of Market Street was burning fiercely, and showers of embers were falling on the roofs

A street in the financial district on the morning of April 18, 1906. The fire engine in the foreground was soon rendered useless by the failure of the city water supply. *(California Historical Society.)*

(Below) Later that same day crowds gathered at the top of the California Street hill and looked on helplessly while the fire ate its way through the wholesale produce district below. *(Roy D. Graves.)*

of buildings to the north and west, kindling numerous new fires in the triangle formed by Market, Powell, and California streets. By nightfall it had become obvious that the entire center of the city was doomed.

As viewed from the Berkeley hills across the bay, the spectacle was thus described by one eyewitness:

> Within half an hour after the earthquake shock, a hump of dark smoke appeared over the City, growing during the succeeding hours until it rose through the quiet air like the clouds made by a volcano. When night came, the whole front of San Francisco was ablaze, the flames shooting upward at particular centers with the glowing discharge of a blast furnace; the light of the conflagration illumined the heavy clouds of smoke with a pink glow . . . The next day (April 19) the clouds of smoke rolled skyward to a height of two miles, their lower layers dark, but the topmost billows sunlit and splendid. As evening came, the wind from the southwest blew smoke over the Bay toward Mt. Tamalpais; the sun, like a red

---

By the morning of the 19th it had become clear that the entire central part of the city was doomed. This view of lower Market Street shows buildings afire on both sides of the street. (*Wells Fargo Bank History Room.*)

The Call=Chronicle=Examiner

SAN FRANCISCO, THURSDAY, APRIL 19, 1906.

EARTHQUAKE AND FIRE:
SAN FRANCISCO IN RUINS

DEATH AND DESTRUCTION HAVE BEEN THE FATE OF SAN FRANCISCO. SHAKEN BY A TEMBLOR AT 5:13 O'CLOCK YESTERDAY MORNING, THE SHOCK LASTING 48 SECONDS, AND SCOURGED BY FLAMES THAT RAGED DIAMETRICALLY IN ALL DIRECTIONS, THE CITY IS A MASS OF SMOULDERING RUINS. AT SIX O'CLOCK LAST EVENING THE FLAMES SEEMINGLY PLAYING WITH INCREASED VIGOR, THREATENED TO DESTROY SUCH SECTIONS AS THEIR FURY HAD SPARED DURING THE EARLIER PORTION OF THE DAY. BUILDING THEIR PATH IN A TRIANGUAR CIRCUIT FROM THE START IN THE EARLY MORNING, THEY JOCKEYED AS THE DAY WANED, LEFT THE BUSINESS SECTION, WHICH THEY HAD ENTIRELY DEVASTATED, AND SKIPPED IN A DOZEN DIRECTIONS TO THE RESIDENCE PORTIONS. AS NIGHT FELL THEY HAD MADE THEIR WAY OVER INTO THE NORTH BEACH SECTION AND SPRINGING ANEW TO THE SOUTH THEY REACHED OUT ALONG THE SHIPPING SECTION DOWN THE BAY SHORE, OVER THE HILLS AND ACROSS TOWARD THIRD AND TOWNSEND STREETS. WAREHOUSES, WHOLESALE HOUSES AND MANUFACTURING CONCERNS FELL IN THEIR PATH. THIS COMPLETED THE DESTRUCTION OF THE ENTIRE DISTRICT KNOWN AS THE "SOUTH OF MARKET STREET." HOW FAR THEY ARE REACHING TO THE SOUTH ACROSS THE CHANNEL CANNOT BE TOLD AS THIS PART OF THE CITY IS SHUT OFF FROM SAN FRANCISCO PAPERS.

AFTER DARKNESS, THOUSANDS OF THE HOMELESS WERE MAKING THEIR WAY WITH THEIR BLANKETS AND SCANT PROVISIONS TO GOLDEN GATE PARK AND THE BEACH TO FIND SHELTER. THOSE IN THE HOMES ON THE HILLS JUST NORTH OF THE HAYES VALLEY WRECKED SECTION PILED THEIR BELONGINGS IN THE STREETS AND EXPRESS WAGONS AND AUTOMOBILES WERE HAULING THE THINGS AWAY TO THE SPARSELY SETTLED REGIONS. EVERYBODY IN SAN FRANCISCO IS PREPARED TO LEAVE THE CITY, FOR THE BELIEF IS FIRM THAT SAN FRANCISCO WILL BE TOTALLY DESTROYED.

DOWNTOWN EVERYTHING IS RUIN. NOT A BUSINESS HOUSE STANDS. THEATRES ARE CRUMBLED INTO HEAPS. FACTORIES AND COMMISSION HOUSES LIE SMOULDERING ON THEIR FORMER SITES. ALL OF THE NEWSPAPER PLANTS HAVE BEEN RENDERED USELESS. THE "CALL" AND THE "EXAMINER" BUILDINGS, EXCLUDING THE "CALL'S" EDITORIAL ROOMS ON STEVENSON STREET BEING ENTIRELY DESTROYED.

IT IS ESTIMATED THAT THE LOSS IN SAN FRANCISCO WILL REACH FROM $150,000,000 TO $200,000,000. THESE FIGURES ARE IN THE ROUGH AND NOTHING CAN BE TOLD UNTIL PARTIAL ACCOUNTING IS TAKEN.

ON EVERY SIDE THERE WAS DEATH AND SUFFERING YESTERDAY. HUNDREDS WERE INJURED, EITHER BURNED, CRUSHED OR STRUCK BY FALLING PIECES FROM THE BUILDINGS AND ONE OF TEN DIED WHILE ON THE OPERATING TABLE AT MECHANICS' PAVILION, IMPROVISED AS A HOSPITAL FOR THE COMFORT AND CARE OF 200 OF THE INJURED. THE NUMBER OF DEAD IS NOT KNOWN BUT IT IS ESTIMATED THAT AT LEAST 500 MET THEIR DEATH IN THE HORROR.

AT NINE O'CLOCK, UNDER A SPECIAL MESSAGE FROM PRESIDENT ROOSEVELT, THE CITY WAS PLACED UNDER MARTIAL LAW. HUNDREDS OF TROOPS PATROLLED THE STREETS AND DROVE THE CROWDS BACK, WHILE HUNDREDS MORE WERE SET AT WORK ASSISTING THE FIRE AND POLICE DEPARTMENTS. THE STRICTEST ORDERS WERE ISSUED, AND IN TRUE MILITARY SPIRIT THE SOLDIERS OBEYED. DURING THE AFTERNOON THREE THIEVES MET THEIR DEATH BY RIFLE BULLETS WHILE AT WORK IN THE RUINS. THE CURIOUS WERE DRIVEN BACK AT THE BREASTS OF THE HORSES THAT THE CAVALRYMEN RODE AND ALL THE CROWDS WERE FORCED FROM THE LEVEL DISTRICT TO THE HILLY SECTION BEYOND TO THE NORTH.

THE WATER SUPPLY WAS ENTIRELY CUT OFF, AND MAY BE IT WAS JUST AS WELL, FOR THE LINES OF FIRE DEPARTMENT WOULD HAVE BEEN ABSOLUTELY USELESS AT ANY STAGE. ASSISTANT CHIEF DOUGHERTY SUPERVISED THE WORK OF HIS MEN AND EARLY IN THE MORNING IT WAS SEEN THAT THE ONLY POSSIBLE CHANCE TO SAVE THE CITY LAY IN EFFORT TO CHECK THE FLAMES BY THE USE OF DYNAMITE. DURING THE DAY A BLAST COULD BE HEARD IN ANY SECTION AT INTERVALS OF ONLY A FEW MINUTES, AND BUILDINGS NOT DESTROYED BY FIRE WERE BLOWN TO ATOMS. BUT THROUGH THE GAPS MADE THE FLAMES JUMPED AND ALTHOUGH THE FAILURES OF THE HEROIC EFFORTS OF THE POLICE FIREMEN AND SOLDIERS WERE AT TIMES SICKENING, THE WORK WAS CONTINUED WITH A DESPERATION THAT WILL LIVE AS ONE OF THE FEATURES OF THE TERRIBLE DISASTER. MEN WORKED LIKE FIENDS TO COMBAT THE LAUGHING, ROARING, ONRUSHING FIRE DEMON.

NO HOPE LEFT FOR SAFETY OF ANY BUILDINGS

San Francisco seems doomed to entire destruction. With a lapse in the raging of the flames just before dark, the hope was raised that with the use of the tons of dynamite the course of the fire might be checked and confined to the triangular sections it had cut out for its path. But on the Barbary Coast the fire broke out anew and as night closed in the flames were eating their way into parts untouched in their ravages during the day. To the south and the north they spread; down to the docks and out into the resident section, in and to the north of Hayes Valley. By six o'clock practically all of St. Ignatius' great buildings were no more. They had been leveled to the fiery heap that marked what was once the metropolis of the West.

The first of the big structures to go to ruin was the Call Building, the famous skyscraper. At eleven o'clock the big 18-story building was a furnace. Flames leaped from every window and shot skyward from the circular windows in the dome. In less than two hours nothing remained but the tall skeleton.

By five o'clock the Palace Hotel was in ruins. The old hostelry, famous the world over, withstood the siege until the last, and although dynamite was used in frequent blasts to drive . . .

Continued on Page Two

BLOW BUILDINGS UP TO CHECK FLAMES

The dynamiting of buildings in the track of the fire, to stay the progress of the flames, was in charge of John Bermingham, Jr., superintendent of the California Powder Works. Several experienced men from the powder works, assisted by policemen and members of the fire department, did the hazardous work of blowing up the buildings. They were razed in sets of threes, but the open spaces where the shattered buildings fell were quickly turned into holocausts of flame. The work was most effective in the business blocks east of Kearny street.

WHOLE CITY IS ABLAZE

As 10 o'clock last night the Occidental Hotel was destroyed by the flames which swept unchecked across Montgomery street and attacked the block bounded by Montgomery, Sutter, Bush and Kearny. The new Merchants' Exchange building was a mass of flames from basement to tower.

The Union Trust building and Crocker-Woolworth Bank were both ablaze and the Chronicle building and other buildings in that block were threatened by the flames.

Shortly after 10 o'clock the fire had eaten its way southward from Portsmouth Square to Kearny and California streets. The entire section fronting on the west side of Kearny street seemed doomed.

All the building adjoining the Hall of Justice were ablaze and the flames were driving in upon the structure by a big dynamite. It is almost a certainty that every building contained in the section bounded by Clay, Kearny, Market and East streets will be consumed.

The flames had eaten their way southward to the rear section and far as Geary street. There is dynamiting blazing after breaks, the financial district. The financing . . .

CHURCH OF SAINT IGNATIUS IS DESTROYED

The magnificent church and College of St. Ignatius, on the northwest corner of Van Ness avenue and Hayes street represents in its destruction, a material loss of over $1,500,000. The actual cost of the great building was over $900,000, but during the years which have elapsed since its erection the church has been enriched by paintings and fine decorations, which were priceless. Some of these were works of art which can never be replaced, however willing those interested in the church might be to meet any expense in the . . .

MAYOR CONFERS WITH MILITARY AND CITIZENS

At 1 o'clock yesterday afternoon 50 representative citizens of San Francisco met the Mayor, the Chief of Police and the United States Military authorities in the police office in the basement of the Hall of Justice. They had been summoned thither by Mayor Schmitz early in the forenoon, the fearful possibilities of the situation having forced themselves upon him immediately after the shock of the earthquake in the morning, and the news which at once recalled him of the completeness of the disaster. He lost no time in making out a list of citizens from whom to seek advice and assistance, and in summoning them to the conference. It was called at the Hall of Justice, as virtually the first news which reached the Mayor regarding the extent of the disaster was that of the ruin of the City Hall. He did not realize that even while the conference was to be going on exercises would be crashing down and windows falling in fragments in the Hall of Justice also, and that before sunset desperate efforts would be made to stay the advance of the flames in the northern section of the down-town district.

Continued on Page Two

With their own plants wrecked, the city's morning newspapers issued this combined edition on the morning of April 19th; it was printed in the shop of the *Oakland Tribune*. On the 20th all three papers resumed publication, the *Examiner* from the pressroom of the *Tribune*, and the *Chronicle* and *Call* from those of two other Oakland papers, the *Herald* and *Enquirer* respectively.

ball, threw a crimson light over the waters and there was more suggestion of horror than at any time. That night the big wooden
houses in the residential portion were burning luridly . . . ; the
sight was one of desolating splendor. On the day following (April
20) the fire had pretty well exhausted itself and the dark murk of
drifting smoke hid the ruins of the once proud city of the Argonauts.

2. A CITY DESTROYED

Throughout the entire three days of the fire determined efforts continued to be made to stay its progress. After the broken water mains had
rendered the usual fire-fighting methods useless, an attempt was made to
check the spread of the fire by dynamiting buildings that lay in its path.
Van Ness Avenue, then lined on both sides with large wooden residences,
was chosen for that experiment, for it was realized that should the fire cross
that wide street it would be likely to continue until it burned itself out
against the natural barriers of the Presidio and the group of cemeteries that
lay several miles beyond.

Squads of regular Army troops from the Presidio were assigned to the
task. Throughout the night of April 18-19 a series of explosions shook the
city as the houses on the east side of the avenue between Jackson and
O'Farrell streets were blown up. However, late that night wind-blown cin-
ders ignited the roofs of houses on the far side of Van Ness, and residents of
the area, along with thousands who had sought refuge there, prepared to
move still farther west. It was at that point, when the prospect looked dark-
est, that a fortuitous shift of the wind forced the fire back, and its further
progress in that direction was halted.

Other parts of the city were not so fortunate. During the three days and
two nights the fire was out of control it consumed an area of four square
miles, including almost the entire central business and industrial sections. In
the end, 514 city blocks were burned over. Some 450 lives were lost, and the
property damage was estimated at $350,000,000. Forests of brick chimneys
stood above masses of twisted pipes and molten metal in the residential
districts. The destruction in the downtown area was hardly less complete.
There the streets were buried beneath many feet of debris where the façades
of burning buildings had collapsed and fallen outward. The walls of other
buildings still stood, but so precariously as to endanger passersby. Rising
above the general desolation were the shells of burned-out skyscrapers.

The outer boundaries of the burned district extended along the bay
front from Townsend Street on the south to the vicinity of Fisherman's
Wharf. From there it ranged in a southwesterly direction over Russian Hill
to Van Ness Avenue and Filbert Street, then down the east side of Van
Ness to Clay. At that point it crossed Van Ness, consumed the five blocks
bounded by Clay, Franklin, and Sutter streets, and continued along Van

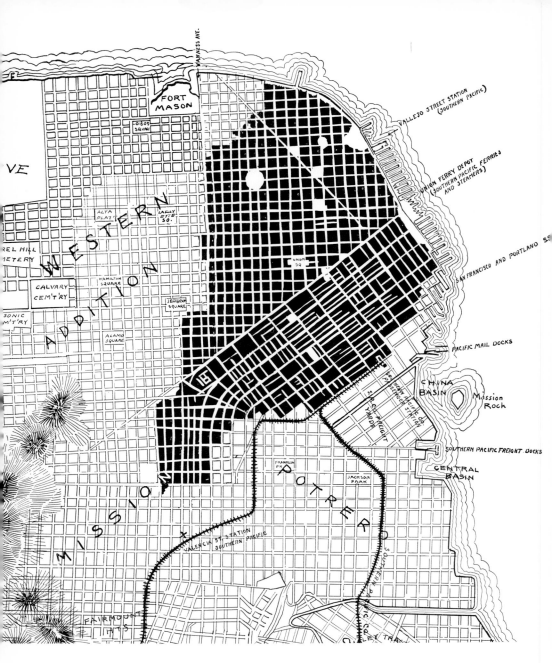

During the 72 hours the fire raged it consumed 28,000 buildings, large and small, in the heart of the city (see the shaded area in the above map) and caused property damage estimated at $500 million. A few spots within the burned district escaped destruction—these are indicated by white spaces on the map. The loss of life was never definitely established; 353 bodies were recovered from the wreckage, and several hundred people were reported as missing.

Ness to Fell Street. There it again crossed Van Ness Avenue and continued out Fell and Oak streets to Market, thence out the south side of Market to Dolores, out Dolores to Twentieth, along Twentieth to Valencia, and obliquely through the Mission District to Howard and Eighteenth streets. From that point it continued along Howard to Fifteenth, crossed the intervening blocks to Bryant and Eighth, followed the east side of Eighth Street to Townsend, and down Townsend to the bay.

Within the perimeter of the burned district a few spots escaped. Chief of these were eleven square blocks on and about Telegraph Hill, and a two-block area on the crest of Russian Hill. They were saved both because of the caprices of the wind and because in each case a supply of water chanced to be available. Several industrial plants at the base of Telegraph Hill had their own wells. Elsewhere in the same locality firemen pumped water from the bay and laid hoses to the edge of the burning area. A reservoir on the top of Russian Hill was used to save the houses there.

In the downtown district, too, a few buildings — including several belonging to the federal government — were saved. Among the latter were the Mint at Fifth and Mission streets, the Main Post Office at Seventh and Mission, and the red brick United States Appraisers Building at Washington and Sansome streets. These owed their survival to the fireproof materials of which they were built, to their location — set back from neighboring buildings — and to their stout defense.

The following eyewitness account described the struggle to save the Appraisers Building:

> In it were stored valuable documents, and by the most heroic efforts it was spared. The Appraiser, General John T. Dare, gathered his few men together as the fire approached, distributing among them any vessels he could obtain which would hold water. A tank on top of the building supplied their needs and all day long they worked, putting out falling embers and woodwork as it ignited.

Another important building in the same area likewise escaped. This building, called Montgomery Block, at the corner of Montgomery and Washington streets, was a venerable, four-story structure that had been built in 1853. It survived until 1958 when it was torn down and its site converted into a parking lot.

3. RELIEF MEASURES

The problems created by the earthquake and its aftermath were on a scale that few cities have ever been called on to face. Close to a quarter of a million were rendered homeless. Utilities of every sort — transportation, water, gas, electricity, fuel — were completely disrupted. Means of feeding and housing the refugees, caring for the sick and injured, and maintaining order had to be improvised. While the fire still raged, the many thousands who had been driven from their homes were welcomed by their more fortunate townsmen and provided with food and shelter. But the emergency was too great to be met by such methods. On the morning of April 18 Mayor Schmitz appealed for help to General Frederick Funston, commander of the troops at the Presidio, who at once dispatched all available soldiers into the threatened areas. For the next three days they aided the hard-pressed police and firemen by patrolling the streets, searching through wrecked buildings for dead and injured, and setting up fire lines to keep unauthorized persons out of the danger zones.

Schmitz also summoned a number of the city's leaders to meet at 3 p.m. of the 18th to consider means of coping with the disaster. The group — which was later increased in size and became known as the Committee of Fifty — gathered in the old Hall of Justice at Kearny and Washington streets, only to be driven out by the near approach of the fire. Thereupon they adjourned and reassembled in Portsmouth Square across the street. Their deliberations had hardly been resumed, however, when the smoke and heat forced them to move again, this time to the still unfinished Fairmont Hotel on Nob Hill. There two urgent problems were taken up: to devise means of suppressing lawlessness, particularly the theft of valuables from deserted buildings in the path of the fire, and to prevent other fires by prohibiting the use of the damaged chimneys and gas and electric appliances. The following notice was hastily drawn up, printed, and posted throughout the city:

Proclamation By the Mayor

The Federal Troops, the members of the Regular Police Force, and all Special Police Officers have been authorized to KILL any and all persons found engaged in looting or in the commission of any other crime.

I have directed all the Gas and Electric Lighting Companies not to turn on Gas or Electricity until I order them to do so; you may therefore expect the city to remain in darkness for an indefinite time.

I request all citizens to remain at home from darkness until daylight every night until order is restored.

I warn all citizens of the danger of fire from damaged or destroyed chimneys, broken or leaking gas pipes or fixtures, or any like cause.

E. E. Schmitz, Mayor

Dated April 18, 1906.

The Fairmont Hotel, along with other Nob Hill buildings, was burned out on the night of April 18-19, and the committee moved its headquarters to the Franklin Hall on Fillmore Street, where it continued to function for several weeks longer.

A third problem—that of caring for the refugees—next presented itself. On the afternoon of the 19th General Funston telegraphed Secretary of War Taft at Washington, fixing the number of homeless at "about 100,000" and urging that "thousands of tents and all the rations that can be sent" be forwarded to the city without delay. Taft's reply, received the next morning, stated that the West Coast Army posts had been ordered to send all needed supplies as rapidly as possible. His wire authorized Funston to "do anything to assist in keeping order, in saving life and property, and in relieving suffering and hunger by the use of troops, materials and supplies under your order."

When the extent of the disaster became known, offers of help flowed in from all parts of the country. Contributions of food and clothing, however, could not be expected to reach the city soon enough to provide for the immediate needs of the homeless. Accordingly, those who were willing to leave the city were encouraged to do so. The Ferry Building had fortunately escaped serious damage, and the transbay ferry service was resumed after a delay of only two hours. Passengers leaving the city either by the ferries or aboard the trains down the peninsula were carried without charge. The trains were subject to frequent delays. Because of the failure of the local water system, the locomotives sometimes left the city with their boilers half empty; moreover, many of the tanks along the line had been shaken down by the quake. An added complication was that telegraph and telephone services had been disrupted, and in places the earth movement had shifted the roadbed slightly, making it prudent for the engineers to proceed cautiously. Despite these handicaps, during the first three days more than a thousand carloads of refugees left the city. The exodus continued, though on a decreasing scale, for several days longer.

After the fires had burned out, the military and civilian authorities directed their major efforts toward easing the lot of the homeless. Most refugees had saved only what they had been able to carry with them when they fled, and few had chosen to take food, blankets, or extra clothing. The most pressing problem, hence, was an acute shortage of such essentials, particularly food. The plants of the produce merchants and the factories and warehouses of the food processors and distributors had been among the first to burn. Moreover, most retail grocery stores and meat markets had also been destroyed, and those that survived had quickly been stripped of their stocks by those who foresaw the coming shortages. The result was that when, on April 20, the remaining food stores were taken over by the

Committee of Fifty and a system of rationing introduced, their shelves were nearly empty.

But no one went hungry. The threat of famine was lessened when, on the morning of the third day, April 20, foodstuffs began to arrive from the near-by Army posts and neighboring communities. Distribution depots were set up in public squares and other points beyond the burned area and milk, bread, and other foods were passed out to all who applied. Later, as the flow of goods into the city increased in volume and variety, clothing, blankets, tents, medicines, and other necessities were distributed.

These were all temporary measures designed to tide the refugees over the critical first days. But those who had lost all possessions needed help over a much longer period of time. Thousands of families were living in tents or improvised shacks in the city parks or vacant lots about the edge of the burned district; these had to be provided with adequate food and shelter. Accordingly, a large-scale emergency housing program was hastily laid out and put into effect. During the first two months more than 8,000 "refugee houses"—most of them long, barrackslike buildings, each containing six or eight family units—were put up and occupied. Many continued in use for several years.

A major part of the cost of this housing project and of food, clothing, and other materials distributed to the destitute was borne by contributions of cash and goods from hundreds of communities both in this country and abroad. More than $10,000,000 was thus donated, as well as vast quantities of supplies. The administration and distribution of these funds and materials were the joint responsibility of the Committee of Fifty and the Red Cross. The extent and complexity of the committee's activities may be realized from this list of its subcommittees: Relief of the Hungry, Relief of the Sick and Wounded, Housing the Homeless, Drugs and Medical Supplies, Transportation of Refugees, Restoration of Water Supply, Restoration of Light and Telephone, Citizen Police, Restoration of Fire in Dwellings, Auxiliary Fire Department, Resumption of Transportation, Relief of Chinese, and Restoration of Retail Trade.

4. "AN' IT'S DOIN' THE BOTH OF US GOOD . . ."

Residents of the shattered city quickly adapted themselves to the profound changes brought about by the emergency. Even for those whose homes had been spared life was changed. During the first six weeks no fires of any sort were allowed inside the houses. Until chimneys could be inspected and repaired and gas and electric services restored, all cooking had to be done outdoors. At first the cooking facilities consisted of no more than a few bricks covered with a grate or piece of sheet iron. Later, the wood-burning kitchen stoves were moved onto the sidewalks and crude shelters built about them to keep out the wind and dust. Streets in the

Refugee camps were established in open spaces throughout the un-burned area, this one was in Golden Gate Park. *(Wells Fargo Bank History Room.)*

(Below) Until damaged chimneys could be inspected and repaired and water, gas and other utilities restored, all cooking was done outdoors. *(California Historical Society.)*

Tents to shelter refugees were pitched on the sites of two Nob Hill residences: that of Charles Crocker in the foreground and of D. D. Colton beyond. To the left are the shells of the Flood mansion and the Fairmont Hotel. *(Wells Fargo Bank History Room.)*

residential districts in the unburned areas were soon lined on both sides with hundreds of such improvised kitchens, many of them displaying homemade signs bearing the names of the Poodle Dog, Delmonico's, and other downtown restaurants.

Cooking under such conditions and lining up at the distributing stations for their daily allotments of bread, milk, and canned goods was an experience shared by all, regardless of what their former financial or social status may have been. The consequence of that leveling process and the spirit with which it was accepted, was thus expressed by a local rhymster, Charles K. Field:

An' Mrs. Van Bergen she greets me these days
With a smile an' a nod of the head;
"Ah, Mrs. McGinnis, how are you?" she says,
"An' do you like Government bread?"
She fetches a bag made of crockydile skin
An' I've got a sack when we meet,
But the same kind of coffee an' crackers goes in,
An' it's all of it cooked in the street.
Sure Mrs. Van Bergen is takin' it fine,
Ye'd think she was used to the food;
We're gettin' acquainted a-standin' in line,
An' it's doin' the both of us good.

The relief of the homeless took, of course, precedence over all other concerns while the fire still burned and for several weeks thereafter. But even during the hours when it appeared that the entire city was doomed, few doubted that it would be promptly rebuilt. So great was the eagerness of merchants and others to resume their normal operations that in many cases the ruins of their former places of business had not fully cooled before they were being cleared so rebuilding could begin.

With the entire center of the city reduced to rubble, however, it was apparent that weeks would have to pass before the downtown streets could be cleared and repaired, water, gas, and other utilities provided, and the tracks of the street-railroad system replaced. Few of the city's business or professional men were content to wait that long. As a result, there was a concerted rush to set up temporary quarters in the unburned districts. Fillmore and outer Mission streets, both former neighborhood shopping centers, were quickly transformed. But the most striking change was on Van Ness. There the baroque mansions lining the avenue's west side— which, except for the five blocks between Clay and Sutter streets, had escaped the fire—were hastily remodeled. For many months these served as temporary quarters for old-established downtown department stores and other leading business firms.

It was a curious experience [wrote Amelia Ransome Neville] to enter a store by a marble vestibule, find yourself in a beautiful great hall, with carved oak staircase and stained-glass windows, to have the goods you desired brought you from the pantry or side-board drawers or from the library shelves, to have them spread before you on a great dining-table . . . or, in another room, to be served at a hastily improvised pine counter. If you wandered up the stairway to look at suits or coats, perhaps you were asked to step into the bath-room to be fitted. It was a topsy-turvy land, but in a few months Van Ness Avenue became a delightful shopping

After the fire many of the big houses on the west side of Van Ness Avenue were taken over by department stores, banks, insurance companies, and other business firms, which continued to occupy them while their burned-out quarters downtown were being rebuilt. This picture shows the City of Paris Dry Goods Company. (*Wells Fargo Bank History Room.*)

street. . . . On the western side, temporary fronts with large windows were built from the houses to the sidewalk. One store, occupying a mansion, built on the terraced garden in the rear a pretty tea house, which became a very popular place with the ladies.

Similar changes took place elsewhere throughout the unburned district. There scores of residences and small shops were taken over by companies that had been burned out downtown, and the living quarters above were converted into the offices of business and professional men. Thus the business of numerous insurance firms, brokerage houses, and other staid enterprises was conducted in the incongruously domestic setting of front and back parlors, bedrooms, and basements.

Meanwhile, the task of clearing away the rubble in the downtown area continued around the clock. The sites of the ruined buildings were covered to a depth of many feet with heaps of brick or stone interspersed with masses of molten metal. But before rebuilding could begin the blocked streets had to be cleared and repaired and lines of communication re-established. Of the thousands of tons of debris removed from this area the greater part was dumped into the shallows of the bay in the North Beach region and in the area south of the Ferry Building. To facilitate that process temporary tracks were laid over the streets of the financial, industrial, and retail shopping centers, over which trains of dump cars shuttled back and forth at all hours of the day and night. Supplementing these, hundreds of horse-drawn wagons were pressed into service. Clearing the burned district so that large-scale reconstruction could begin occupied an army of workers for many months; its cost was estimated at more than $20,000,000.

5. RECONSTRUCTION

One matter that caused concern while the fire was still raging, and for some days thereafter, was uncertainty how the vaults of banks and other business houses had withstood the intense heat. Some time passed before that question could be answered. For to open them before they had cooled sufficiently would have caused their contents to burst into flame on contact with the outer air. Fears for the safety of valuables so stored were for the most part unfounded. In every case where adequate precautions were taken when the vaults were opened—and when the vaults themselves had been properly constructed—their contents were found to be undamaged. Thus not only were large stores of currency, securities, jewels, and other property saved, but also valuable company records that made it easier for burned-out business firms to resume operation.

The question of whether the fire-insurance companies would be able to pay the extremely heavy losses sustained by their policyholders was another source of anxiety. Here again the losses were far less heavy than

This photograph, taken from the tower of the Ferry Building, shows rebuilding operations getting under way amid the wreckage on lower Market Street. Temporary railroad tracks are being laid on both sides of that thoroughfare to help remove debris.

many had feared. A survey made several months after the fire revealed that the claims filed with the insurance companies totaled approximately $175,000,000. While not every carrier was able to pay its claims at once, and a few companies repudiated their debts entirely, by far the greater number discharged their obligations in full. In the final reckoning a total of $167,000,000 was paid, leaving a net loss of only about $8,000,000.

Such insurance payments failed by a wide margin to cover the entire property loss, which was estimated at from $350,000,000 to $500,000,000. However, they helped finance a massive building boom that got under way in the summer of 1906 and continued for many months. This in turn created so heavy a demand for workmen and building materials of every sort that costs rose sharply. At the beginning of 1906 the building trades had employed fewer than 20,000 workers; by the end of the year their number had more than tripled, and the wages of skilled artisans had reached $20 for an eight-hour day, a figure comparable to that paid during gold rush days.

But soaring costs were a lightly regarded detail in the endeavor to make the city once more the West Coast's leading financial, commercial, and cultural center, and to lose no time in the process. The work went on without interruption seven days a week. One writer stated that in the downtown district "there was hardly a period in the twenty-four hours of day and night when the sharp drumming of the steam riveter could not be heard."

During the first three years the value of buildings put up in the burned area exceeded $150,000,000. In January, 1906, the number of Class-A buildings—that is, those with steel frames and brick, stone, or concrete walls and floors—was 27. None was so badly damaged that it had to be razed; by 1909 all had been restored and were again in use. During that same period 77 new Class-A buildings had been completed and occupied. Besides the 104 new or restored structures of that type, 115 Class-B, and 1,500 Class-C buildings had been put up. (Class-B buildings had concrete or brick walls and floors reinforced with steel bars and beams; in Class-C buildings only the outer walls were of brick or stone, the floors and partitions being of wood.)

In the region beyond the central business and industrial sections, but still within the burned district, 19,000 new wood-frame buildings were built. Many were residential units of two or more stories, each floor having accommodations for a single family. Of the 28,000 buildings destroyed, 20,500 had been replaced by the end of the third year. Moreover, the new structures were, in general, superior in design, workmanship, and materials to those they replaced.

The determination and energy with which the citizens set about rebuilding their city were widely admired, yet among the San Franciscans themselves many were dissatisfied. They had urged that before reconstruction began a comprehensive new plan for the city's future development be drawn up and adopted. These saw in the disaster an opportunity to correct some of the faults in the city's original design, and thereby to add immeasurably to its convenience and beauty. Interest in the Burnham plan, which had been rejected earlier because its cost was considered prohibitive, was revived. A number of other suggestions were made. One was to widen several of the heavily traveled downtown streets, including Montgomery and Kearny; another to cut through new cross-town streets to speed the flow of traffic between the areas to the north and south of Market Street.

While the merits of these and other proposals were widely recognized, the city's businessmen were eager to move back to their old locations. Thus none of the suggested changes was made, and a rare opportunity was lost.

On one point, however, all segments of the population agreed: every precaution must be taken to prevent a repetition of the catastrophe. The building code was revised and strengthened to lessen the likelihood of extensive damage by future fires or earthquakes. The fire department was reorganized; its personnel was increased, new firehouses were built, and engines and other equipment of the latest design were installed. Most important of all, steps were taken to assure an adequate supply of water should the distribution system again be destroyed. This was accomplished both by providing additional storage reservoirs and by building beneath street intersections in many parts of the city scores of cisterns from which water could be pumped if the regular system should again fail.

6. BUBONIC PLAGUE

In the fall of 1907, while the rebuilding of the city was at its height, the residents were called on to cope with yet another emergency. This time it was a dangerous health problem: the sudden appearance of bubonic plague.

Because of the city's extensive trade with the Orient, San Franciscans had long been aware that the plague might gain a foothold in this country. Accordingly, the local authorities, with the co-operation of state and national health agencies, had taken precautions to minimize that possibility. Their efforts had been redoubled in the mid-1890s when the dread disease — which under the name of the Black Death had periodically swept over Europe and the Orient since the Middle Ages — broke out in Bombay and from there spread to Hong Kong, the Philippines, and Japan. For a time its further progress eastward seemed to be checked. Then in December, 1899, two cases were reported among the Chinese at Honolulu, whereupon the entire population of that city's Oriental quarter were removed and placed under quarantine, and their houses burned.

Word that the plague had spread to within two thousand miles of the mainland heightened the concern of health officials all over the nation. On orders of the surgeon general, a group of physicians who had made a special study of the disease were assigned to the San Francisco quarantine station on Angel Island. Thereafter the passengers and crews of ships arriving from trans-Pacific ports were subjected to rigid tests before they were permitted to land. These precautions, however, failed of their purpose. Early in January, 1900, several deaths occured in the local Chinatown under circumstances that aroused the suspicion of the city health officers. Post-mortem examinations confirmed that the deceased had been victims of the plague.

When these findings became known, they set off a controversy that divided the city for several months. For it was realized that the news, if widely publicized, could have a serious effect on the local economy. There was, indeed, a strong likelihood that a quarantine would be imposed, shutting the city off from the rest of the country for an indefinite period. Determined efforts were made by some city and state officials and by some

California newspapers to discredit the findings of the physicians who had made the diagnosis or, failing that, to minimize their importance.

The situation was thus described by Frank Morton Todd, author of *Eradicating the Plague in San Francisco:*

> Instead of being confronted by a united authority with intelligent plans for defense, the question . . . became the subject of factional dispute. There was open hostility to the work of the sanitarians, and war among City, State, and Federal health authorities. . . . Eugene Schmitz, while mayor, refused to approve the printing of health reports and vital statistics, and attempted to remove from office four members of the Board of Health who persisted in the statement that the plague existed in the city.

In the end all such attempts to suppress the truth failed. By the winter of 1900 San Franciscans in general had belatedly been awakened to the seriousness of the situation. At a mass meeting held in early December an organization called the Mercantile Joint Committee was formed and a vigorous campaign was launched to stamp out the disease. So well did the committee do its work that "after eighteen months of unremitting toil" on the part of a numerous corps of physicians, technicians, and sanitary workers the spread of the disease was halted. During this visitation, the plague was confined to twenty square blocks in the Chinese quarter. It claimed 121 victims, nearly all of whom were Asians; of that number only 8 survived.

In 1907, the plague broke out again. Its reappearance at that time was the more unexpected because Chinatown, the center of the earlier contagion, had been destroyed in the 1906 fire, and it had been assumed that this had eliminated any probability of its return. When in early April the first new case was reported, it aroused no great concern, nor did a second two months later. During the final two weeks of June, however, when fourteen persons were stricken, the seriousness of this new outbreak became apparent. Again the city officials were reluctant to acknowledge that the plague had appeared, and for several weeks little was done. It was not until mid-July, when Mayor Charles Boxton resigned and was succeeded by Edward R. Taylor, that effective countermeasures were taken. By then the number of cases had risen to fifty-five.

Taylor, himself a physician, realized the gravity of the situation. One of his first official acts was to ask President Theodore Roosevelt for help from the federal health officials. Roosevelt responded by directing Surgeon General Walter Wyman of the U. S. Public Health Service to render all necessary assistance. Accordingly, sixteen Public Health officers, headed by Assistant Surgeon General Colby Rucker, were dispatched to the city, and a vigorous campaign got under way. Headquarters were established on Fillmore Street; a central laboratory was installed there, and the city was

In April, 1907, while the city was in the midst of its massive reconstruction program, an outbreak of bubonic plague confronted the citizens with a new emergency. Thousands of buildings were rat-proofed as part of the war against the disease-carrying rodents.

divided into thirteen sanitary districts. Each district had a field office in charge of a surgeon and a staff of inspectors, foremen, and laborers.

Then began what Frank Morton Todd described as "the most intensive rat hunt in history." For rats were known to be the chief carriers of the disease, and it was only by hunting out and destroying the infected rodents that the plague could be controlled. During the months-long campaign more than 150,000 rats were caught, all of which were subjected to bacteriological examination at the central laboratory. Of the many thousands examined during September, the first full month this program was in operation, only two infected rats were found. In October, however, their number increased to twenty-three, in November to thirty-seven, and in December to forty-three.

By year end a definite pattern had been established: as the number of diseased rodents captured and destroyed increased, the number of human victims declined. During the last three months of 1907 the total of humans stricken was forty-four, thirty-four, and ten respectively. Throughout the first part of 1908 the decline continued, but at an accelerated pace. In January sixty-four infected rats were destroyed, and only four human cases were reported. In February the number of disease-carrying rodents increased to eighty-nine while only one person was stricken. The latter proved to be the plague's last victim. Nonetheless, the war of extermination continued. Only three infected rats were found in June, one each in July and August, and none in September and October. On November 1 it was officially announced that the plague had been eradicated, and the campaign came to an end.

Some idea of the magnitude of that operation may be gained from the following figures. To trap or poison the infected rats, four hundred paid workers, plus several times that number of volunteers, were recruited and remained in the field for the better part of a year. More than half a million buildings were inspected, of which 11,234 were disinfected and 1,713 destroyed. Six and a half million square feet of wooden sidewalks and floors of homes, stables, stores, and factories were torn up and replaced with concrete; 700,000 pieces of printed instructions were distributed, 14,608 traps were set out, and $12,375 was paid out to individuals who trapped rats and brought them to the health centers, for which they received a bounty of ten cents each.

Between September 24, 1907, and March 1, 1909, 160 San Franciscans were stricken with the disease; of that number 77 died.

The final report of the Citizens' Health Committee, which had over-all charge of the campaign, summed up its activities in these words:

That San Francisco made a new record in sanitation, that the plague ceased and no trace of it can now be found on this peninsula, are sufficient evidence that, with the help of the public, the Committee discharged the obligation placed upon it; for without that concerted action of the whole people . . . no such fortunate outcome would have been possible.

FASTEN THIS UP IN YOUR KITCHEN.

Citizens' Health Committee,
Headquarters, Room 1233 Merchants' Exchange.

TO GET RID OF RATS.

KITCHEN RULES.

Keep all supplies in rat-proof bins.
Keep meats in safes or in refrigerators.
Keep uncooked vegetables in crates on shelves. Never on the floor.

IF COOKING IS DONE WITH A COAL FIRE.

Burn in your kitchen fire all refuse (trimmings of meat, bones, parings of vegetables, egg shells, all platter and plate scrapings, and all waste food) as it occurs. This means the putting into the fire of small amounts at a time, when they will readily burn. This is known to be a practical method. By it there is no garbage.

IF COOKING IS DONE WITH A GAS FIRE.

Keep all garbage in covered metal cans.
Keep the cans closely covered.
Have the garbage removed at least twice a week.
Have scavenger carry your garbage can to his wagon.
Report all scavengers who do not do so.
Don't put garbage in slop hoppers.
Always clean up your own premises.
Throw no garbage into the street nor on vacant lots.
Admit authorized Health Inspectors to your premises. They are there for your benefit.
Tell your neighbors to do all the above—and see that they do.
Report to the Committee all cases of insanitary conditions.
These rules to be in force during the existence of plague and afterwards.

Here is one of 700,000 pieces of printed instructions issued by the Citizens' Health Committee during what has been called "the greatest rat hunt in history." Throughout the intensive, year-long campaign, 400 paid workers were in the field, plus numerous volunteers. So well did they do their work that the disease was eventually stamped out and, on November 1, 1908, the campaign ended.

X

Growing Pains

1. THE GRAFT TRIALS

The 1906 earthquake and fire created a variety of new problems and solved a number of old ones. Their effect on still others, however, was merely to force them temporarily into the background, from which they reappeared in aggravated form after the emergency had passed. Of such problems the most important by far was that of breaking the rule of the political machine that had gained control of the city government during the years before the fire and of forcing the bribe-taking officials from office.

The political situation as it existed on April 18, 1906, was outlined in Chapter VIII. Eugene E. Schmitz had been elected mayor on the Union Labor ticket in 1901, and re-elected in 1903 and 1905, each time by larger majorities. The election of 1905 put Abe Ruef, who had managed all three of Schmitz's campaigns, in complete control at the City Hall. Thereupon he — who until then had been content with relatively minor forms of extortion — branched out into more lucrative fields including the granting of special privileges to utility companies, for which he received "legal fees" of as much as $200,000.

The last-named sum was paid Ruef by the United Railroads, which operated most of the city streetcars, in return for his having obtained authorization from the Board of Supervisors for the company to abandon the underground cables on several of its lines and to substitute overhead trolley wires. This move was made in the face of opposition from many residents who wished to retain the traditional cable cars. Indignation over the supervisors' authorization was still strong when the 1906 fire caused it, along with other controversial issues of the day, to be forgotten.

But not for long. Early in May, the supervisors, again at Ruef's behest, granted the company permission to install overhead trolleys on all city car lines under its control. Ruef answered the protests that greeted this move by explaining that only by that means could streetcar service be restored within a reasonable time. This latest evidence of the Ruef-Schmitz group's disregard of the wishes of the majority so aroused the public that a meeting was called at which plans were laid to drive the politicians from office.

James D. Phelan   Fremont Older

That meeting marked the beginning of the celebrated "graft trials" that were to occupy the center of the stage in San Francisco for several years, and were being followed with interest in all parts of the nation. Among the leaders of the reform movement were James D. Phelan, the former mayor; Fremont Older, the editor of the *Evening Bulletin*; and Rudolph Spreckels, a wealthy businessman who became the chief financial backer of the prosecution forces.

As the first step in their campaign Fremont Older secretly visited Washington to enlist the support of President Roosevelt and, if possible, secure the services of Francis J. Heney as chief prosecutor. Heney, who had recently gained renown for his successful prosecution of timber fraud cases in Oregon, proved willing to undertake the assignment provided William J. Burns, a government investigator who had worked with him in Oregon, was also appointed. Older returned to San Francisco with word that President Roosevelt had agreed to release the two men from government duties for the duration of the investigation.

Thereupon District Attorney William L. Langdon, who had been working closely with the Phelan-Older-Spreckels group, announced his intention of asking the newly impaneled grand jury to indict the mayor and members of the Board of Supervisors on charges of bribery. When Ruef learned of this he countered with a bold move. Presumably on his orders Schmitz had fled to Europe while the investigation was getting under way, and had appointed James L. Gallagher, chairman of the Board of Supervisors, to serve as mayor during his absence. At Ruef's prompting, Gallagher issued an order removing Langdon from office and appointing Ruef in his place. Langdon challenged the legality of Gallagher's order and refused to give up the post until the matter had been passed on by the courts. A few days later Superior Judge James M. Seawell rendered a decision sustaining Langdon's position and barring Ruef from assuming the office. Langdon then named Heney assistant district attorney and put him in charge of the prosecution.

Early in November, 1906, Heney appeared before the grand jury and filed charges against Schmitz and Ruef. Ruef was accused with having solicited and received a bribe of $8,500 from the owners of a number of resorts frequented by prostitutes and other underworld characters, and euphemistically termed French restaurants. Heney contended that in return for the bribe, the owners had been granted licenses to operate for another year. On hearing the evidence the jury ordered the pair arrested and tried for extortion. Schmitz was still absent from the city and so was temporarily out of reach. Ruef, however, was arrested, posted bond in the amount of $50,000, and was released. Three months later the two men were brought into court; both entered pleas of not guilty.

"HE'S MINE."

"Tad" Dorgan's cartoon pictures Mayor Schmitz imprisoned in a cage shaped like the City Hall, with Boss Ruef holding the key. Such cartoons were part of the relentless campaign waged against the corrupt politicians by the *Bulletin* and the *Examiner*.

Meanwhile further evidence of corruption was brought to light. The Board of Supervisors then had under consideration an ordinance sharply increasing the license fees charged the owners of skating rinks and imposing burdensome restrictions on the conduct of their businesses. Such ordinances had been a money-making device frequently employed by the bribe-hungry supervisors; in this instance, however, the plan backfired. One owner, angered at the size of the fee the supervisors had demanded to withdraw the proposed ordinance, reported the matter to District Attorney Langdon. A meeting was arranged between the rink owner and three supervisors, during which the officials accepted the proffered bribe money, unaware that the transaction was observed by witnesses in an adjoining room. Using the trapped trio as a lever, the prosecutors set about trying to force confessions from the entire board. This they eventually accomplished, mainly by promising the bribe-takers that they would be leniently treated when they were brought to trial.

The confessions of the supervisors revealed the full extent of the ring's operations. Their testimony before the grand jury made clear that in addition to pay-offs from gamblers and brothel keepers, they had been exacting tribute from the owners of legitimate businesses, including several large public-service corporations. The customary procedure in all such cases was for Ruef to collect the pay-offs, and after taking his substantial cut to pass on the remainder to Supervisor Gallagher, who distributed it among his fellow members. In his confession Gallagher stated that the total amount he had received from Boss Ruef was $169,350, of which he had retained $27,275 for himself. How much Ruef profited by such deals was never determined; estimates made at the time fixed the sum at not less than $500,000.

2. END OF AN ERA

The revelations of the supervisors greatly widened the scope of the investigation. Until then the chief aim had been to break Ruef's political power and to force Schmitz and the other bribe-taking officials from office. The second of these objectives was speedily accomplished. On June 13, 1907, Schmitz was found guilty of extortion and sentenced to five years in prison. Following Schmitz's conviction, one of the discredited supervisors, Charles Boxton, served briefly as mayor, but a month later he too was forced from office and was succeeded by Edward Robeson Taylor. At the same time the remaining members of the old board resigned and were replaced by men of Taylor's selection.

This marked the end of one phase of the campaign. The graft trials, however, had hardly begun. For by then the aim of the prosecution was not only to expose and punish the bribe-takers, but also those who had tendered the bribes — including the so-called higher-ups who had been buying special privileges for the corporations they represented. Schmitz's conviction had been obtained largely on the testimony of his former confederate, Ruef. The latter had pleaded guilty of extortion on a promise that the prosecution — which felt that only by his testimony could the bribe-givers be convicted — would recommend to the court that he be granted amnesty. In the subsequent trials Ruef repudiated his promise to co-operate, and the immunity agreement was canceled.

Up to that joint the Langdon-Heney group had had comparatively smooth sailing. While they were exposing the rascality and greed of the City Hall politicians, public support had been virtually unanimous. However, when the investigation turned against those who had paid the bribes and benefited by them, some of that support began to drop away. For among the bribe-givers were men of standing and influence in the commercial and social life of the city, including officials of street-railroad, telephone, gas and electric utility companies, and other staid business enterprises. Hence, the remaining phases of the long-drawn-out litigation — the last cases were not disposed of until 1912, more than five years later — were conducted in an atmosphere of growing hostility.

Evidences of this changing attitude became apparent as early as 1907. As the municipal election of that year approached, several local newspapers withdrew their support of Mayor Taylor, District Attorney Langdon, and the rest of the reform ticket and backed the candidates of the Union Labor party. During the campaign much was made of the fact that the trials, which by then were being closely followed all over the country, were giving the city a bad name and hence were "hurting business." Nonetheless, Taylor and his fellows were re-elected — though by a narrow margin — and the trials continued.

The successful candidates began their new terms on January 8, 1908. On the following day the appellate court handed down a decision reversing the conviction of Schmitz. That decision, which was later confirmed by the State Supreme Court, also freed Ruef, who, like Schmitz, had been convicted of extortion.

Notwithstanding that set-back, the prosecution forces continued the fight. Ruef was rearrested and brought to trial on a new charge — that of bribing a supervisor to vote for a streetcar franchise. During Ruef's second trial Chief Prosecutor Heney was shot down in the courtroom by a prospective juror whom Heney had rejected because of a prior conviction on a felony charge. For a time Heney's injuries were believed to be fatal; however, he eventually recovered and resumed his duties. Meanwhile, his place was taken by a young attorney, Hiram Johnson, who was then at the beginning of his political career.

Heney's shooting revived public interest in the trials — which had begun to lag following Schmitz's release from jail — and temporarily silenced critics of the reform group. Ruef's second trial ended in his conviction, and he was sentenced to a fourteen-year term in San Quentin. The trials of the "higher-ups" then began. First on the list of alleged bribe-givers was a utility-company official, Louis Glass, vice president of the Pacific States Telephone Company. After lengthy hearings Glass was found guilty of having paid Ruef a bribe on behalf of his company in return for favorable legislation by the supervisors and was sentenced to five years in prison. (Glass' conviction was later set aside by the State Supreme Court, "on grounds so technical that the man in the street made no pretense at understanding the tortured reasoning.")

Next to be tried were officials of the United Railroads. This time the prosecution's efforts were less successful. Tirey L. Ford, the company's chief counsel and the man accused of having paid the bribe money, was tried on three separate counts. On the first count the jury failed to agree, and on the second and third they returned verdicts of not guilty. Attempts to convict Ford's superior, Patrick Calhoun, president of the railroad company, fared no better. During Calhoun's protracted trial his staff of attorneys, which included a number of eminent legal lights of the day, resorted to a wide variety of devices in order to hamper the prosecution. Key witnesses were spirited out of the state; others refused to testify; documents introduced as evidence mysteriously disappeared, and several jurors told of pressure being brought to bear on them to influence their votes. The five-month-long trial ended in a hung jury, and the charges were dismissed.

Undeterred, the prosecution moved for a retrial, and the wearisome process of selecting a new jury got under way. This was still in progress when the municipal election of 1909 was held. District Attorney Langdon had refused to run again, and Heney was chosen as the reform party's candidate for the office. As had happened two years earlier, the chief issue of the campaign was the question of whether the graft trials should continue. The 1909 election was the first to be held under the state's new direct primary law. Three parties — the Republicans, Democrats, and Union Labor party — all had candidates in the field. For the mayoralty the Republicans nominated William W. Crocker; the Democrats, T. B. W. Leland; and the Union Labor party P. H. McCarthy. Heney, candidate for district attorney, had received the endorsement of the Democrats only; his opponent, Charles M. Fickert, was supported by both the Republican and Union Labor organizations. McCarthy and Fickert were elected.

✦   ✦   ✦

The defeat of Heney marked the virtual end of the graft trials. Although some months passed before the last of the indictments were dismissed, no attempt was made to bring the remaining defendants to trial. During the nearly five years since the Phelan-Spreckels-Older group had launched their campaign public sentiment had changed radically. In the beginning the cleanup movement had the support of all segments of the population save only those who stood to benefit by maintaining the status quo. Church groups, civic clubs, and associations of business and professional men had passed resolutions endorsing the campaign and pledging their support. So, too, had the leading daily newspapers and all but one or two of the local weeklies.

By 1909, however, the man on the street had become tired of reading about the endless courtroom battles. The feeling grew that to continue the trials would be a futile waste of public funds. One by one the newspapers withdrew their support, leaving only the *Bulletin* to continue the fight.

But notwithstanding the limited success of its efforts to punish the wrongdoers — for of all those convicted of giving or accepting bribes only Ruef was sent to prison — the graft prosecution should not be considered a failure. Ruef's political machine was permanently broken up, and the venal city officials had been forced from office. Thereafter, those doing business with the city were not obliged to pay tribute to a grasping boss. Moreover, the law-abiding citizens had been shaken from their complacency by the revelations of widespread corruption and made to realize that only by constant vigilance on their part could the city be prevented from again falling into the hands of bribe-hungry politicians.

The administration of Mayor Taylor and his fellow officials, covering the years 1907-1909, had marked the beginning of the city's regeneration. When in 1910 the Union Labor candidate, P. H. McCarthy, succeeded Taylor, some quarters feared that this meant a return to boss rule. One of McCarthy's campaign promises had been to make San Francisco "the Paris of America." This proved to be shrewd politics, for the public, weary of the austerities of the reconstruction period, welcomed the prospect of a return to the light-hearted gaiety that had long been a characteristic of the city. But many came to realize that what the new mayor and some of his backers had in mind was a return to the practices of the era before the fire when gambling, prostitution, and other rackets had flourished virtually without hindrance. Although the public was in favor of preserving those qualities that had given the earlier town its charm, it was in no mood to incorporate into the new San Francisco the worst features of the old.

The task of rebuilding their ruined metropolis had awakened in the residents a sense of civic pride. The 1906 disaster had marked a major turning point in the city's evolution, and those who had been through the ordeal were able to look back on the earlier period with some degree of objectivity. Many of its characteristics they were determined to preserve: its variety and color, the carefree spirit of its people, its picturesque foreign quarters, its traditional fêtes and celebrations, its theaters, restaurants, bars and hotels, and other adjuncts to gracious, convivial living. But they also felt that the new city had no longer a place for those manifestations of organized vice that had long been tolerated there, as in other world seaports. McCarthy's attempt to reintroduce them when he became mayor in 1909 contributed to the defeat of his administration two years later.

3. WATER FROM THE SIERRA

With the municipal election of 1911 San Francisco politics entered a period of tranquility that was in marked contrast to the tumult and contention of the previous decade. In McCarthy's bid for a second term he was defeated, his successful rival being James Rolph, Jr., who polled 47,427 votes to the other's 27,067. Rolph had based his campaign on a promise to clean up the city's two main trouble spots, the Barbary Coast and the "uptown tenderloin." The first was a street of dance halls, bars, and like resorts frequented mainly by visiting seamen; the second, which centered on Turk, Eddy, and Ellis streets, west of Powell, was the haunt of pickpockets, street-walkers, and other underworld characters.

The new mayor lost no time carrying out his promise to rid San Francisco of the criminal element; at the same time, however, he resisted pressure from those who insisted that the laws be enforced so rigidly as to make the city a completely "closed town." Rolph's policy of closely supervising the resorts on the Barbary Coast and elsewhere rather than shutting them down entirely was evidently acceptable to most residents, since they returned him to office for nine consecutive terms. It was not until his election as governor of California in 1931 that "Sunny Jim", as he was called, finally relinquished the office he had held for nearly two decades.

At the time of Rolph's first election, nearly six years had passed since the earthquake and fire of 1906. By then the enormous task of reconstruction had been almost completed. The more than five hundred square blocks of the burned area — which many believed would remain scarred and battered for years to come — had been so thoroughly rebuilt that only here and there could any trace of the disaster be seen. In addition to private capital and private enterprise, which had been replacing thousands of residences and hundreds of stores, office buildings, and factories, the city had been carrying on a far-reaching rehabilitation program. Virtually all public buildings had been heavily damaged, and many were completely destroyed. The latter included the City Hall and Hall of Records in the Civic Center, the city jail and hospital, as well as firehouses, police stations, schools, and other facilities throughout the city.

The work of replacing the destroyed buildings with temporary structures so the city could resume its normal functions was looked on as an emergency measure and was carried through as rapidly as possible. Meanwhile plans were being laid to meet future needs. The aim of the planners was not only to restore the damaged buildings but eventually to replace them with facilities appropriate to the handsome new city they visualized. The consequence of this movement was that by the time Mayor Rolph had completed his first term, the city was well embarked on a large-scale public-works building program.

San Franciscans of the day recognized that if their city were to grow and prosper one major problem would have to be solved: a supply of water, sufficient in quantity and quality to meet present and future needs, must be found. This problem had existed ever since the first settlements had been established on the peninsula — for in the San Francisco area rain rarely falls during eight months of the year. In the days before the gold rush the villagers had depended on several springs adjacent to the cove, the largest of which was in a depression called Mill Valley, near the present intersection of Powell and Washington streets. But the flow from these springs was so small that ships visiting the harbor usually had to cross to the Marin shore to refill their water casks.

The arrival of the first gold hunters in 1848 had made it evident that new sources of supply had to be found. For a time water was brought in barges from springs near Richardson's Bay and retailed at dockside for as much as $1 per bucket. In 1849 two water companies were formed. One got its supply from Lobos Creek, several miles to the west, and brought it into the town in a series of open ditches and wooden flumes. These were only temporary measures, however, for as the population continued to grow, the demand usually exceeded the supply, and rationing had to be imposed. The next step was to dam the streams of the lower peninsula to form artificial lakes from which water was pumped to reservoirs in the city. As time passed, these sources, too, proved inadequate. In the late 1880s two pipe lines were laid beneath the southern end of the bay to carry water from the Alameda Creek watershed into the peninsula lakes. During the next two decades other streams on both sides of the bay were tied into the system. By 1910, however, the city's water consumption, which then amounted to forty million gallons a day, was again taxing existing facilities to the limit. Moreover, no other major source of supply was available within many miles of the city.

Long before 1910 it was obvious to those responsible for maintaining the city's water supply what the ultimate solution to this perennial problem would have to be. In 1901 Mayor Phelan had appointed a committee of engineers to make a survey of the Sierra Nevada range — which at its nearest point lies 150 miles to the east — and choose a spot from which mountain water could be piped to the city. The committee's choice fell to the watershed of the Tuolumne River, which is within the boundaries of Yosemite National Park. Phelan thereupon applied to the Interior Department for permission to build dams, reservoirs, and other facilities on two tributaries of the Tuolumne at a point twenty miles north of the Yosemite Valley.

When this plan was announced, strong opposition developed from two directions. Spokesmen from organizations of mountaineers denounced the "desecration" of the natural beauties of the region, and farmers of the San

Joaquin Valley protested that the waters of the Tuolumne were needed to irrigate their orchards, vineyards, and fields. These two groups mustered enough strength at Washington to delay the beginning of the project for more than a decade. In 1908 Secretary of the Interior R. A. Ballinger ordered Mayor Taylor to furnish proof that water from the Sierra was vital to the city's future. The following year President Taft appointed a board of Army Engineers to make a thorough study of the matter; the board's report upheld the city's claim and recommended that its request be granted. This, however, served only to increase opposition to the project and to force a further delay. In December, 1912, a group of city officials went to Washington and conferred with Walter A. Fisher, President Taft's new Secretary of the Interior, in an attempt to break the deadlock. When their mission failed, the city carried its plea to Congress. The enabling legislation, called the Riker Act, was introduced early in 1913. After prolonged hearings, and in the face of determined opposition, the bill was passed by both houses. It received President Wilson's signature on December 19.

Meanwhile, plans to start work on this project, by far the largest publicly financed enterprise the city had yet undertaken, were well advanced. In January, 1910, the voters had approved by a margin of 20 to 1 a bond issue of $45,000,000 to get the project under way. Between 1914 and 1917 much preliminary work was done. A 70-mile-long railroad was built into the mountains from the floor of the San Joaquin Valley, over which workers, materials, and equipment were carried to the sites of the future dams and reservoirs. The floors of the reservoirs were cleared, tunnels were bored to divert the mountain streams from their beds while the foundations of the dams were laid, and the route of the 156-mile aqueduct that would carry the water to the distant city was surveyed and right-of-way privileges secured.

That was the status of the project when, in April, 1917, the United States entered World War I. During the next eighteen months work on this project — along with work on many other public projects not connected with the war effort — was suspended. But with the coming of peace, building operations were resumed — and continued with scarcely a pause for close to half a century.

Some of the high points of that complex operation are described in the next chapter.

4. THE "MUNI" RAILWAY

One provision of the new charter adopted by the voters in 1900 committed the city to a policy of municipal ownership of public utilities. The campaign for a city-owned water system was in keeping with that policy. Another civic project that had long been advocated — and which, like the Sierra water plan, was accomplished only after years of effort — was that of a city-owned and -operated street railway system.

The need for a unified system of public transportation had been recognized for several decades. Since the early 1870s half a dozen privately owned companies had been operating the cable and horse-drawn cars, each competing with the others for a share of the public patronage. The earnings of such concerns were small and, as time passed, the quality of their service steadily deteriorated. This state of affairs eventually led to a proposal that the city take over the various companies, replace their uneven tracks and outmoded rolling stock, and, having consolidated them into a single system, introduce universal tranfer privileges.

The initial step in that plan — which was to make San Francisco the first American city to operate its own street transportation system—was taken in November of 1911. That year the voters approved a bond issue to buy the Geary Street Railroad, one of the city's busiest lines. During most of 1912 service was suspended while the roadbed was reconstructed, the under-

A municipally owned and operated streetcar system had long been advocated by the citizens. This view, taken from the corner of Geary and Powell streets, shows part of the crowds that greeted the inauguration of service on the Geary Street line on December 28, 1912. *(Roy D. Graves.)*

ground cables replaced by trolleys, and electric cars of the latest design built. When this first unit of the Muni system began functioning on December 28, 1912, it extended from Thirty-ninth Avenue on the west to the downtown terminus at Kearny and Market streets.

The goal of placing the entire system under city ownership was eventually realized, though progress was tantalizingly slow. In 1913 a second bond issue, this one for $3,500,000, was approved. Its purpose was to extend the Geary Street line from Thirty-ninth Avenue to the Ocean, and to provide improved service to the Marina District, where an exposition honoring the completion of the Panama Canal was then building. Meanwhile, efforts to buy out the United Railroads, the company that operated most of the other lines, had been stalled because of a failure to agree on the purchase price. When negotiations for the use by the municipal cars of the United Railroad Company's tracks on Market Street likewise failed, the city laid parallel tracks the entire length of that thoroughfare. For a number of years thereafter the cars of the competing lines thundered down the busy street, two abreast.

The need to provide better service to outlying parts of the city, and in particular to the fast-growing Richmond and Sunset districts and the area on the far side of Twin Peaks, was the main reason for the growth of the municipal system during the next two decades. To serve those living west of Twin Peaks, the two-and-a-quarter-mile Twin Peaks Tunnel was built. Completed in 1917 at a cost of $4,500,000, the tunnel reduced the time of transit to and from the city's center from one hour to twenty-five minutes, and thereby hastened the development of several new residential districts in that area. Later the flow of traffic was speeded by building other tunnels under the city's hills. Some, like that under Twin Peaks, were exclusively for the use of streetcars; others, including the Stockton Street and Broadway tunnels, were also for pedestrians and automobiles.

Over the years the municipal system was extended as the remaining privately owned lines were taken over one by one, some by purchase and others when their franchises expired. It was not until 1952, however, that the last of this group, the long-established California Street Cable Railroad Company, was acquired, and the entire system came under city control.

One civic project that was widely discussed during the years just before 1906 was the so-called Burnham Plan. As mentioned earlier, when this ambitious scheme for the beautification of the city was first presented, it was rejected as too costly. During the first weeks after the fire the plan was again put forward by its sponsors, and was once more rejected, this time because to put it into effect would have caused many months of delay.

But the years of discussion of Burnham's grandiose conception had not been entirely wasted. For it had brought the citizens to an awareness of the

The City Hall, completed in 1915, occupies the two blocks bounded by Van Ness Avenue, McAllister, Polk, and Grove streets. Designed by Arthur Brown, Jr. and John Bakewell, Jr., it has come to be recognized as one of the most successful examples of classic architecture in the country. This view across the courtyard between the Municipal Opera House and the Veterans Memorial Building shows the City Hall's Van Ness Avenue entrance and the 308-foot dome. (*Redwood Empire Association.*)

city's shortcomings from the standpoints of beauty and convenience. The result was that when in later years other less sweeping plans were proposed they received sympathetic hearings. Thus, in 1912, when an $8,000,000 bond issue to finance the first units of the new Civic Center was submitted to the voters, it was approved by more than the necessary two-thirds majority.

This ambitious project, which its sponsors described as "a monument to the city's cultural tradition, its achievements in democratic government, and its proud position among the commercial centers of the nation," had been in the planning stages since the beginning of the reconstruction period six years earlier. The site selected included that of the ruined City Hall and Hall of Records, as well as most of the area bounded on the north by Golden Gate Avenue, by Hayes Street on the south, and on the east and west by Market and Franklin streets.

The focal point of the entire scheme was the Civic Center Plaza, which occupied the four city blocks facing McAllister, Grove, Polk, and Larkin streets. About its sides eventually arose an impressive group of city, state, and federal buildings. First to be built was the present City Hall, which was completed in 1915 at a cost of $3,500,000. Designed by architects John Bakewell and Arthur Brown, Jr., this handsome four-story building, faced with California granite, occupies two city blocks. Its most striking feature is a lofty 308-foot dome which — as the city's exuberant mayor, "Sunny Jim" Rolph, delighted to point out to visitors — is 16 feet, 3 inches higher than that of the Capitol at Washington.

One of the impr
group of buil
fronting on the
Center Plaza, th
Francisco Publ
brary stands o
southeast corn
Larkin and McA
streets. It wa
signed by Geor
Kelham and co
ed in February,
Besides the ma
brary, there are
twenty-five bra
(*Redwood Emp*
sociation.)

The Exposition Auditorium, which faces the plaza on the south, was also completed in 1915. Its opening coincided with that of the Panama Pacific International Exposition, and its three connecting halls, with a combined seating capacity of 15,000, have since then been the scene of many notable public gatherings.

Third of the group facing the plaza is the Public Library, which occupies part of the site of the City Hall of pre-fire days; that is, the block bounded by Larkin, Fulton, Hyde, and McAllister streets. Built in a style that harmonizes with other buildings of the group, and like them faced with California granite, the Library was completed in 1917 at a cost of $1,000,000.

The block-long California State Building faces the plaza from the McAllister Street side. It was completed in 1926. Ten years later the Federal Office Building, containing 422 rooms and costing $3,000,000, was put up on the block bounded by Hyde, Fulton, McAllister, and Leavenworth streets.

Over the years further additions have been made to the Civic Center group. Among the most important are the Opera House and the Veterans' Memorial Building, which face the City Hall from the west side of Van Ness Avenue and are separated by a memorial court. The Opera House, the only municipally owned structure of its kind in the country, was completed in 1932. It was there that, on June 26, 1945, representatives of fifty countries signed the charter of the United Nations. The Veterans' Memorial Building, dedicated to those San Franciscans who served in World War I and in earlier wars, provides a meeting place for local veterans' organizations and, on the upper floor, houses the San Francisco Museum of Art, one of three major art galleries maintained by the city.

More recent additions to the complex of buildings housing departments of the city, state, or national governments that have been put up on or adjacent to the original Civic Center include an eight-story wing to the California State Building facing on Golden Gate Avenue, which dates from 1958, and a twenty-two-story, block-square Federal Office Building fronting on Golden Gate Avenue, Turk, Polk, and Larkin streets. At the time of its completion in 1965 it was the largest office building on the Pacific Coast.

5. "THE EVANESCENT CITY"

Yet another civic enterprise, delayed — but not abandoned — because of the 1906 fire, was a plan to sponsor a world's fair to commemorate the completion of the Panama Canal. By January of 1906 preparations for that event were so far advanced that Congress had been asked to pass a bill naming San Francisco the official exposition city and appropriating $5,000,000 of federal funds to help finance its building. The bill was still pending three months later when the events of April 18 forced it into the discard.

But not for long. Early in 1907 a group of leading citizens formed a non-profit corporation called the Pacific Ocean Exposition Company, and during the next several years the interrupted plans again moved forward. In December, 1909, the organization's name was changed to the Panama Pacific International Exposition Company. Then, on April 18, 1910 — the fourth anniversary of the fire — a city-wide fund-raising meeting was held at which San Franciscans registered their support of the venture by subscribing to more than $4,000,000 of exposition bonds.

Meanwhile, several other cities were vying for the honor of celebrating the opening of the canal, and a spirited rivalry developed as each sought the endorsement and financial support of the federal government. The choice eventually narrowed to two cities, San Francisco and New Orleans. In preparation for the meeting at Washington at which the choice would be made, San Franciscans strengthened their bargaining position by voting the exposition company $5,000,000 in city funds and by securing a pledge of the same amount from the State Legislature. This assurance of ample financing decided the issue. On January 31, 1911, Congress passed a resolution naming San Francisco the exposition city and asking President Taft to invite the nations of the world to participate.

Meanwhile the question of where the fair should be built had been much debated. Several locations were considered, among them the Golden Gate Park, the Presidio, and an area of unimproved tidelands on the bay front between Fort Mason and the Golden Gate. The last-named place was eventually chosen, and the work of preparing the 635-acre site began. This formidable task required the building of a sea wall parallel to the shore, then filling the enclosed area with sand pumped from the bottom of the bay, and finally adding a three-foot-deep layer of topsoil over the entire area.

The filling-in process started early in 1912 and was completed eighteen months later. Meanwhile, scores of architects, engineers, painters, sculptors,

The Panama Pacific International Exposition, commemorating
the completion of the Panama Canal, was held in San Francisco
in 1915. Despite the war then raging in Europe, the fair was both
an artistic and financial success, drawing close to 20 million
visitors. The 432-foot Tower of Jewels, at the right, was the dominant architectural feature.

and landscape gardeners had been preparing plans for the building and
ornamentation of what has come to be considered one of the most impressive
and artistically successful world's fairs. The ten main exhibit palaces were
built in the form of a huge rectangle opening onto a series of courtyards.
Machinery Hall, which covered more than eight acres of floor space, occupied one end of the rectangle, and the Palace of Fine Arts the other. Midway
in this group, and dominating the whole, stood the 435-foot Tower of Jewels.
Buildings housing the exhibits of twenty-nine states and twenty-five foreign
nations were grouped to the west of the Palace of Fine Arts. Beyond were
the agricultural and livestock exhibits, a race track, a stadium, and — what
at the time was still a novelty — an airfield. The amusement area, called The
Zone, was at the eastern end of the grounds — a seven-block-long boardwalk
extending from Van Ness Avenue to Fillmore Street, lined with attractions
ranging from refreshment booths, curio shops, and roller coasters to an
elaborate working model of the canal itself.

While the city was preparing to play host to the world in 1915, war
broke out in Europe. Many feared that this would cause a sharp drop in
attendance, and the possibility of postponing the opening until after the

war was seriously considered; however, the fair was so far advanced that it was decided to open it as scheduled on February 20, 1915. As it happened, this proved to be a wise decision. Although several European nations withdrew and others reduced the size of their exhibits, still others carried out their original plans. One of the latter was France. Notwithstanding the fact that Paris was so seriously threatened that the civilian government had fled to Bordeaux, the handsome French Building—a replica of the Palais de la Légion d'Honneur—was completed and a shipload of paintings, sculpture, and other arts and crafts of the hard-pressed homeland were put on display there.

During the eight and a half months the exposition remained open 18,756,148 visitors passed through its gates. It closed for the last time on the night of December 4, 1915, whereupon the work of demolishing the buildings and tearing up the gardens and courtyards began. After the site had been cleared, streets were laid out; during the next few years the area was solidly built up with the apartment houses, shops, and single-family dwellings that comprise the present Marina District.

Three features of the exposition have been preserved: the Auditorium in the Civic Center downtown and, on the former grounds, the Yacht Harbor and the Palace of Fine Arts. Nearly fifty years later the impressive but fast deteriorating Palace of Fine Arts was in the process of being rebuilt of permanent materials thereby making it a lasting reminder of what one of San Francisco's favorite poets, George Sterling, called "The Evanescent City."

6. MOONEY AND BILLINGS

During the months between the close of the 1915 exposition and this country's entry into World War I the labor troubles that had plagued the city for more than half a century started again, and in aggravated form. In the numerous strikes of that period—of the longshoremen in June, 1916, followed closely by that of the culinary trades, tugboat crewmen, and structural steel workers—the battle lines between workers and employers were sharply drawn, and both sides prepared for yet another test of strength.

At a meeting of employer groups on July 10, 1916, an organization called the Law and Order Committee was formed. It announced as its purpose the bringing of permanent industrial peace to the strife-torn city. One of the first moves of the committee was to adopt an open-shop policy in all trades where the workers were on strike, and to replace their striking employees with nonunion workers. This decision was challenged by the organized workers and their partisans, whose resentment was further increased when the Board of Supervisors adopted an ordinance prohibiting the picketing of businesses where strikebreakers were employed.

During this period of acute industrial unrest an event took place that profoundly shocked the city. Because of the war in Europe and the likelihood that this country would eventually become involved, a campaign to make the nation militarily strong had for some time been in progress. In California and elsewhere, however, a small but vocal minority had bitterly opposed the rearmament program, terming it a device by which the "warmongers" planned to lead the country into war. When plans for a massive Preparedness Day parade on July 22, 1916, were first announced, those in charge of the arrangements were warned that violence might result. The warnings were disregarded; the parade was held on schedule, and as the miles-long column was passing up Market Street a bomb exploded among the sidewalk crowd near the Ferry Building. Six persons were killed outright, three subsequently died, and upwards of fifty were injured.

San Franciscans of all shades of political belief were deeply stirred by the tragedy. Four days later six thousand gathered at the Civic Auditorium and pledged themselves to the "relentless pursuit" of those responsible. City, state, and federal law-enforcement agencies joined in a concerted manhunt. From the first, suspicion was directed toward those who had made no secret of their opposition to the rearmament program. Two days before the bombing, this group had held a protest meeting in a downtown hall, at which speakers had denounced those sponsoring the parade and demanded that it be canceled.

Among the first suspects to be arrested were two men closely identified with the militant wing of the labor movement: Thomas J. "Tom" Mooney and Warren K. Billings. Both had previously been tried for sabotage— Mooney for dynamiting transmission towers during a strike of electrical workers, and Billings for the unlawful possession of explosives. Mooney had been acquitted of the charge, but Billings had ben sentenced to two years in prison, from which he had only recently been released.

Two long and bitterly contested trials followed. In September, 1916, Billings was convicted of second-degree murder and given a life sentence. The following February, Mooney was found guilty of first-degree murder and sentenced to be hanged.

At the time, few doubted the justice of the verdicts, for evidence presented at the trials seemed to leave no doubt of the guilt of the accused. However, evidence was later uncovered that shook the public's belief in the fairness of the trial. Photographs were produced that placed Mooney not near the scene of the explosion—as several witnesses had testified—but on a rooftop several blocks distant. Serious doubts were cast, too, on the testimony of other prosecution witnesses. As a result of these and other revelations, many came to believe that the two were innocent.

As time passed, the Mooney case ceased to be a matter of purely local concern and was attracting wide attention both in this country and abroad.

While Mooney was being held at San Quentin while the date of his execution was fixed a campaign was launched to secure his release, or, failing that, to have his sentence reduced to life imprisonment. The matter hung fire for more than a year, while interest in the case grew from month to month. Then, in November, 1918, at the urging of President Wilson (who based his plea in part on the ground that "the case has assumed international importance"), Governor William D. Stephens reduced Mooney's sentence to life imprisonment.

During the years that followed, Mooney and Billings—the one at San Quentin and the other at Folsom—became to many symbols of injustice on the part of enemies of the labor movement, and thus wielded considerable influence in the political life of the city and state. Finally, in January, 1939, nearly a quarter century after Mooney's arrest, Governor Culbert Olson, in fulfillment of a campaign pledge, granted the aging prisoner his unconditional release. Once freed, his importance as a symbol of labor's martyrdom rapidly faded; he died in 1942, virtually forgotten. Later in 1939 Billings—who as a "two-time loser" was not eligible for a full pardon —was given his freedom on parole; he, too, quickly disappeared from the public view.

During World War I and for some time thereafter a temporary truce marked the relations between management and labor. But the animosities built up during years of contention still smoldered beneath the surface and needed only the hard times that followed the stock market crash in 1929 to break out again in all their former vehemence. Thus during the early and middle 1930s the city was kept in intermittent turmoil by a new series of strikes.

In the spring of 1934 members of the International Longshoremen's Association, led by Australian-born Harry Bridges, walked off the docks following the rejection of their demand for higher wages and better working conditions. Other unions presently joined the strike, completely tying up the waterfront, and when the employer groups sought to break the embargo by bringing in non-union workers the Embarcadero became the scene of almost daily pitched battles.

These reached a climax on July 5—"Bloody Thursday"—when a clash between police and strikers resulted in two deaths and more than a hundred injuries. This in turn brought on a general strike in which an estimated 140,000 union members took part and which for three days all but paralyzed the city. Finally, some three months after the original walk-out, the employers and union leaders agreed to mediate their differences, and in October the longshoremen, having gained most of their objectives, returned to work and an uneasy peace was restored.

XI

The Twenties, Thirties and Forties

1. EXPANSION

San Francisco's role in World War I was a repetition, though on a much larger scale, of the part it played during the war with Spain nearly two decades earlier. Throughout the two emergencies peacetime activities were curtailed as many of the city's industrial plants and a major share of its shipping facilities were diverted to wartime uses. On the bay front shipbuilding plants were enlarged and new yards established to help meet the need for combat craft and for ships to carry men and supplies to the fighting zones. For many months crews of shipbuilders and dock hands worked twenty-four hours a day, seven days a week. At the same time factories and mills were busy producing food, munitions, and other essentials for the armed forces at home and abroad.

Under the provisions of the Selective Military Conscription Bill, which was signed by President Wilson on May 18, 1917, 11,256 San Franciscans were inducted into the Army; in addition, thousands of volunteers joined the Navy, Air Corps, or other branches of the service. The establishment of Camp Fremont on the peninsula and the quartering of thousands of recruits at the Presidio and on Yerba Buena and Angel islands, added to the wartime atmosphere of the city. Soldiers and sailors on leave crowded the downtown streets, particularly on weekends. Volunteer groups were formed to aid in feeding, housing, and entertaining them. In addition to these activities, San Franciscans gave liberal support to successive war-bond drives and to fund-raising campaigns of the Red Cross, Y.M.C.A., and other welfare agencies.

Workers needed to man the shipyards and other war-stimulated industries were drawn to the city in such numbers as to overtax existing facilities. The result was an acute shortage of housing, as well as overcrowded restaurants, shops, streetcars, and places of amusement. In the spring of 1918 the situation was further complicated by an outbreak of influenza which claimed many victims. In an effort to control the infection, all who appeared in public places were required to wear "flu masks" covering the nose and mouth. Perhaps because of that precaution, San Francisco suffered less from the outbreak than other American cities. Nonetheless, during the height of the epidemic so many were incapacitated that the war effort was seriously slowed down.

The signing of the armistice on November 11, 1918, set off a spontaneous celebration that lasted all day and most of the night. Other concerns were forgotten as workers poured from the downtown buildings and formed impromptu parades through the streets. Church bells rang, factory whistles blew, cannon boomed from the Presidio and from ships in the bay, and thousands of servicemen were given leave and joined the merrymakers. In the months that followed, several hardly less tumultuous celebrations greeted California contingents returning from the fighting fronts.

World War I brought about two changes that years of effort on the part of local reform groups had failed to accomplish—the revocation of the licenses of the Barbary Coast dance halls and the final end of legalized prostitution. Both steps were made possible by the enactment in 1917 of a state red-light abatement law.

News of the passage by Congress in December, 1917, of the Eighteenth (Prohibition) Amendment, was received with a marked lack of enthusiasm in San Francisco, where the freedom of the individual had been a tradition since gold-rush days. During the years the act remained on the statute books attempts to enforce its provisions were even less successful in San Francisco than in other parts of the country.

*   *   *

Notwithstanding recurrent labor troubles, a highly unstable economy due to the fighting in Europe, and the almost complete suspension of civilian building during the nineteen months of this country's participation in World War I, the decade ending in 1920 brought great material progress. The city's population increased from 416,912 in 1910 to 506,676 ten years later. This rise of more than twenty per cent was mainly caused by thousands of workers drawn to the city during the war years, who chose to remain permanently. To these were added numerous members of the armed forces who had been stationed in or near the city, and who elected to return after the fighting was over.

The rapid growth of population, plus the general prosperity of the postwar years, was reflected in many ways. Through the early and middle 1920s building operations were on a scale not known since the years following the 1906 fire. On California, Montgomery, and other streets of the financial district a group of imposing new office buildings arose, most of them replacing temporary structures put up during the reconstruction period. In the retail shopping area centering on Union Square and along Market Street from Third to Eighth Street, the number and size of hotels, stores, restaurants, and motion picture houses increased year by year.

This is the third of the city's three mints. The first, built in 1854, was supplanted in 1873 by the "Old Mint" that still stands at the southwest corner of Fifth and Mission streets. It served until 1937 when it was succeeded by the building pictured here.

Meanwhile the main industrial district, which had long been confined to the area fronting on the bay between Market Street and Hunters Point, had been solidly built up, and as more space was needed new plants were established farther down the peninsula, most of them beyond the city's southern boundary.

In the Richmond and Sunset districts many acres of formerly barren sand hills were covered with long rows of almost identical cottages, each with a lawn in front and with garage doors beneath the livingroom bay window. To serve these growing residential districts streetcar and bus lines were extended and schools, parks, and shopping centers built. In the South of Market district new streets were cut into the steep Potrero and outer Mission hillsides, where each year the upper tiers of houses climbed closer toward their crests. The completion of the Twin Peaks Tunnel in 1917 had opened a large area of unimproved land in the southwestern part of the city, and during the next decade several hundred acres of former cow pastures and vegetable gardens were transformed into attractive new residential districts.

While the built-up area was spreading toward the west, south, and east, changes were taking place in the older districts closer to the city's center. On Jackson Street, Broadway, Pacific Avenue, and other streets of Pacific Heights, the large wooden mansions built during the period when domestic servants were plentiful and cheap were torn down and replaced by apartment houses, flats, and single-family dwellings.

Yet another project initiated and carried through during the first decades of the century was the removal of the bodies from the early-day cemeteries in the western part of the city and using the land for residential and commercial purposes. This task was accomplished only after a long struggle and in the face of spirited opposition by many old-time San Franciscans. For all four burial grounds—Laurel Hill, Calvary, and those of the Odd Fellows and the Masons—dated from the 1850s, and in them were buried many who had been prominent in the business and political life of the early city. The Laurel Hill, or as it was originally called, the Lone Mountain Cemetery, which fronted on Presidio Avenue from California Street to Geary, was the oldest and best known of that group. When in 1912 the Board of Supervisors ordered all cemeteries within the city limits vacated, the protests were so numerous that Laurel Hill was temporarily spared. Not until 1937, a quarter-century later, was it closed, its ornate stone monuments and massive vaults razed, and the bodies transferred to a new burial ground on the peninsula.

Throughout the active postwar period city-sponsored enterprises kept pace with those financed by private capital. Mention has been made of three major public-works projects that got under way in the early 1900s: the new Civic Center, the beginning of the municipal water system, and the building of the first city-owned streetcar lines. As we have seen, the Municipal Railway began operating in 1912 when the city took over the old Geary Street cable line. Over the years the system was steadily extended: by the purchase of privately owned companies and by laying tracks to serve newly settled districts about the city's perimeter. From the beginning the "Muni" has been operated on the principle of service rather than profit and it therefore has received annual subsidies from city funds. To keep the yearly deficits within bounds, passenger fares have been increased from time to time. When service began in 1912 the fare was five cents. This was increased to seven cents in 1944, to ten cents (or three trips for twenty-five cents) in 1946, to a straight ten cents in 1949, and to fifteen cents in 1952. The total number of passengers carried during 1964 was 203,312,521.

2. HETCH HETCHY

In 1919 the award of a contract for building the 430-foot-high O'Shaughnessy Dam across Hetch Hetchy Canyon in the high Sierra marked the beginning of the second phase of San Francisco's program of municipal ownership of public utilities — the procurement of a supply of water adequate for the city's current and future needs.

The preliminary phases of that complex and costly enterprise, including the ultimately successful struggle to gain permission for the use of water from federal lands in the Yosemite National Park, have been outlined in Chapter X. After these matters were settled, work began on other phases of the project. The next step was the construction of an aqueduct that would convey the water from the mountains and across the intervening foothills and valleys to the distant city. The magnitude of that operation is illustrated by the fact that the water, during its passage from the Sierra reservoirs to San Francisco, travels more than 150 miles, dropping from an altitude of 3,800 feet at its source to below sea level at the point where the aqueduct passes beneath the southern arm of San Francisco Bay. At no point in its passage does the water flow in open canals. It is brought down from the mountains through a series of tunnels. From the Oakdale portal at the base of the Sierra it is conveyed in underground conduits across the San Joaquin Valley. It then enters a 25-mile-long tunnel through the Coast Range mountains, dips beneath the lower bay, and empties into a series of lakes on the lower San Francisco Peninsula. From that point it is pumped as needed into reservoirs within the city itself.

The size and complexity of the operation made it both costly and time-consuming. It was not until 1934 — more than a third of a century after application for the use of Sierra water was first made to the federal government — that water began flowing into the city's distribution system. Up to that time the voters had approved water bonds in the amount of $89,600,000. That, however, was only a beginning. In the years that followed an almost continuous expansion of facilities was necessary to keep pace with the needs of the growing population of the communities served. Between 1930 and 1960 the amount of water consumed rose from 52,000,000 to 168,000,000 gallons daily. During the same period the city's capital investment in its water system and in the generation of hydroelectric power — which from the beginning has been a related activity — increased from $89,600,000 to $277,000,000, or, if bond interest payments are included, to more than $400,000,000.

In 1961 it became evident that the needs of the consumers would soon exceed the system's capacity, which then was 180,000,000 gallons daily. Accordingly, plans were made for another major expansion of facilities. In October of that year the voters approved a bond issue of $115,000,000 — until then the largest in the city's history — for that purpose. The work was to be done in two parts. First, the capacity of the aqueduct and of reservoirs within the city was to be enlarged to the point where they could deliver a maximum of 300,000,000 gallons daily. Second, the height of the existing dams was to be raised, thereby increasing the amount of water impounded

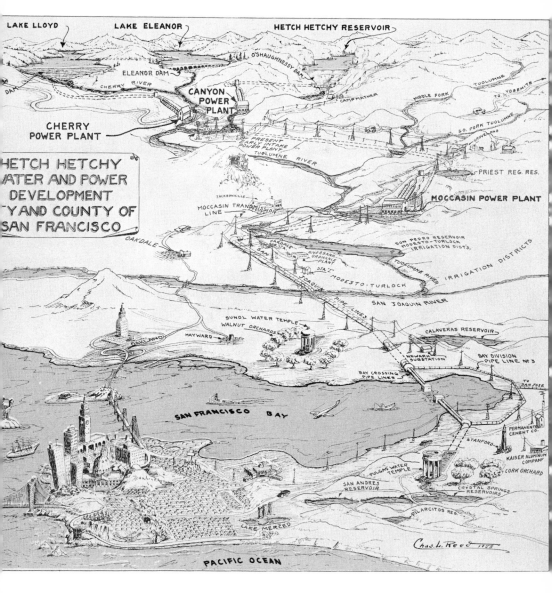

LAKE LLOYD   LAKE ELEANOR   HETCH HETCHY RESERVOIR

O'SHAUGHNESSY DAM
ELEANOR DAM
CHERRY RIVER
DAM
CANYON POWER PLANT
CAMP MATHER
TUOLUMNE
TO YOSEMITE
MIDDLE FORK
CHERRY POWER PLANT
SO. FORK TUOLUMNE
GROVELAND
PRESENT INTAKE EARLY POWER PLANT
TUOLUMNE RIVER
PRIEST REG. RES.
JACKSONVILLE
HETCH HETCHY WATER AND POWER DEVELOPMENT CITY AND COUNTY OF SAN FRANCISCO
MOCCASIN TRANSMISSION LINE
MOCCASIN POWER PLANT
OAKDALE
DON PEDRO RESERVOIR MODESTO-TURLOCK IRRIGATION DISTS.
OAKDALE
RIVERBANK ORDNANCE PLANT
STA. TID MODESTO-TURLOCK
TUOLUMNE RIVER
IRRIGATION DISTRICTS
SAN JOAQUIN PIPE LINES
MODESTO-TURLOCK
SAN JOAQUIN RIVER
CALAVERAS RESERVOIR
SUNOL WATER TEMPLE
WALNUT ORCHARDS
OAKLAND
HAYWARD
NEWARK SUBSTATION
BAY DIVISION PIPE LINE Nº 3
TO SAN JOSE
BAY CROSSING PIPE LINES
SAN FRANCISCO BAY
PERMANENTE CEMENT CO.
STANFORD
KAISER ALUMINUM COMPANY
CORK ORCHARD
PULGAS WATER TEMPLE
SAN ANDRES RESERVOIR
CRYSTAL SPRINGS RESERVOIRS
LAKE MERCED
PILARCITOS RES.
Chas. L. Reed 1955
PACIFIC OCEAN

How to obtain a supply of water adequate for the needs of the city has long presented a problem. In the beginning the only source was several nearby springs; later water was piped from reservoirs down the peninsula. Finally, when these two proved inadequate, work began on the vast Hetch Hetchy development by which water is brought from a group of artificial lakes in the high Sierra. As the water flows down to the lowlands it generates the electric power used to light the city and operate the municipal streetcar system. (*S. F. Water Department.*)

in the mountain lakes so as to provide a daily flow of 400,000,000 gallons. It was estimated that the first of these objectives would meet the city's needs until 1985, and the second until the year 2000.

As the water descends to the floor of the San Joaquin Valley it is used to generate electric power. The first city-owned powerhouse, a small plant known as the Intake Station, was completed in 1918; its output was used exclusively for building dams, tunnels, and other early construction works. A second and larger powerhouse, that at Moccasin Creek, which develops 100,000 horsepower, was completed in 1925. The Moccasin Creek plant remained the chief source of municipal power until the completion of the Cherry River powerhouse in 1960. The last-named, which was built at a cost of $30,000,000, has a capacity of 187,000 horsepower. Yet another large plant, the Canyon powerhouse, is scheduled for completion in the late 1960s; it will produce an additional 106,000 horsepower, bringing the total to nearly 400,000 horsepower.

The energy thus produced is brought to the city over a number of transmission lines and is put to a variety of public uses. It furnishes power to operate the city-owned streetcar and bus lines, to pump water from the peninsula lakes into the city reservoirs, and to light the streets and public buildings. In addition, electrical energy is sold to irrigation districts in the Central Valley and to communities near which the transmission lines pass.

From the inception of the plan to bring Sierra water into the city the intention was to take over the properties of the Spring Valley Water Company, which owned the local distribution system, and thus bring the entire operation under municipal control. As was the case when the city sought to buy the privately owned streetcar lines, this purchase was a long-drawn-out process. Between 1910 and 1928 five bond issues designed to finance the purchase of the water company's property were submitted to the voters. In each case the asking price was considered too high, and all were rejected. Not until 1930 did a sixth bond issue, this one for $41,000,000, receive the two-thirds majority necessary for the measure to carry.

During the three decades that have passed since the city took over the entire system, the amount of water delivered to consumers in San Francisco and parts of San Mateo and Alameda counties increased threefold. By the mid-1960s the watersheds of the high Sierra were furnishing more than 60 per cent of the city's water supply; most of the remainder comes from city-owned lands on the lower San Francisco Peninsula. The city's total investment in its water system then amounted to more than $400,000,000. In recent years, however, no part of its cost has been borne by the taxpayers. Receipts from the sale of water and electrical energy have made the operation self-supporting.

3. THE CITY BUILDS AN AIRPORT

Those who sponsored the 1898 charter, which committed the city to ownership of public utilities, could hardly have foreseen that less than thirty years later it would be operating a complex and fast-growing facility known as a municipal airfield. For when the new charter was adopted the historic flights of the Wright brothers were still eight years in the future, and another lengthy period was to elapse before the full significance of their feat came to be recognized. As early as 1911, however, two local events served to forecast the new invention's value as a military weapon. In the spring of that year, the first live bombs were dropped from an airship near San Francisco, and later that same year a primitive biplane took off from an improvised platform on the deck of a warship anchored in the bay.

It was the rapid rise of commercial aviation following the close of World War I that put the city in the airport business. The initial step toward the establishment of a municipal flying field was taken in 1927 when funds were voted to buy 1,376 acres of bay-front land in northern San Mateo County. At the same time the city took an option on an adjoining 1,000-acre tract, much of which lay in the shallows of the bay. To finance the development of Mills Field, as the site was originally called, two additional bond issues were submitted to the voters. The first, in the amount of $1,700,000, was for the construction of runways, hangars, and other facilities, and the second, a $4,000,000 issue, for the increase of the size of the field by the purchase of the land under option. Both measures were defeated. One reason for their rejection was that the recent stock-market crash had made the voters reluctant to increase the city's bonded indebtedness. Another and perhaps weightier reason was that at the time it was thought that a site closer to the center of the city would become available — the man-made island then being reclaimed in mid-bay, on which the Golden Gate International Exposition of 1939-40 was built.

Thus, during the 1930s the development of the peninsula airport proceeded slowly. It was not until Treasure Island was taken over by the Navy in 1940 that a comprehensive program for the expansion of the former Mills Field — now known as the San Francisco International Airport — got under way. This work was materially aided by a grant of $10,000,000 in federal funds paid to the city in return for its having relinquished its claim to the bay island. In the next dozen years the runways, hangars, shops, terminals, and other facilities needed to keep pace with the rapid increase in airborne traffic were continuously enlarged. That trend has continued ever since. In November, 1956, a $25,000,000 bond issue was approved; of that amount, $14,000,000 was allotted to build a second terminal, and most of the balance was used to lengthen runways so as to accommodate the new jet liners. By 1965 the total investment in the airport, including that of the airlines it

The San Francisco International Airport in northern San Mateo County is owned and operated by the city. Founded in 1927 and originally called Mills Field, it has since seen an almost continuous expansion of facilities. Today it is one of largest and busiest air terminals on the West Coast. (*S. F. Public Utilities Commission.*)

served, had reached $170,000,000, and an extensive program of future expansion was in the planning stage.

More than 2,000 acres, much of it land reclaimed from the bay, were then in use, and an additional 3,100 acres of tidelands were being held in reserve for future expansion. During the fiscal year from July 1, 1964 to June 30, 1965, 8,349,365 passengers passed through the airport; the amount of air express totaled 13,525,155 pounds, and of air freight 281,854,465 pounds. Operating revenue for the same twelve-month period was $9,700,000, an increase of 15 per cent over the previous year. These figures made clear that San Francisco's airport, like the city's street-transportation and water systems, had become a major operation, one that gave every indication of increasing in size and complexity with each passing year.

4. BRIDGING THE BAY

San Francisco's position at the tip of the peninsula had long posed a transportation problem by separating the city by several miles of water from the east and north sides of the bay. Until comparatively recent times, however, that was looked down on as no very severe handicap. From the late 1860s on, fleets of ferryboats had provided frequent service to and from the Alameda and Marin shores, and the leisurely morning and evening crossings were looked on by commuters as pleasant breaks in the daily routine.

But as the population of the bay area continued to increase it became clear that the ferries would one day be unable to handle the transbay traffic. Accordingly, plans for bridging the bay were advanced from time to time. Among the earliest of such proposals was that of "Emperor Norton," one of the city's bumper crop of eccentric characters, who in 1869 stood on the crest of Rincon Hill and issued this imperial edict: "The bridge shall be built!" The "Emperor's" command was eventually carried out — but only after a long delay. More than half a century was to pass before a work of

Bridging the Golden Gate was one of the engineering marvels of the 1930s. This view shows the huge concrete fender that enabled workmen to lay the foundation of the south tower. A suspension type bridge 4200 feet long connects the two 751-foot towers. (*Redwood Empire Association.*)

that magnitude would be feasible either from the engineering or the economic standpoints.

First of the major transbay bridges to become a reality was the San Francisco-Oakland Bay Bridge, which at the time of its completion was the world's longest and most costly suspension-type bridge. After several years of preliminary planning, construction began in May, 1933, and the bridge was completed and opened to traffic on November 12, 1936. The 8½-mile structure is in two sections which are connected in midbay by a tunnel through Yerba Buena Island. The western half, a high-level suspension bridge with a clearance of 216 feet above water, passes in a series of arches from the San Francisco side to Yerba Buena Island. The second part, a cantilever-type structure, extends from the island to the Alameda County shore. The Yerba Buena tunnel, the largest ever bored, is 76 feet high and 58 feet wide — large enough to permit a four-story house to be drawn through it. The total cost of the bridge and its approaches was $77,000,000.

One problem encountered during the planning of this great structure was the fact that San Francisco and Yerba Buena Island are separated by two miles of deep water, a distance much too long to be crossed by a single span. That difficulty was overcome by the construction of a hugh concrete pier midway between the two points to serve as an anchorage for the cables. This required sinking the foundations down to bedrock, 200 feet below the water's surface, and building upward to the level of the bridge's lower deck, giving the pier an over-all height of more than 400 feet. To the east and west of this man-made island, four 518-foot towers were built to support the cables from which the two decks were suspended. Originally the six-lane upper deck was used exclusively by passenger automobiles; on the lower deck three lanes were reserved for trucks and busses and the remaining space for tracks over which the interurban trains ran. Later the transbay trains were abandoned and replaced by motor busses, whereupon the tracks were removed and both levels opened to automobiles. In recent years the westbound traffic has used the upper deck, and the eastbound the lower.

From the beginning automobile traffic was so heavy that the revenue from tolls — which were originally fixed at sixty-five cents per car — was more than ample to make the bridge self-supporting. The tolls were accordingly reduced, first to fifty cents, then to twenty-five cents. When the bridge was completed in 1936 its capacity was believed to be large enough to handle the anticipated traffic for at least fifty years. Less than half that time had passed, however, before it grew evident that additional facilities would become necessary long before the half-century mark was reached. Whether these should take the form of a second bridge, or of a tunnel beneath the bay, or of a revival of the ferryboats — or perhaps a combination of all three — was a much debated subject during the late 1950s and early 1960s. The steps taken to solve the problem are described in Chapter xii.

When the San Francisco-Oakland Bay Bridge was opened in 1936, it marked the virtual end of the picturesque ferries. Shown here is the western half of the structure, which extends from Yerba Buena Island to the waterfront. The two sections are connected by a tunnel through the midbay island. *(Redwood Empire Association.)*

✓ ✓ ✓

The Golden Gate Bridge, spanning the entrance to the bay, is the second of the great bridges put up during the 1930s. This is much the shorter of the two, yet its building posed problems fully as difficult as those encountered on the bay span. For the north and south portals of the Golden Gate are separated at their nearest point by a mile and a half of turbulent water that at each turn of the tide flows through the channel with the speed of a mountain torrent. As was the case with that section of the Bay Bridge connecting San Francisco and Yerba Buena Island, the distance is too great to be crossed by a single span. Hence, it was necessary to build towers some distance offshore at the north and south ends.

Laying the foundations of these towers, particularly that on the San Francisco side, taxed the ingenuity of the designer of the bridge, Joseph B. Strauss, and of its builders. The depth of the water at the site of the southern tower, and the swiftnes of the currents, made the usual methods of underwater construction impracticable and called for the development of new techniques. After other experiments had been tried and failed, a great wall, or fender, enclosing an area equal to that of a football field, was built

Part of the city as seen from the observation plaza at the southern end of the Golden Gate Bridge. The statue is that of Joseph
B. Strauss, the engineer who designed the bridge. *(S. F. Convention & Visitors Bureau.)*

on the site; the water was then pumped out and the pier foundation laid.
Afterward the water was let into the enclosed space and the fender — a
forty-foot-thick wall of concrete — remained in place to protect the pier from
damage by storms or shipping.

The following statistics indicate the structure's size. The two towers
rise 746 feet above the surface of the water. The over-all length of the
bridge is 8,940 feet. The distance between the two towers is 4,200 feet,
which at the time of its construction and for more than twenty-five years
thereafter made it the longest single span in the world. Its six-lane deck is
220 feet above the surface of the channel, a height that permits ships of any
size to pass beneath it. The cables supporting the runway are 36½ inches in
diameter; each is made up of 27,572 strands of steel wire, each with the
thickness of a lead pencil. The combined lengths of the strands would pass
three times around the earth.

The financing of the big structure posed problems almost as complex as
those faced by its builders. While it was still in the planning stages strong
opposition developed from several sources. Engineers were by no means
unanimous in their opinion that the bridge *could* be built. Others prophe-
sied that the amount of traffic it would attract would be insufficient to pay
the cost of building and maintaining the costly structure, and that it consequently would be a burden to the taxpayers for years to come. Besides, high-

ranking officers of the Army and Navy expressed concern at the possibility that in time of war the bridge might be blown up and so block the entrance to the harbor.

Proponents of the enterprise, however, disregarded these gloomy prognostications. At their urging, the State Legislature early in 1929 passed an act creating the Golden Gate Bridge and Highway District, composed of San Francisco and the five north-bay counties of Marin, Sonoma, Napa, Mendocino, and Del Norte. On November 4, 1930, voters of the district approved an issue of $35,000,000 of bridge bonds, the measure carrying by a ratio of three to one. Meanwhile, test borings were made, preliminary plans were drawn up, and permission was obtained from the War Department to route the bridge approaches through military reservations on the San Francisco and Marin County sides. The first construction contracts were let on June 17, 1931, and the bridge was opened to traffic six years later, on May 25, 1937.

As was the case with the San Francisco-Oakland Bay Bridge, which was completed several months earlier, fears that the Gate span would prove a bad investment were quickly dispelled. From the beginning the income from tolls (originally fifty cents for automobiles, and later reduced to twenty-five cents) proved more than enough to retire the bonds and meet operating expenses. During the first full year of operation the number of vehicles passing through the toll gates averaged 9,073 daily; during the 1964-65 fiscal year the daily average was 69,267.

By the middle 1960s it was recognized that the time was not far distant when the bridge would be unable to accommodate this rapidly growing volume of traffic. Accordingly preliminary plans to add a second deck to the existing structure, or, should that prove impracticable, to build a second San Francisco-Marin bridge, got under way. By the fall of 1966 no definite decision on this matter had been reached.

6. TREASURE ISLAND

Once the building of the bay bridges was under way, San Franciscans —who rarely pass up an opportunity for a civic celebration—began laying plans for a festival to commemorate their completion. Out of that movement grew the decision to stage a world's fair, one that would duplicate the success of the fairs of 1894 and 1915. In the summer of 1933 Mayor Angelo J. Rossi appointed a committee to draft preliminary plans and choose an appropriate site. The spot selected was an area of shallow water known as Yerba Buena Shoals, which lay to the northwest of the island of that name. The committee's decision was influenced by the fact that the area would be easily accessible from San Francisco and the cities on the east shore by means of the new transbay bridge which would pass through the island. Another factor favoring the site was that, after the exposition closed, the site could be used as a municipal airport. The belief was that its central location would give it a marked advantage over the peninsula airfield. An engineering survey of the shoals, which were owned by the state, was made. When test borings showed that a stratum of clay beneath the surface would provide a solid foundation for the projected buildings, the city set about acquiring title to the property.

Early in 1934 a nonprofit corporation, the San Francisco Bay Exposition Company, was formed. Although the city was just emerging from a severe business depression, the project moved steadily forward. The work of building Treasure Island, as the man-made island was called, began early in 1936. This required filling in an underwater area covering four hundred acres, which varied in depth from two to twenty-six feet, and building it up to a height of thirteen feet above the surface. This task was accomplished by surrounding the entire site with a rock fill three miles in length and filling the enclosure with sand and silt pumped from the bay. An elaborate drainage system reduced the amount of salt in the dredged-up material, and a surface coating of loam made possible the growing of trees, lawns, and flowerbeds on the grounds.

The Golden Gate International Exposition, the third of the city's world fairs, was built on man-made Treasure Island in midbay. This view was taken from nearby Yerba Buena Island, to which it is connected by a causeway.

The Golden Gate International Exposition opened on February 19, 1939. Its total cost, including the reclamation of land, amounted to $18,900,-000. This sum was raised by a municipal bond issue, by contributions from individuals and organizations, and by a grant of federal funds through the agency of the Works Progress Administration.

The prime purpose of the exposition was to emphasize the city's close cultural and commercial relations with the countries of the Orient and the Pacific islands. This theme was symbolized by its subtitle, "A Pageant of the Pacific," and by a huge statue, "Pacifica," the work of sculptor Ralph Stackpole, which dominated the great central courtyard. The exposition remained open from late February to the end of October, 1939, was closed during the winter months, and reopened in May of the following year. The final closing ceremonies were held on the night of September 2, 1940. During the two sessions seventeen million visitors passed through its gates.

6. WORLD WAR II AND THE UNITED NATIONS CONFERENCE

When Hitler's invasion of Poland set off World War II, the exposition on Treasure Island was nearing the end of its first season. As events were to prove, the war changed the city's plans for the future of the island. When, slightly more than a year later, the gates were closed for the last time, the country was in the midst of a massive preparedness program, and the island was taken over for use as a naval base. A number of the exposition buildings were converted into temporary barracks, storage warehouses, and the like, and the remainder of the site was rebuilt with hangars, shops, offices, and other facilities, including an airstrip. During the war years the island served as a major naval training, outfitting, and embarkation center through which thousands of servicemen passed on their way to the Pacific battle fronts.

The war activities at Treasure Island were typical of those in many other places throughout the bay area. In San Francisco the years from 1941 to 1945 were marked by an unprecedented growth in population, and by the rapid expansion of industrial plants, shipping, housing, and recreational facilities. World War II had as great an impact on the city's economy as any event since the gold rush nearly a century earlier. During the war years the number of factories increased by one-third, while the number of industrial workers more than doubled. The influx of workers to man the shipbuilding plants and other war industries, and to handle the immense quantities of supplies being dispatched across the Pacific, quickly outran facilities for housing and feeding them and for transporting them to and from their jobs.

Conditions in the already overcrowded city were further complicated by the many servicemen passing through the port. For San Francisco and other points on the bay became the chief embarkation centers from which men and supplies were forwarded to the Pacific fighting fronts. During the three years and ten months between the attack on Pearl Harbor and the capitulation of Japan, 1,644,243 military personnel and 23,389,000 tons of war materials passed through the Golden Gate. Many thousands of men and vast quantities of goods were embarked not only on the San Francisco waterfront, but at Treasure Island, Fort McDowell on Angel Island, the Oakland Army Base, Camp Stoneman near Antioch, and at Richmond, Sausalito, Stockton, and Vallejo.

The critical need for ships, both combat vessels and cargo carriers, was met in part by the expansion of navy yards at Hunters Point and Mare Island and private shipbuilding plants about the bay, including San Francisco's long-established Union Iron Works. However, by far the greater amount of wartime shipping produced in the area was built at two new yards, one at Richmond in the East Bay, and the other at Sausalito. So great was the demand for workers that within a few months both these once quiet towns were transformed into cities. At the peak of its activity the Richmond yard employed more than ninety thousand, and at Marinship in Sausalito the number was only slightly less; together, the two produced well over one thousand vessels. At both yards freighters and tankers were built, launched, equipped, and put to sea in greater numbers and at greater speed than ever before.

During the first months after Pearl Harbor there was widespread concern that San Francisco might itself be attacked, and elaborate precautions were taken to prepare for that eventuality. A Civilian Defense Corps, manned by volunteers, was recruited and trained, air-raid sirens were installed, and provisions made to impose black-outs at the approach of enemy planes, submarines, or surface vessels. Antisubmarine nets were laid across the harbor's entrance, additional guns were mounted at points commanding the approaches to the bay, and a constant offshore naval and air patrol was maintained. It was not until the war entered its final phases and the likelihood of such attacks became remote that these precautionary measures were relaxed.

San Francisco shared with other West Coast cities the effects of another wartime measure; that is, the removal of persons of Japanese ancestry from the coastal areas and their internment in "relocation centers" at Tule Lake, Manzanar, and other remote spots. This involved severe hardships for the internees, the great majority of whom were either native-born citizens (Nisei) or loyal supporters of their adopted country. However, they bore the ordeal with fortitude and at the war's end all but a few returned and again became useful and respected members of their old communities.

✓   ✓   ✓

Fighting in the Pacific was still in progress when, early in 1945, President Roosevelt, Prime Minister Churchill, and Joseph Stalin met at Yalta and laid the groundwork for a conference to draft the charter of a new world organization. On February 12 San Francisco's Mayor Roger Lapham received this message from Acting Secretary of State Joseph C. Grew:

It is my great pleasure to inform you that San Francisco has been selected as the site of the United Nations Conference to take place beginning about April 25, 1945, for the purpose of preparing a charter for a United Nations Organization for the maintenance of international peace and security. Representatives of the Department of State will get in touch with you in a day or so in order to confer with you with regard to the necessary arrangements for the Conference.

From Sacramento, on March 26, Governor Earl Warren issued this public announcement:

All Californians join in extending a welcome to the delegates to the United Nations Conference on World Security. We are fully conscious of the honor conferred upon us by the selection of one of our great cities as the meeting place for the representatives of the allied countries.

We welcome these distinguished guests, knowing that their efforts will be directed toward guiding the steps of mankind in the ways of peace. We know that the welcome which we extend is shared by peace-loving peoples throughout the world, and that everywhere in the lands from which the delegates have come, there are prayers that this historic meeting will promote greater tolerance and understanding among all nations for generations to come.

The conference, which was attended by representatives of forty-five nations, opened on April 25 with a preliminary meeting in the War Memorial Opera House and continued until June 26, when the charter was formally adopted. During the two months while the delegates were framing the document the attention of the free world was focused on their deliberations. The full facilities of the city were put at the disposal of the visitors. Suites of rooms in the leading hotels were reserved for the delegates and their staffs, and the Opera House, Veterans Building, and other meeting places were made available to them. Because of the nature of their task and because the world was still at war, official functions welcoming the guests were held to a minimum. Nonetheless, they were given ample opportunity to enjoy the city's traditional hospitality during their limited hours of leisure. "We shall ask nothing of you," Mayor Lapham had stated in his welcoming address, "realizing that you are charged with a great task . . . and we know you will realize that San Francisco is carrying a heavy responsibility as the main war port of the Pacific Coast."

The fact that the charter of the United Nations, mankind's hope for world peace, was drawn up and signed in their city has ever since been a source of pride to San Franciscans.

The modern city from the air. This panoramic view, looking toward the north, shows the tall office buildings of the downtown area and the hotels and apartment houses on Nob and Russian hills. The wooded hills of the Presidio and the Golden Gate Bridge are visible in the upper left, with Point Reyes in the distance. Alcatraz Island and Belvedere are at the far right and beyond are the Marin County hills, topped by Mount Tamalpais. (*Redwood Empire Association.*)

XII

The Contemporary Scene

1. THE CITY IN MID-CENTURY

San Francisco has a consolidated city and county government with legislative powers vested in an eleven-member Board of Supervisors, five or six members of which are elected every two years for four-year terms. The mayor, who has the power of veto over legislation passed by the supervisors, also serves a four-year term, as do the city treasurer, assessor, city attorney, sheriff, district attorney, public defender, and judges of the municipal and superior courts. Two officials, the chief administrative officer and the controller, are appointed by the mayor; the controller, however, is subject to confirmation by the supervisors. Both officials have permanent tenure. The mayor also appoints members of the following boards, commissions, and agencies who, with a few exceptions, serve at his pleasure: art, city planning, fire, housing, library, recreation and park, permit appeals, police, public utilities, redevelopment, retirement, and welfare. The chief administrative officer has jurisdiction over the departments of finance and records, public works, public health, purchasing, real estate, electricity, weights and measures, county welfare, and the offices of coroner and public administrator.

The charter under which the city government functions was adopted by the voters in 1932. There were four earlier charters, those of 1850, 1856, 1861, and 1898.

Of the city and county's total area of 129 square miles, only about one-third is above water. Included in its boundaries are three bay islands — Alcatraz, Yerba Buena, and the man-made Treasure Island — as well as the Farallon group which lies some thirty miles offshore; the latter was made part of the city in 1872. Save for the annexation of the Farallon Islands, San Francisco's boundaries have not been changed in more than a century. Its land area of less than 45 square miles makes it the most compact of the country's large cities; only Buffalo, with 39.4 square miles, is smaller. San Francisco is by far the most densely populated city in California. According to the 1960 census it had an average of 15,553 persons per square mile; this compares with 6,935 in Oakland, 5,451 in Los Angeles, and 2,979 in San Diego. In addition to its permanent residents, an estimated 125,000 persons

245

(Left) The observation platform atop Coit Tower on Telegraph Hill affords a sweeping view of the city and bay. The tall, fluted column was a gift to the city from Lillie Hitchcock Coit, a lifelong admirer of the city's volunteer firemen.

(Right) Three familiar San Francisco landmarks appear in this photograph: the tower of Old St. Mary's on the right, a glimpse of Chinatown on the left, and, in the foreground, a cable car descending the California Street hill.

(Left) This view of the Ferry Building tower—which was modeled on the famous Giralda Tower in Seville, Spain — was taken from the shadow of the controversial Embarcadero Freeway. (Three photos from S. F. Convention & Visitors Bureau.)

(Left) In recent years several blocks of old buildings centering about Jackson and Sansome streets have been restored by a group of wholesale dealers in furniture, fabrics, and related materials. The result is Jackson Square, a district reminiscent of the city as it was a century and more ago. *(S. F. Convention & Visitors Bureau.)*

(Right) From the beginning its water-borne commerce has occupied an important place in San Francisco's economy. In and adjacent to the Maritime Museum have been assembled numerous relics of the city's seafaring heritage. Shown here are two coastal schooners and a transbay ferry tied up to the old Hyde Street pier. *(Redwood Empire Association.)*

(Left) The city's hills at night. Above the street of wooden residences in the foreground the illuminated dome of the City Hall is visible. Beyond is the facade of the block-long Federal Office Building, with a group of tall hotels and apartment houses in the distance. *(Redwood Empire Association.)*

Two of the city's three major art museums are pictured here: the third,
the San Francisco Museum of Art, is in the Veterans Memorial Building in the Civic Center. The M. H. De Young Memorial Museum
(above) fronts on the Music Concourse in Golden Gate Park. Below
is the Palace of the Legion of Honor which is in Lincoln Park. *(S. F.
Convention & Visitors Bureau.)*

daily commute to the city from the suburbs, giving it a daytime population of approximately 855,000.

The cosmopolitan nature of the population, which has been characteristic of the city from its beginning, has been maintained through the years. Among the 740,383 residents in 1960 were 74,383 Negroes, 36,445 Chinese, 12,326 Filipinos, 9,404 Japanese, and 2,226 Koreans. There were numerous other minority groups, including 1,068 American Indians. In addition to its famous Chinatown, which is the largest concentration of Chinese outside the Orient, modern San Francisco retains several of its early-day "foreign quarters." North Beach is largely inhabited by persons of Italian descent, and a considerable Japanese colony centers about Post, Buchanan and Laguna streets. A majority of the now numerous Negro population lives in the Fillmore and Hunters Point areas. Although only 4.7 per cent of California's population live in San Francisco, the city in 1960 had more than 10 per cent of the state's foreign-born residents.

This diversity of population is evidenced in many ways: in the variety of foods served in its restaurants, in its frequent festivals celebrating the national holidays of other nations, in its numerous foreign social clubs and other organizations, and in the multiplicity of its places of worship. Among the latter are churches serving virtually every creed and faith, including Chinese temples and Buddhist shrines. Further evidence of the city's cosmopolitanism is the fact that more than twenty of its newspapers and periodicals are in foreign languages. Among these are journals printed in Chinese, Japanese, Italian, Spanish, Russian, French, German, Swiss, Greek, Portuguese, Yiddish and Scandinavian.

Throughout its history the educational and cultural life of the city has kept pace with its advances in other fields. In 1965 there were 130 city-operated public schools, some 50 adult-education centers, and 25 child-care centers, with a combined daily attendance of more than 108,000 and with 4,275 full-time teachers. In addition to kindergarten, elementary, and junior and senior high schools, the public school system maintains a number of continuation, vocational, and trade schools. There are also numerous private parochial schools and business and technical colleges, which in 1962 had approximately 30,000 students. Closely allied with the educational system are the public libraries, which consist of the main library in the Civic Center and 27 branches serving virtually every sector of the city.

The largest of the city's institutions of higher education is the San Francisco State College, which in 1965 had an enrollment of more than 13,000. Among other schools of college rank are the long-established University of San Francisco and the San Francisco College for Women, both Catholic schools, and the city-sponsored City College of San Francisco. Several departments of the University of California are based in San Francisco. Foremost among these is the Medical Center on Parnassus Avenue, where the university's schools of medicine, dentistry, pharmacy, and nursing are situated. Other local divisions of the state university include Hastings College of the Law and the San Francisco Art Institute.

San Francisco's interest in the arts is evidenced not only in its support of musical activities and the theater but by its many art galleries, both public and private. The three major galleries are the M. H. de Young Memorial Museum in Golden Gate Park, the San Francisco Museum of Art in the Civic Center, and the Palace of the Legion of Honor in Lincoln Park. Other important collections of artistic, historical, or scientific materials are on display at the San Francisco Maritime Museum, the California Academy of Sciences, the Wells Fargo Museum, the California Historical Society, and the Society of California Pioneers.

Musical organizations supported wholly or in part by the city include the San Francisco Symphony Orchestra and the San Francisco Opera Association, both of which have long been known for the quality of their productions. The city also maintains a municipal band and a municipal chorus, gives financial aid to the San Francisco Ballet Guild, and through its Art Commission sponsors an annual International Film Festival and an Outdoor Art Festival.

2.   URBAN RENEWAL

Less than three months after the close of the United Nations Conference in 1945, the capitulation of Japan brought the fighting in the Pacific to a close and San Francisco began its return to a peacetime footing. This was a difficult transition. For the better part of five years, wartime activities had been the city's chief concern. Throughout that period many civilian works, including both private and public construction, had been held to a minimum. The result was that by the time peace came large areas of the overcrowded city had taken on a shabby, run-down appearance.

This state of affairs had aroused the concern of some while the fighting was still in progress. Early in 1945, Mayor Lapham appointed a committee to study the city's current situation and future needs. The committee's report, rendered later that year, listed a number of problems that urgently needed attention. Among them were: the decline of certain older residential districts, mounting traffic congestion in the downtown area, and a need to overhaul agencies charged with health, education and the protection of life and property.

In the postwar rehabilitation program, first priority was given to clearing away outmoded buildings in certain blighted areas and replacing them with modern facilities. One of the largest of such areas was the Western Addition, a 200-acre residential district closely built with wooden structures during the 1880s and 1890s. Many of the thousands of

This air view of the financial district shows the man-made canyon of Montgomery Street, "the Wall Street of the West," lined on both sides with multi-story buildings housing banks, insurance companies, brokerage houses, and many others. (*S. F. Convention & Visitors Bureau.*)

(Upper left) One o
city's newer skyscr
is the glass-walled C
Zellerbach Build
which occupies th
angular lot bounde
Market, Sansome,
Bush streets. The r
building on the Ma
Sansome corner
branch bank. (Ed
T. Haas.)

(Above) In the fa
1966 work began o
new Head Office o
Bank of Americ
model of which is s
here. The build
which is schedule
completion in 1968
be the tallest on
West Coast.

(Opposite) A night
of Grant Avenue
shopping center of
Francisco's far
Chinatown. (Red
Empire Association

Negroes who had arrived during the war years had settled in the part centering around Fillmore Street. According to the 1945 survey, the number of persons living there exceeded 200 per acre; only in parts of Chinatown did similar conditions prevail. In clearing this site not only were thousands of dwellings, shops and other structures razed, but also some streets were widened to speed traffic between the downtown area and residential districts further west. One feature of redevelopment was the Japanese Cultural Center. The first of its kind in the country, it consists of several blocks facing the widened Geary Boulevard and features hotels, restaurants and shops offering products of the Orient.

Another part of the city badly in need of rehabilitation was the wholesale-produce district. This was a region of ramshackle, one-story buildings, many dating from the 1906 fire. During early morning hours its narrow streets were cluttered with produce trucks and at all hours the sidewalks were piled high with stacks of fruit and vegetables. Because of the area's proximity to the financial district it has long been recognized as one of the most desirable in the city and since the 1930s proposals had been made to relocate the fruit and vegetable brokers to better utilize the site. This was not feasible until 1949, however, when legislation was enacted permitting federal loans for up to two thirds of the cost of such works. Thereupon city officials, in cooperation with state and federal agencies, set about acquiring title to the property and finding suitable quarters for the ousted produce merchants. Redevelopment of the site began and since then, work on the Golden Gateway, as the new district is called, has been almost continuously under way. Today it is an attractive area of tall office buildings and apartment houses grouped about court-yards and malls fronting on tree-lined streets. Over much of the district are elevated arcades extending from block to block, with restaurants and shops opening onto miniature parks.

A third major redevelopment, one that after long delay was getting under way as the 1980s opened, is that known as the Yerba Buena Center. Like the Golden Gateway it lies close to the city's center and is an area of outmoded factories, hotels and other buildings to the south of Market Street. Legal difficulties, including that of finding suitable hous-ing for residents of the demolished hotels, long prevented rebuilding the cleared site. However, a start was made in 1979 when work began on the main exhibit hall of the George Moscone Convention Center, a much-needed facility if the city was to maintain its position as a favorite place for national conventions.

3. LOOKING AHEAD

By the beginning of the 1980s San Francisco was well along on its campaign to rebuild its rundown commercial and residential districts.

The downtown skyline in 1980, as seen from Treasure Island, the man-made island in midbay. *(S. F. Convention & Tourist Bureau.)*

Big league baseball became a reality in San Francisco in 1958 when the former New York Giants moved to the city. This view of the Giants' new home, Candlestick Park, indicates the popularity the game has attained. *(Redwood Empire Association.)*

But much more needed to be done if the city were to become the modern metropolis its leaders envisioned. In recent years changes had taken place at an accelerated rate, creating problems that could hardly have been foreseen a generation earlier. In particular, World War II had created conditions common to many war-swollen communities: housing shortages; traffic congestion; overcrowded schools, hospitals, shops, restaurants and places of recreation.

In San Francisco the city's small area had made such problems acute. During the years from 1910 to 1940 the Richmond and Sunset Districts, and the area west of Twin Peaks—the only substantial undeveloped sections of the city—had gradually filled up. This brought a steady rise in value of vacant space which remained and set off a movement which has continued ever since: the moving of middle-income families to the suburbs, where ample space was available and the cost of homes much less. One consequence was the city's population. For more than a century it had been rising steadily, but between 1950 and 1980 it had shown a small but continuing decline.

One purpose of the city's urban-renewal program had been, by providing adequate housing at moderate cost, to slow down this movement to the suburbs; an effort that has met with only limited success. At the same time it came to be recognized that San Francisco's ultimate position was to be that of a headquarters' city; that is, the business,

Train of the Bay Area Rapid Transit System (BART) which connects San Francisco with the eastbay counties of Alameda and Contra Costa. *(S. F. Convention & Visitors Bureau.)*

---

financial and cultural center for the large and populous region it serves. To carry out that role, a major publicly and privately financed building boom got under way. Throughout the 1960s and 1970s the face of the city has been changed by the rise of lofty apartment houses on Telegraph, Nob and Russian Hills; by scores of high-rise office buildings on California, Market and other downtown streets; and by new hotels and shops in the Union Square area.

At the same time steps were being taken to relieve a situation that had steadily become more acute: that of providing fast and comfortable transportation both within the city and to suburban communities. By the mid-1960s, the two bay bridges, which at the time they were built were expected to serve until the end of the century, were already taxed to their fullest capacity. It was realized that if the city was to retain its traditional position of leadership, means must be found to supplement the bridges. A major step toward bringing that about was taken in 1962, when the Bay Area Rapid Transit System (BART) was formed. The voters of San Francisco, Alameda and Contra Costs counties approved a bond issue of $793 million to finance its building. Work on this large project, which connects the three counties with frequent, high-speed electric trains, began soon after and by 1975 was in operation over its full length. Trains from eastbay communities enter the city through a three-mile-long tunnel beneath the bay, then pass under Market and Mission streets and end at

Daly City. The Market Street section of the subway is on two levels, with BART trains operating on the lower level and the local streetcars above. This placing of much of its vehicular traffic underground has permitted redesigning Market Street over much of its length. Broad brick sidewalks and a double line of ornamental trees have added much to the attraction of this, the city's main thoroughfare.

With its program of urban renewal well advanced and BART and other means of speeding transportation completed and functioning, San Francisco entered the 1980s in a forward-looking mood. True, a variety of problems remained. During rush hours the amount of traffic made downtown streets almost impassable, vacant piers along the waterfront attested to the decline of the city's once active maritime commerce, and year by year efforts of the law enforcement agencies to control crime have met with indifferent success. Nonetheless, substantial progress has been made on so many fronts that as the decade of the 1980s opened, San Francisco looked forward with confidence to the opportunities and challenges of the future.

One of three ferries plying between the city and Marin County, designed to alleviate traffic on the Golden Gate Bridge. *(Redwood Empire Association.)*

ing calls for the construction of seventy-five miles of high-speed electric railroad in Alameda and Contra Costa counties, and to connect it with the city by means of a tunnel beneath the bay. The system is expected to be completed in 1971. Meanwhile, tentative plans were being made to extend the facility to Marin County on the north, and down the peninsula as far as San Jose. The ultimate aim is to provide fast and frequent transportation linking the entire bay area more closely together.

By this vast and costly project, together with the comprehensive rehabilitation program being carried out within the city itself, San Franciscans of the mid-1960s prepared to meet the opportunities and challenges of the future.

Most recent of the city's skyscrapers, the 42-story Wells Fargo
Bank Building, which was completed in 1966, adds a striking
new note to the downtown skyline. *(Edward T. Haas.)*

Bibliography

This listing of books pertaining to San Francisco is intended as a convenient guide for those who wish to read further about one phase or another of the city's history. It is by no means a complete catalog of San Franciscana; to include all such works would require many pages. But although a number of useful and instructive books have been omitted—some because they are long out of print and difficult to come by, and others because they discuss subjects adequately covered here—the works that follow form a reading list comprehensive enough to serve the needs of students and general readers alike. All are authoritative treatments of their subjects, and nearly all may be found in most well-stocked libraries. Moreover, the great majority are written in a manner that makes for interesting as well as informative reading.

For the convenience of users, the titles have been grouped under a number of headings, each dealing with a different phase of the city's evolution. Although each book is listed only once, a number of them cover several periods. The dates given are those of the books' first publication; many, however, are available in later editions.

DISCOVERY AND EXPLORATION: 1572-1769

Bancroft, Hubert H. *History of California*. 7 vols. San Francisco, 1884-1890.
Bolton, Herbert E. *Anza's California Expeditions*. 5 vols. Berkeley, 1930.
Eldredge, Zoeth S. *The Beginnings of San Francisco*. 2 vols. New York, 1912.
Kroeber, Alfred L. *Handbook of the Indians of California*. Washington, D. C., 1925.
Teggart, Frederick J., ed. *Narrative of the Portolá Expedition of 1769-1770 by Miguel Costanso*. Berkeley, 1910.
Wagner, Henry R. *Spanish Voyages to the Northwest Coast of North America*. San Francisco, 1929.

THE MISSION PERIOD: 1769-1833

Beechey, Frederick W. *An Account of a Visit to San Francisco, 1826-27*. San Francisco, 1941.
Bolton, Herbert E. *Outpost of Empire*. New York, 1931.
Chevigny, Hector. *Lost Empire; the Life and Adventures of Nicolai Petrovich Rezanov*. New York, 1937.
Dana, Richard Henry. *Two Years Before the Mast*. New York, 1840.

Engelhardt, Fr. Zephyrin. *The Missions and Missionaries of California,* 1st ed. 4 vols. San Francisco, 1908-1915.

Forbes, Alexander. *California: A History of Upper and Lower California.* London, 1839.

Geiger, Maynard J. *The Life and Times of Fray Junípero Serra.* 2 vols. Washington, D. C., 1959.

Kotzebue, Otto von. *A Voyage of Discovery to the South Sea and Beering's Straits.* London, 1821.

YERBA BUENA: 1835-1849

Brown, John Henry. *Reminiscences and Incidents of "the Early Days" of San Francisco.* San Francisco, 1886.

California Star, The. Vol. I, 1847-1848. Facsimile. Berkeley, 1965.°

Hittell, John S. *A History of the City of San Francisco.* San Francisco, 1878.

Phillips, Catherine Coffin. *Portsmouth Plaza: The Cradle of San Francisco.* San Francisco, 1932.

Revere, Joseph Warren. *A Tour of Duty in California.* New York, 1849.

Robinson, Alfred. *Life in California.* New York, 1846.

Simpson, Sir George. *Narrative of a Journey Round the World During the Years 1841 and 1842.* London, 1847.

THE GOLD RUSH: 1848-1856

Bancroft, Hubert H. *Popular Tribunals.* 2 vols. San Francisco, 1887.

Benard de Russailh, Albert. *Last Adventure.* San Francisco, 1931.

Borthwick, J. D. *Three Years in California.* Edinburgh, 1857.

Delano, Alonzo. *Pen Knife Sketches.* San Francisco, 1853.

Helper, Hinton Rowan. *The Land of Gold.* Baltimore, 1855.

Marryat, Frank. *Mountains and Molehills.* New York, 1855.

Royce, Josiah. *California From the Conquest in 1846 to the Second Vigilance Committee.* Boston, 1886.

Soulé, Frank, Gihon, John H., and Nisbet, James. *The Annals of San Francisco.* San Francisco, 1855.

Taylor, Bayard. *Eldorado, Or Adventures in the Path of Empire.* New York, 1850.

Wierzbicki, Felix P. *California As It Is and As It May Be.* San Francisco, 1849.

THE CITY GROWS UP: 1856-1880

Bowles, Samuel. *Across the Continent.* Springfield, Mass., New York, 1865.

Clemens, Samuel L. (Mark Twain). *The Washoe Giant in San Francisco.* San Francisco, 1938.

Cole, Cornelius. *Memoirs.* New York, 1908.

Harpending, Asbury. *The Great Diamond Hoax.* San Francisco, 1913.

Lewis, Oscar and Hall, Carroll D. *Bonanza Inn.* New York, 1939.

Lyman, George D. *Ralston's Ring.* New York, 1937.
Prieto, Guillermo. *San Francisco in the Seventies.* San Francisco, 1938.
Rae, William Fraser. *Westward by Rail,* 2d ed. London, 1871.
Williams, Samuel. *The City of the Golden Gate.* San Francisco, 1921.

TURN OF THE CENTURY: 1880-1906

Asbury, Herbert. *The Barbary Coast.* New York, 1933.
Beebe, Lucius, and Clegg, Charles. *San Francisco's Golden Era.* Berkeley, 1960.*
Burgess, Gelett. *Bayside Bohemia.* San Francisco, 1954.
Hart, Jerome. *In Our Second Century.* San Francisco, 1931.
Kipling, Rudyard. *Letters From San Francisco.* San Francisco, 1949.
Kroninger, Robert H. *Sarah & the Senator.* Berkeley, 1964.*
Levy, Harriet Lane. *920 O'Farrell Street.* New York, 1947.
Mighels (Cummins), Edna Sterling. *The Story of the Files.* San Francisco, 1893.
Neville, Amelia Ransome. *The Fantastic City.* Boston, 1932.

DESTRUCTION AND REBUILDING: 1906-1912

Bonnet, Theodore. *The Regenerators: A Story of the Graft Prosecution in San Francisco.* San Francisco, 1911.
Bronson, William. *The Earth Shook, the Sky Burned.* New York, 1959.
Hulme, Kathryn. *We Lived As Children.* New York, 1938.
Irwin, Will. *The City That Was.* New York, 1906.
MINING & SCIENTIFIC PRESS, (Rickard, T. A., ed.) *After Earthquake and Fire.* San Francisco, 1906.
Older, Fremont. *My Own Story.* San Francisco, 1919.
Reedy, William Marion. *The City That Has Fallen.* San Francisco, 1933.
Thomas, Lately. *A Debonair Scoundrel: An Episode in the Moral History of San Francisco.* New York, 1962.

THE CONTEMPORARY SCENE: 1912-1966

Atherton, Gertrude. *My San Francisco.* New York, 1946.
Caen, Herb. *Baghdad-by-the-Bay.* New York, 1949.
Camp, William Martin. *San Francisco: Port of Gold.* New York, 1947.
Dobie, Charles Caldwell. *San Francisco; A Pageant.* New York, 1933.
Duffus, R. L. *The Tower of Jewels.* New York, 1960.
Gentry, Curt. *San Francisco and the Bay Area.* New York, 1962.
Gilliam, Harold, and Palmer, Phil. *The Face of San Francisco.* New York, 1960.
Older, Cora (Mrs. Fremont). *San Francisco: Magic City.* New York, 1961.
Writers' Program, California (American Guide Series). *San Francisco: The Bay and Its Cities.* New York, 1940.

---

*Published by HOWELL-NORTH BOOKS.

When it was opened in 1937 the Golden Gate Bridge, which links the city with the populous communities on the north side of the bay, was the longest single-span suspension bridge in the world and remained so for many years. The approach to the bridge from the Marin County side affords a spectacular view of both city and bay. *(Redwood Empire Association.)*

Index

*denotes illustration